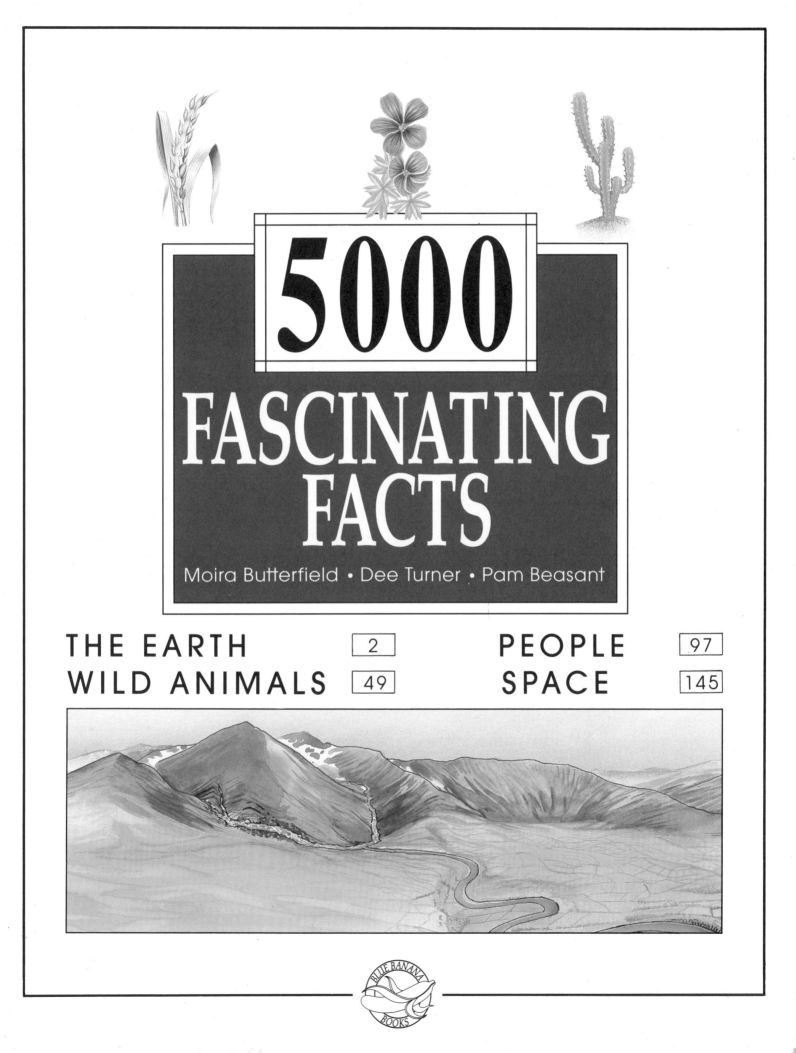

5000 FASCINATING FACTS

Moira Butterfield • Dee Turner • Pam Beasant

THE EARTH 2

WILD ANIMALS 49

PEOPLE 97

SPACE 145

To help you pick out the things you want
to read about in this book, some key words are
printed in bold type like this: **volcano**.

Look out too for <u>spot facts</u> (which start with a ●)
<u>strange-but-true facts</u> in their special boxes,
and <u>mini-facts</u> at the top of each page.
At the end of each Part,
you'll find lists of records and an index.

<u>Part One</u>

THE EARTH

The Earth in Space	4
The Earth from Birth	6
The Earth's Surface	8
Inside the Earth	10
Volcanoes and Geysers	12
Earthquakes	14
Mountains and Valleys	16
Rivers and Lakes	18
Oceans	20
Coastlines	22
The Sky	24
Weather	26
Wild Weather	28
Climate and Seasons	30
Plant Life	32
Rainforests	34
Deserts	36
Polar Regions	38
Saving the Earth	40
Earth Facts and Lists	42
Index	46

Introduction

Welcome to our world! You can find out here all about the planet Earth, and how scientists think it came to be formed.

At the bottom of the Earth's crust, the rocks are red-hot. At the centre of the Earth, the temperature could be 45 times hotter than the temperature of boiling water.

Mountain building takes millions of years. Volcanoes and earthquakes continue to change the shape of the Earth's surface. Did you know that there can be more than 20 volcanic eruptions (mostly under the sea) and a similar number of large earthquakes each year?

Places like rainforests, deserts and the polar regions have very different plants and creatures. Antarctica is the coldest and windiest place on Earth. Although birds, whales and seals live around its coast, the largest animal to be found inland is a small fly!

The Earth's oceans make up 97 per cent of the water on the planet.

The world's weather ranges from burning sunshine and beautiful rainbows to fierce thunderstorms, hurricanes and tornadoes. Some tornadoes can even lift a train into the air.

The Earth in Space

Our world is a **planet** travelling through Space. It journeys around a giant ball of fiery hot gases called the **Sun**.

The Sun is a **star**. It produces **light** and **heat** which reach the Earth.

The Earth is the only known planet that has **life** on it. It is ideal for living things because it has **water** and **air**.

The Solar System

The Earth is part of the **Solar System**, a group of nine planets that travel through Space around the Sun.

● The Earth takes one year to travel round the Sun, a distance of 958 million km.

Mercury

Venus

Earth

Mars

Jupiter

The Solar System (not to scale)

Saturn

Uranus

Neptune

Pluto

● The Earth is the fifth biggest planet in the Solar System, but it is tiny compared to the Sun. If the Sun were the size of a beachball, the Earth would be the size of a pea!

Earth facts

● The top and bottom of the Earth are called the Poles.

● An imaginary line around the middle is called the Equator.

Northern hemisphere

North Pole

Polar diameter – 12,714 km

Equatorial Diameter – 12,756 km

Equator

Circumference – 40,075 km

Southern hemisphere

South Pole

● The Earth is divided into two imaginary halves called hemispheres.

● It weighs 6 sextillion metric tonnes (which is 6 plus 21 noughts).

Earth's orbit

The Earth's path around the Sun is called its **orbit**. It travels in a long oval shape called an **ellipse**. As it travels through Space it spins around on its **axis**, an imaginary line through the centre of the planet from Pole to Pole.

- The Earth spins on its axis once a day. When your part of the Earth turns away from the Sun, darkness falls.

- As the Earth travels round, your home begins to face the Sun again and daylight arrives.

- During the day the Sun looks as if it is moving across the sky. In fact, it is the Earth that is moving, not the Sun.

This side is in darkness.

Axis

The Earth spins this way . . .

This side is in daylight.

Earth's orbit

An ellipse shape

Sun

The Moon

The Moon is a **satellite** of the Earth, which means it orbits around our planet. It orbits once every 27 days, 7 hours, 43.25 minutes.

- Some scientists think that the Moon was once part of the Earth. It may have been broken off when a huge asteroid collided with our planet billions of years ago.

- Half of the Moon always faces away from the Sun, so it is constantly in shadow. This dark side cannot be seen from the Earth but it has been photographed by spaceships.

Strange but true

- The ancient Greeks thought that stars were lamps hanging above the Earth.

- People used to believe that the Earth was flat. They thought that ships would fall over the edge.

- For centuries people believed that the Sun orbited the Earth.

- The Earth gets heavier each year because it picks up dust from space.

5

The Earth from Birth

Blue-green algae

The Solar System was probably formed about 4.6 billion years ago from a huge cloud of gas and dust, perhaps caused by the explosion of a giant star.

The gas and dust began to spin around the Sun, which formed in the middle of the cloud. Gradually the remaining dust may have joined together to form the **planets.**

The **Earth** probably began as a mass of rock which was surrounded by a thick mist of gases. It is at least 3000 million years old, and it may be much older. Since its birth it has changed in many ways.

Earth's beginnings

The development of the Earth is divided into five lengths of time called **Eras**. The first two Eras, the **Archeozoic** and the **Proterozoic**, lasted for four billion years, which is almost **80%** of the Earth's history.

● During the Archeozoic Era the Earth was born. Water and gases such as oxygen were formed. Tiny and very simple creatures called bacteria developed about 3.5 billion years ago, along with tiny algae plants.

● During the Proterozoic Era, about 700 million years ago, the first animals appeared in the sea. They were simple animals without backbones, such as worms and jellyfish.

● The Paleozoic Era lasted from about 590 million years ago to 248 million ago. During this time the Earth was covered in swamps. Larger plants, fish and amphibians appeared.

● The Mesozoic Era lasted from about 248 million years ago to 65 million years ago. In this period many animals developed, including giant reptiles called dinosaurs. The first mammals and birds also appeared.

● The Cenozoic Era began about 65 million years ago and is still going on. The plants and animals we know today developed during this time.

Strange but true

● Fossilized footprints of early humans have been discovered in rocks.

● Supersaurus was one of the biggest dinosaurs. It weighed as much as 10 elephants.

● People once thought that fossils were the remains of dragons and giants.

● The Stegosaurus was 9 metres long, but had a brain the size of a walnut.

Microscopic plants called algae were amongst the first life forms.

How life began

When the Earth was young, a mixture of different chemicals covered its surface. The Sun's radiation acted on the chemicals and they formed new materials called **amino acids** and **sugars**.

The amino acids and sugars linked up and eventually living **cells** were created. Cells are the smallest units of life, from which all living things are made.

Fossils

Scientists can tell what early plants and animals were like by looking at **fossils**. A fossil is the hardened remains or shape of an animal or plant preserved in rock.

● A fossil forms when a dead animal, for example, gets covered in mud or clay.

● The soft parts of the body decay, leaving the hard parts such as bone.

● Over thousands of years, the mud hardens into rock, preserving the animal.

● Some animal and plant fossils have been found in pieces of amber, a fossilized resin which oozed from pine trees millions of years ago and then hardened.

Fossil in amber.

● Fossils of microscopic cells have been found in Greenland. They date from 3800 million years ago, which makes them the oldest known forms of life.

Greenland

Evolution

Evolution is the theory that animals and plants have gradually changed shape and form over millions of years, to enable them to survive in their surroundings. For instance, human beings may have evolved from apes.

Dinosaurs

Dinosaurs were the biggest animals that ever lived. They were reptiles with scaly skins.

● Plant-eating dinosaurs were huge. Brachiosaurus and Diplodocus were some of the biggest, up to 30 metres in length.

● Meat-eating dinosaurs were smaller and ran on hind legs. The largest was Tyrannosaurus, which stood about 5 metres tall.

The dinosaurs **disappeared** about 65 million years ago. No-one knows exactly why. They may have died out because:

● An asteroid hit the Earth, throwing up so much dust that the Sun's rays were blocked out, leading to the death of plants and some of the biggest animals.

● The Earth's temperature heated up and became too warm for the dinosaurs.

● The mammal population grew bigger and took most of the dinosaurs' food.

The Earth's Surface

The Earth has an outer shell called the **crust**. It is divided into 20 huge pieces called **plates** that fit together rather like a jigsaw. They float on top of hot, partly molten rock.

On top of the crust there is **land** and **ocean**. The land is split into seven parts called **continents**.

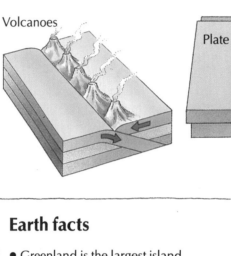

Land

Ocean

Plate

Molten rock

The Earth's plates

The Earth's **plates** move around very slowly as they float on top of hot rock. As they move, they carry the land and the ocean floor with them. Sometimes the plates:

- Collide, pushing up mountains or creating deep ocean trenches and volcanoes (see p12 and p21).

- Slide slowly past each other, producing so much strain that they cause earthquakes (see p14).

- Move apart so the ocean floor splits between them and molten rock rises up through cracks.

Volcanoes

Plate

Plate

Floor spreads apart

Strange but true

- In the past people thought that the oceans and continents were a result of Noah's flood.

- The Earth's plates move between 1.3 cm and 10 cm a year.

- The world's oceans are widening by between 1 cm and 10 cm a year.

- Pangaea comes from an ancient Greek word meaning 'whole Earth'.

Earth facts

- Greenland is the largest island in the world. It may possibly be several islands covered by a sheet of ice.

Greenland

- The northernmost point of land in the world is the islet of Oodaq near the North Pole. It is covered in ice.

- The southernmost point of land in the world is the Amundsen-Scott South Polar Station in Antarctica.

- The highest point of land in the world is Mount Everest in the Himalayan mountain-range.

The continents

The Earth's **continents** move around on top of the plates that float beneath them. The movement is very slow; it has taken millions of years for the continents to reach where they are today.

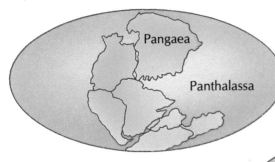

- About 120 million years ago there were two continents: Laurasia and Gondwanaland.
- Laurasia broke into North America, Europe and Asia.

- The continents began as one big mass of land called Pangaea. It started to break up about 200 million years ago.
- Pangaea was surrounded by a single vast ocean called Panthalassa.

- Gondwanaland broke up to become Africa, South America, Antarctica, Australia and India.
- The continents are still moving. For instance, North America moves away from Europe at a rate of about 3 cm a year.

The past and the future

Here are some examples of the shape of continents in the **past**:

- The eastern coast of South America and the western coast of Africa were joined. Their modern shapes could fit together like a jigsaw.
- The continents of Africa and Antarctica were also joined. There is proof of this because fossilized remains of tropical African plants and animals have been found in modern Antarctica.

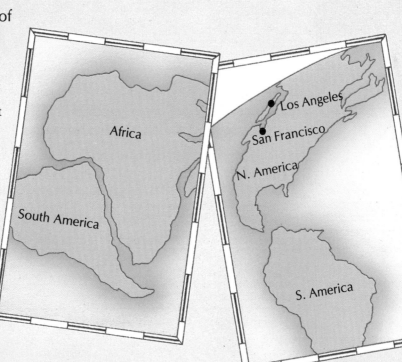

Here are some examples of what may occur in **50 million years** time:

- The two American continents will have broken apart.
- Africa and Asia will have broken apart.
- Part of California, including the city of Los Angeles, will have broken off from America. It will float north, past San Francisco on the mainland.

9

Inside the Earth

The Earth is made up of four different layers. The layer of hot, partly-molten rock beneath the **crust** layer is called the **mantle**.

Beneath the mantle there is a layer of liquid metal called the **outer core**.

Beneath the liquid metal, in the centre of the Earth, there is a ball of very hot solid metal called the **inner core**.

Crust
Mantle
Outer core
Inner core

The Earth's layers

Scientists have worked out what is likely to be inside the Earth by analyzing **rocks** and by studying the **shock waves** that travel up to the surface during earthquakes (see p14/15).

- The temperature in the middle of the Earth is thought to be about 4500° C, which is 45 times hotter than the temperature of boiling water!

- New crust is being made all the time, as molten rock bubbles up through huge cracks between plates in the ocean floor (see p8).

- There are two kinds of Earth crust – ocean crust beneath the seas and continental crust beneath the land.

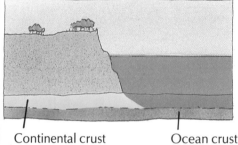

Continental crust   Ocean crust

- The deepest borehole ever drilled into the Earth's crust is more than 12 km from the surface.

Strange but true

- Diamond is harder than any other natural substance.

- Children playing on a river bank in South Africa discovered the first diamond.

- The largest diamond ever found weighed over half a kilogram.

- Diamonds are made of carbon, the same material as coal soot.

Rocks

There are three different types of rock on Earth. They are given the names **igneous**, **sedimentary** and **metamorphic**.

- Igneous rocks are formed when hot molten material called magma bubbles up from beneath the crust and hardens.

- Some sedimentary rocks are made from pieces of other rock types that are pushed down under the Earth's surface and altered by pressure.

- Other sedimentary rocks form from layers of dead animals and plants on the seabed. The layers harden over many millions of years.

- Metamorphic rocks are formed deep beneath the Earth's crust, where igneous or sedimentary rocks are changed by heat and pressure.

Sedimentary rocks:
Sandstone
Limestone   Shale

Igneous rocks:
Pumice   Granite   Obsidian

Metamorphic rocks:
Marble   Slate

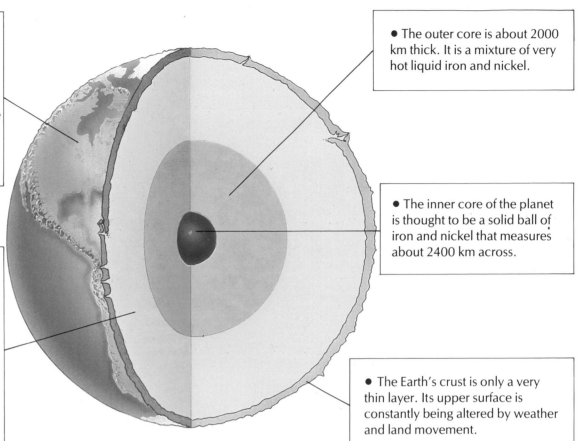

- The Earth's crust stretches about 40 km below the surface. It is made of light rock. The temperature of the crustal rock increases by about 30°C for every kilometre downwards. At the bottom of the crust, the rocks are red-hot.

- The outer core is about 2000 km thick. It is a mixture of very hot liquid iron and nickel.

- The Earth's mantle is about 2900 km thick. At the top it is made of solid rock. Deeper down it is so hot that the rock melts and becomes molten. The rock in the mantle layer is composed mainly of iron and magnesium.
  There is a definite boundary line between the crust and the mantle.

- The inner core of the planet is thought to be a solid ball of iron and nickel that measures about 2400 km across.

- The Earth's crust is only a very thin layer. Its upper surface is constantly being altered by weather and land movement.

Riches from the Earth

Our main sources of **heat and power** come from beneath the Earth's surface. Oil, gas and coal are called **fossil fuels**.

- Oil is made from the bodies of tiny sea creatures that lived millions of years ago. The bodies gathered on the seabed and they were gradually squeezed down under rocks that formed above them. Eventually they turned into oil.

- Coal is made from trees that died millions of years ago. Layers of the dead plant material were squeezed down until they turned into carbon.

- Natural gas is made when animal and plant bodies decompose. It is usually found in the same place as oil.

Ocean oil platform

Gemstones

Precious stones are mined from beneath the Earth's surface.

- Gems form as crystals in igneous rock. They vary in colour, shape and size. Because they are rare, they have been prized for centuries.

- The rarest diamonds are blue or pink. Rubies are the rarest gems of all. The finest ones come from Myanmar (Burma).

- The best sapphires come from Burma, Kashmir and Montana, USA.

- The finest emeralds come from Colombia in South America.

Volcanoes and Geysers

Volcanoes occur when hot liquid rock seeps up through cracks in the Earth's crust. Most volcanoes are found where two **plates** are pushing against each other or moving apart (see p8).

Volcanoes that erupt are called **active**. Many of them are found in an area around the Pacific Ocean called the '**Pacific Ring of Fire**'.

Volcanoes in the Pacific Ring of Fire

Pacific Ocean

Volcanoes that might erupt are **dormant**. Volcanoes that have stopped erupting are **extinct**.

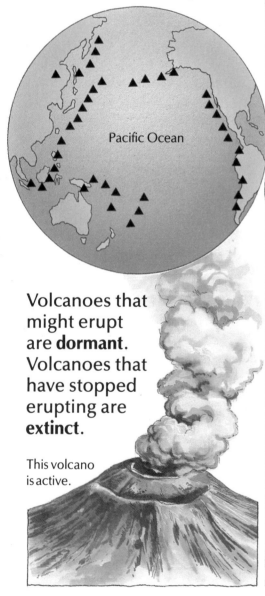

This volcano is active.

How a volcano forms

Pressure builds up underground and pushes molten liquid rock up from a chamber beneath the surface. It spews out of a crack in the ground as **lava**.

Crater formed by the explosion.

Dome

Layers of ash and lava.

- Ash, lava and rocks build up to form a hill with a crater on top. Sometimes the lava comes out through side exits called domes.

- Gas, lava and pieces of solid rock (called tephra) spew out. Large molten lumps of tephra are called volcanic bombs.

Magma chamber

Hot springs and geysers

Hot springs occur when underground water is heated up by hot rocks beneath the Earth's surface. The boiling water rises up through cracks in the ground.

Geysers are hot springs that spout water and steam at regular intervals.

- Yellowstone Park in the USA has over 2500 geysers, including a world-famous one nicknamed 'Old Faithful'.

- New Zealand and Iceland are the other main areas of geyser activity.

- A fumarole is a crack in the ground that releases more acid gases than water. These often occur on volcano slopes.

A fumarole

Make-up

Bath cleaner

Road surfacing material

Volcano shapes

A **volcano shape** depends on the type of eruption that caused it and the sort of material that comes out.

● Shield volcanoes are shaped like upturned saucers, with gentle slopes.

● Cinder cone volcanoes are high, with steep slopes.

● Stratovolcanoes are cone-shaped mountains.

Types of eruption

Eruptions are given different names, depending on how strong they are.

● Hawaiian eruptions are not very violent. They pour out liquid lava in fiery rivers.

● Strombolian eruptions pour out thicker lava, but not very violently. Strombolian volcanoes erupt continuously.

● Vulcanian eruptions produce violent explosions and throw out tephra, dust, gas and ash.

● Peléean eruptions are gigantic explosions which throw out a huge cloud of gas and lava.

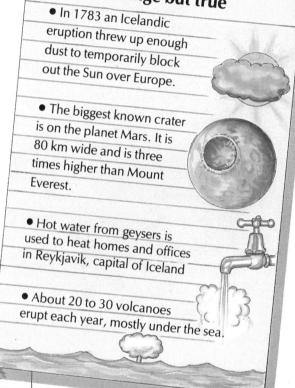

Strange but true

● In 1783 an Icelandic eruption threw up enough dust to temporarily block out the Sun over Europe.

● The biggest known crater is on the planet Mars. It is 80 km wide and is three times higher than Mount Everest.

● Hot water from geysers is used to heat homes and offices in Reykjavik, capital of Iceland

● About 20 to 30 volcanoes erupt each year, mostly under the sea.

Volcanic islands

Many **ocean islands** have been formed by volcanic eruptions beneath the sea. First ash is blown above the water and then a pile of rock and lava builds up until it appears above the waves.

● In 1963 the volcanic island of Surtsey appeared near Iceland. It took three weeks to rise from the waves.

● In 1883 the volcanic island of Krakatoa, near Java, blew up. Rock blasted 80 km into the air.

Pompeii

In AD 79 the Italian volcano **Vesuvius** erupted and buried the Roman cities of **Pompeii** and **Herculaneum**.

● The cities were hidden for nearly seventeen centuries, until a farmer discovered some ruins in 1748.

● Vesuvius is still an active volcano. If it erupted in the future the nearby city of Naples would have to be evacuated.

Earthquakes

Pigeons

Earthquakes are severe shocks that happen when powerful **vibrations** pass from underground up to the surface through solid rock. The ground shakes violently and huge cracks may appear, sometime wide enough to swallow cars.

Earthquakes happen where two of the Earth's **plates** meet. The pressure of the plates pushing against each other causes deep cracks in the rock called **fault lines.**

The rocks on either side of a fault line sometimes slide up or along. This makes them bend and shatter, causing earthquake **shock waves.**

Rock moves along the line.

Fault line

Centre of the earthquake

Earthquake profile

An earthquake begins beneath the ground at the point where the rocks move.

The movement creates **waves of energy** which travel up to the surface.

• The point where the earthquake begins underground is called the focus.

• The point on the surface above the focus is called the epicentre.

Epicentre on the surface

Shock waves

Focus underground

• There may be lots more minor earthquakes called aftershocks after the first earthquake. These occur because the rocks beneath are falling back into place.

Earthquake areas

• Most earthquakes happen around the edges of the Pacific Ocean or in mountainous areas such as the Himalayas and the Alps.

• The San Andreas Fault runs down California. In 1906 the rocks on one side of the fault moved 4.6 metres, causing an earthquake.

San Francisco

San Andreas Fault line

Los Angeles

Earthquake buildings

• Earthquake-proof buildings are built with reinforced steel or concrete frames on a solid platform. Many skyscrapers in San Francisco are built this way.

Earthquake effects

An earthquake can cause:

• A series of gigantic fast-moving waves called tsunami. The biggest one this century was 67 metres tall, the height of about 9 houses!

• Dangerous mud and rock avalanches that engulf the surrounding land.

• Fires set off by broken gas pipes and electrical cables.

Measuring earthquakes

Earthquakes are measured using the **Richter Scale** or the **Mercalli Scale**. The Richter Scale has 8 numbers that measure earthquake energy. Each number denotes 10 times more energy than the number before. The Mercalli Scale has 12 numbers measuring the effect of an earthquake on objects and buildings.

Examples of Richter numbers:

1·2	5	7	8
Barely noticeable	Some damage	Like a nuclear bomb	Total devastation

Examples of Mercalli numbers

II	V	VII	XII
Lamps swing and windows shake	Dishes smash	Walls collapse	Total damage

Earthquake instruments

Seismograph

Instruments called seismographs are used to measure earthquakes.

- A seismograph uses a pen attached to a frame to draw a line on a drum. The line shows the force of the earthquake.

- The first seismograph was made in China in AD 150. It was a pot with dragon heads sticking out. Tremors made balls fall from the dragons' jaws into the mouths of frogs below. The side that the balls fell showed the direction of the quake epicentre.

Ball falling

Predicting earthquakes

Scientists monitor earthquake areas to predict tremors. There are **monitoring stations** all over the world that measure Earth movement. Some early signs of earthquakes are shown below:

- A radioactive gas called radon is released from rocks. Scientists monitor well water to detect increases in radon traces.

- Small tremors called foreshocks happen just before an earthquake. The ground swells up and cracks.

- Animals behave oddly. They are often very sensitive to tremors.

Strange but true

- Aftershocks may continue for days after a major earthquake.

- There are thousands of earthquakes a year. Only 20 to 30 are large ones.

- In 1975 the Chinese city of Haicheng was evacuated 2 hours before an earthquake because people noticed their animals behaving oddly.

A mountain is a mass of rock that rises steeply above its surroundings. Mountains occur in groups or chains. They cover about one quarter of the Earth's surface.

A mountain range

Most of the world's tallest mountain ranges were built when two of the Earth's **plates** collided with each other, slowly pushing up the rock above. Mountain building takes millions of years. It is still going on today.

Mountains pushed up

Plate

Plate

Types of mountain

There are four different types of mountain, called **fold**, **block**, **volcanic** and **dome**.

Fold mountain

Block mountain

Volcanic mountain

Dome mountain

Magma pushes up.

- Fold mountains occur when two of the Earth's plates push against each other. The rock in the middle is pushed up in folds.

- Sometimes two faults (deep rock cracks) run alongside each other. Pressure heaves up the block of land in the middle.

- A volcanic mountain grows when lava, dust and ash gradually build up in a cone shape around an eruption.

- Dome mountains are created when hot volcanic material rises upwards from deep in the Earth and pushes the rocks above into a dome shape.

Mountain areas

There are **mountain ranges** all over the world. The largest ones are shown on the map below.

Rocky Mts
Urals
Altai Mts
Alps
Carpathian Mts
Pyrenees
Appalachians
Tien Shan
Caucasus
Himalayas
Atlas Mts
Andes
East African Highlands
Brazilian Highlands
Great Dividing Range
Drakensberg Mts

Mountain ranges

K2 Himalayas 8611 metres	**Kangchenjunga** Himalayas 8586 metres	**Makalu** Himalayas 8475 metres	**Dhaulagiri** Himalayas 8172 metres

Mountain profile

At the bottom of a mountain there may be a forest of **deciduous trees**, which lose their leaves in winter. In warm areas there may be **rainforest**.

Further up, there are likely to be **coniferous trees**, which keep their needles all year round.

The place where the trees stop growing is called the **tree line**. Above this line only hardy alpine plants, grasses and mosses grow.

Finally, the temperature gets too cold for plants to grow. On the top of high mountains it is so cold that there is snow all year round. Below this the snow will melt in summer. The line between the two areas is called the **snow line**.

Snow stays all year round

Snow line

This snow melts in summer

Alpine plants, grasses and mosses

Coniferous fir trees

Deciduous trees (rainforest in hot areas)

Strange but true

● The Andes and the Himalayas are still rising upwards.

● The lowest officially-named hill stands 4.5 metres high on a golf course in Brunei.

● Mount Everest is 20 times higher than the world's tallest building, the Sears Tower in Chicago.

Glaciers and valleys

A **glacier** is a huge mass of ice that travels down a mountainside. A glacier:

● Carves out a U-shaped valley as it travels along.

● Moves along very slowly.

Sometimes a **river** forms when summer snow melts on a mountainside. A river:

● Carves out a V-shaped valley as it travels.

● May carve a steep-sided valley called a gorge.

River valley

Glacier valley

17

Rivers and Lakes

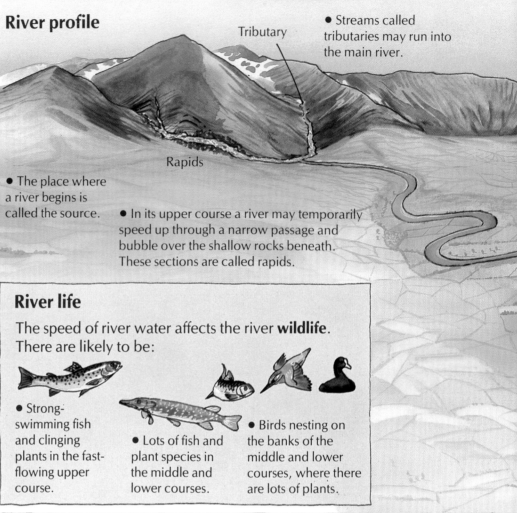

Nile
Africa
6695 km long

Rivers begin high up on mountains and run downhill to the sea. They start from **underground springs** or **melting glaciers**.

A river's route is divided into three parts. The first part is called the **upper course**, where the river flows steeply downhill and the current is fast. The water carries sand, gravel and rocks down with it.

River profile

Tributary

● Streams called tributaries may run into the main river.

Rapids

● The place where a river begins is called the source.

● In its upper course a river may temporarily speed up through a narrow passage and bubble over the shallow rocks beneath. These sections are called rapids.

River life

The speed of river water affects the river **wildlife**. There are likely to be:

● Strong-swimming fish and clinging plants in the fast-flowing upper course.

● Lots of fish and plant species in the middle and lower courses.

● Birds nesting on the banks of the middle and lower courses, where there are lots of plants.

Upper course

Middle course

Lower course

In the **middle course** the river flows along a gentler slope. It travels more slowly but it still wears away rock and sand from its banks.

In the **lower course** the river slows down and gets wider. The sand and rock it has been carrying are now worn down to tiny particles called **silt**.

Lakes

A **lake** is a large area of water that has collected in a valley. It may be caused by rainwater, melted snow or an underground stream. Lakes can be:

● Very large. The world's biggest freshwater lake is Lake Superior in the USA and Canada. It covers a vast area of over 82,000 sq km.

● Very deep. The world's deepest lake is Lake Baykal in Russia. Its deepest crevice goes down 1940 metres.

Amazon
S. America
6570 km long

Mississippi
N. America
6020 km long

Yangtze
Asia
5530 km long

● A river joins the sea at its mouth. Here there is an area where freshwater and seawater mix, called an estuary.

Deltas

When a river reaches its mouth it is moving very slowly. Sometimes it is carrying lots of mud and silt which may pile up in the river mouth to form areas of land called **deltas**.

● The Ganges and the Brahmaputra Rivers meet in India and Bangladesh to form the world's largest delta. It is 480 km long and 160 km wide.

● In its middle course a river slows down and travels around bends called meanders.

● As the river cuts through a valley it may leave shelves on either side called river terraces.

Meander

Oxbow lake

Estuary

Delta

● Sometimes a river meander changes course, leaving behind a small lake called an oxbow lake.

Mouth

Waterfalls

Waterfalls occur when a hard band of rock crosses under a river. The water cannot wear the hard rock down, but it wears down soft rock further on. Eventually this creates a steep drop.

● The world's highest waterfall is the Salto Angel Falls in Venezuela. It plunges down a cliff 807 metres high.

Strange but true

● A huge underground river runs underneath the Nile, with six times more water than the river above.

● Lake Bosumtwi in Ghana formed in a hollow made by a meteorite.

● Beaver Lake, in Yellowstone Park, USA, was artificially created by beaver damming.

● The world's shortest river with a name is the Roe River, Montana, USA. It is 61 metres long.

Oceans

There are four large oceans on the Earth. They join together to form one huge mass of water. They are called the **Pacific**, the **Atlantic**, the **Indian** and the **Arctic**.

Parts of the oceans are divided into smaller areas called **seas**. These are mostly around coastlines and islands.

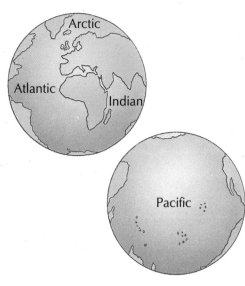

The **temperature** of seawater varies across the world. For instance, most of the water in the Arctic is permanently frozen, whereas in hot tropical areas the sea can reach the temperature of a warm bath.

Ocean floor profile

If you were able to look beneath the ocean surface you would see:

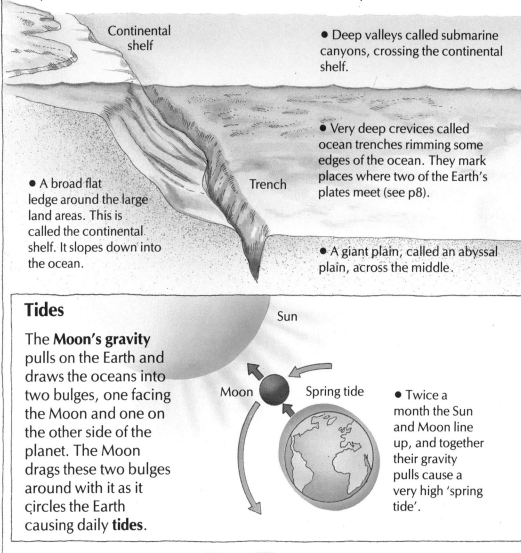

Continental shelf

Trench

- Deep valleys called submarine canyons, crossing the continental shelf.

- Very deep crevices called ocean trenches rimming some edges of the ocean. They mark places where two of the Earth's plates meet (see p8).

- A broad flat ledge around the large land areas. This is called the continental shelf. It slopes down into the ocean.

- A giant plain, called an abyssal plain, across the middle.

Tides

The **Moon's gravity** pulls on the Earth and draws the oceans into two bulges, one facing the Moon and one on the other side of the planet. The Moon drags these two bulges around with it as it circles the Earth causing daily **tides**.

Sun

Moon

Spring tide

- Twice a month the Sun and Moon line up, and together their gravity pulls cause a very high 'spring tide'.

Coral reefs

Coral reefs are found in warm shallow seas. They are built by tiny animals called **polyps**. Each polyp builds a small stone cup to live in. When a polyp dies, it leaves its cup behind. New polyps build on top and gradually the reef grows.

Fringe reef

Barrier reef

Coral polyp

Coral atoll

- Fringe reefs grow around the shores of continents or islands.

- Barrier reefs grow several kilometres offshore. The Australian Great Barrier Reef is the biggest example.

- A coral atoll is a broken ring of coral islands with water in the middle.

Atlantic	Indian	Arctic
82,217,000 sq km	73,481,000 sq km	14,056,000 sq km

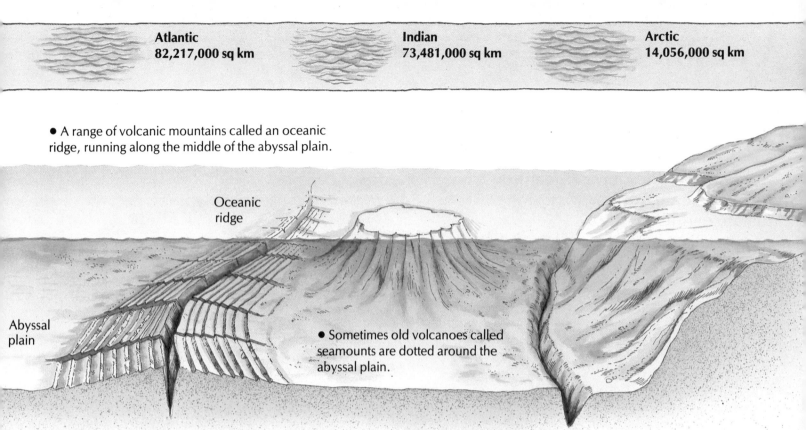

● A range of volcanic mountains called an oceanic ridge, running along the middle of the abyssal plain.

Oceanic ridge

Abyssal plain

● Sometimes old volcanoes called seamounts are dotted around the abyssal plain.

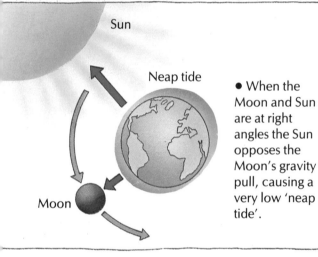

Sun

Neap tide

Moon

● When the Moon and Sun are at right angles the Sun opposes the Moon's gravity pull, causing a very low 'neap tide'.

Currents

Ocean water travels around the world in regular paths called **currents**. They are caused by **winds** and by **warm water** moving away from the Equator and **cold water** flowing in from polar regions to take its place.

● The world's largest current is the West Wind Drift, which flows between America and Antarctica.

Strange but true

● Off the coast of Florida there is an underwater hotel. Guests have to dive to the entrance.

● There are 4 grams of gold in every million tonnes of seawater.

● The biggest storm wave ever recorded was 34 metres high from crest to trough.

● The biggest iceberg ever seen had a bigger surface area than the country of Belgium.

Sea riches

● Oysters, seaweed and fish can be farmed in the sea. Some scientists have managed to build artificial reef 'farms' and colonize them with lobsters and shellfish.

● Underwater communities could be built for marine farm workers. Some experiments have already been carried out using prototype underwater houses.

● On the deep ocean floor there are millions of rock lumps called manganese nodules. Manganese is used for hardening steel.

Coastlines

A coastline is the place where the land meets the ocean. Coastlines vary in shape and they have different features – for instance, one coastline might have gentle sloping **beaches**, whereas another might have rocky **cliffs** and **caves**.

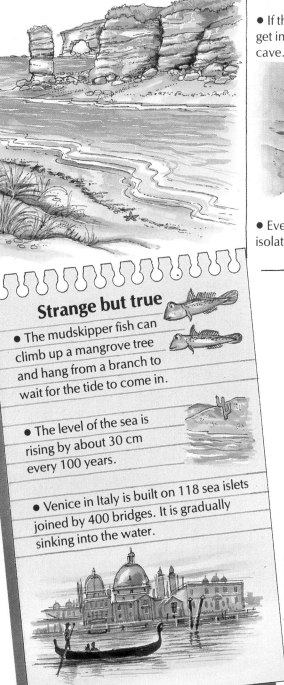

Strange but true

- The mudskipper fish can climb up a mangrove tree and hang from a branch to wait for the tide to come in.

- The level of the sea is rising by about 30 cm every 100 years.

- Venice in Italy is built on 118 sea islets joined by 400 bridges. It is gradually sinking into the water.

Coastal features

Coastlines do not always stay the same shape. As the sea pounds against the shore it gradually wears down the rock to form features such as **caves** and **arches**.

- If there is a crack in a cliff, seawater will get into it and gradually hollow out a cave.

- Sometimes waves pound both sides of a headland and wear away an arch in the middle.

- Eventually arches collapse, leaving isolated rocks called stacks.

- Sometimes waves enlarge a cave so much that a crack appears in the roof. In rough weather water sprays out of the crack, called a blowhole.

Beaches

The sea gathers loose rocks and stones as it wears away at the coastline. The waves grind them into tiny particles and then drop them onto the shore, forming **beaches**.

- The Hawaiian Islands have beaches made of black sand, formed by volcanic lava.

- The Bermuda Islands have pale pink beaches. The sand is made from fragments of red shell.

- The dazzling white beaches of Barbados are made of tiny shell fragments worn down by the sea.

- A stretch of beach on the Namibian coast in Africa provides an important supply of loose diamonds. They are hidden amongst the sand and gravel.

● Cliffs are sometimes made up of layers of different rock. You can often see the layers, called bedding planes, running along a cliff face.

Marshes and estuaries

● An estuary is the area of muddy land where a river meets the sea. River and sea water wash over it creating mudflats, creeks and salty marshes. Seabirds like to nest here.

● In hot tropical places the coastal marshes are often swamps filled with mangrove trees. They can survive in salty water because their roots are partly above the ground and can absorb oxygen from the air.

Coastal life

Beaches provide a home for lots of different **animals** and **plants**. You might find:

● Seaweed, which is a plant without roots or a stem. It is made up of fronds and a root-like 'holdfast' at the bottom for anchoring the seaweed firmly on to rocks.

A limpet shell

● Limpets anchored firmly to the rocks. A limpet has a very powerful foot which works like a suction cup and clamps the shell firmly to the rock surface.

Worm casts

● Worm casts, which are small piled-up cones of wet sand. They are made by lugworms that burrow beneath the surface. The tiny worms swallow sand and digest the minute particles of food mixed up with it. Then they push out the waste, making casts on the sand surface.

● Marram grasses and other hardy salt-tolerating plants. They grow on sand dunes, which are blown into sloping shapes by the wind.

Marram grasses

● A bubble in the sand. Underneath, there may be a cockleshell. It burrows down and then it sticks two tiny siphons above the surface. One takes in seawater along with food particles. The other expels the waste water, creating the bubble that you can see.

A cockleshell

The Sky

The Earth is surrounded by a blanket of **gases** called the **atmosphere**. It is made up of five main layers. Each layer is a different **temperature** and is made up of a mixture of different gases.

The boundaries between the different layers are not clear-cut.

In the air

The atmosphere is made up of:

78.09% nitrogen

20.95% oxygen

0.93% argon

0.03% carbon dioxide, helium, hydrogen, methane, krypton, neon, ozone, xenon and water vapour.

Sky colours

Sunlight is made up of different **light waves**. The visible ones are red, orange, yellow, green, blue, indigo and violet. These colours are called the **spectrum**. You can see them in a rainbow, or if you pass light through a specially shaped piece of glass called a prism. The spectrum causes:

- Blue skies. When the Sun's rays reach the Earth's atmosphere, the blue light waves scatter in all directions. Provided the light is not obscured by cloud, it shows across the sky.

- Red sunrises and sunsets, when blue light waves are blocked out by dust in the air and only red light waves get through. Dust tends to be most common in the morning and evening.

Strange but true

- Some early hot-air balloons were so heavy that the passengers stripped off to help keep the weight down.

- The Ancient Egyptians worshipped a sky goddess called Nut.

- The world's windiest place is Commonwealth Bay, Antarctica.

- In 1934, a gust of wind reached 371 km/h on Mount Washington in New Hampshire, USA.

Air pressure

The layers of gases around the Earth press down on the surface. This force is called **air pressure**. It is strongest at ground level and gets weaker with height.

- High up on mountains the air pressure is weak and the air has less oxygen content than air down below.

- Aircraft cabins are artificially pressurized so that the passengers can breathe comfortably even though they are flying high up in the atmosphere.

Low pressure

High air pressure

Force 6 – strong breeze
Large tree branches move

Force 9 – strong gale
Chimney pots crash down

Force 12 – hurricane
Whole areas devastated

Atmosphere layers

The atmosphere is made up of these layers:

● The exosphere – height 500 to 8000 km. Here it is intensely hot, a minimum of 2200°C.

Weather satellites orbit in the exosphere

● The thermosphere – height 80 to 500 km. The temperature of this layer increases with height. At the top it is about 2200°C.

When spaceships re-enter orbit, their heat shields burn up in this layer, due to friction

● The mesosphere – height 50 to 80 km. The temperature of this layer gets colder with height. It varies from 10°C to −80°C.

Unmanned balloons have measured the temperature in this layer

● The stratosphere – height 8 to 50 km (varies from place to place). This layer is cold, but the temperature increases with height. Within this layer is a band of ozone gas, which filters out the Sun's harmful rays.

Aircraft fly in this layer to avoid rough weather

● The troposphere – height up to 16 km over the Equator, 8 km over the Poles. This layer contains nearly all the water vapour and most of the other gases in the atmosphere. It gets colder with height.

Weather occurs in this layer

The wind

Wind is air that is moving. The Sun's rays are reflected upwards from the ground, warming the air above. **Warm air** is light and it rises upwards. **Cold air** is heavier and it sinks into the space left by the rising warm air.

● Some winds blow constantly in regular patterns around the world. They are caused by warm air rising up from the Equator and cold air from polar regions flowing into the space beneath.

● A current of rising warm air is called a thermal. Some birds like to find thermals. They spread out their wings and let the moving air carry them along. Gliders work in the same way.

● Anemometers are used to measure wind speed. The most common kind has three cups fixed onto a shaft. The stronger the wind, the faster the cups spin around. Their movement controls a dial that indicates speed.

Weather

Here are some unusual weather facts and records:

Rainiest place: on Kauai, Hawaii. Rains for 350 days a year

When water is warmed it **evaporates**, which means that it changes into an invisible gas called **vapour**. When vapour gets cold it changes back into **liquid droplets**. When it gets very cold it becomes solid **ice crystals** that form snowflakes.

Six-sided snowflakes

Strange but true

- Some people say they can smell rain. The smell may be gases produced by the damp soil.

- Italian farmers shoot fireworks into clouds to shatter hailstones that damage crops.

- Sea fog was once thought to be the breath of an underwater monster.

- At the North and South Poles the snow never melts.

The water cycle

The **Sun** heats up the world's **oceans** and **rivers**. It makes water evaporate and rise upwards. As the vapour gets higher it gets colder and changes into **water droplets**, which gather around specks of salt and dust in the air. Billions of droplets together form a **cloud**. The droplets grow bigger until they are so heavy that they fall as **rain** back into the oceans and rivers.

Cloud

Ocean

Types of weather

Apart from rain, water vapour in the air causes:

- Snow, which occurs when it is very cold. Water droplets in the air freeze into ice crystals and fall to the ground.

- Fog, which occurs when the ground is cold and the air above it is warmer. The vapour in the air changes into a cloud of water droplets.

- Hailstones, which begin as icy pellets in high storm clouds. They are buffeted about inside the cloud and gradually grow bigger as layers of ice freeze around them. Eventually they grow so heavy that they fall to the ground.

Air masses

An **air mass** is formed when a vast area of air stays in the same place for some time. It gets warm or cold, depending on the temperature of the land or sea beneath.

When an air mass moves it brings weather changes.

Rain

● No new water is ever made in the atmosphere. Instead, the existing water recycles again and again. So any rain you see is likely to have fallen many times before!

● Rainbows, which appear on rainy days when the Sun is shining. You can only see one if you are standing with your back to the Sun. The sunlight shines on the raindrops in the air and is split up into the seven colours of the spectrum (see p24).

● Dew, which occurs when air cools down at night and water vapour condenses into droplets of dew on the ground. The dew evaporates in the morning when the air warms up again.

Clouds

There are ten different **kinds of cloud**. Each different shape gives a clue to the sort of weather you can expect.

● Cumulus clouds are fluffy, white puffs. They signal fine weather.

● Cirrus clouds are wisps with flicked-back tails. They may signal rain.

● Cirrostratus clouds thinly veil the Sun. They can bring rain or snow.

● Stratocumulus clouds spread out in uneven patches. They can mean dry weather.

● Cirrocumulus clouds look like ripples in the sky. They signal weather changes.

● Altostratus clouds make patchy thin layers. They may grow into rain clouds.

●Stratus clouds spread out in a low grey layer. They mean rain or snow.

● Cumulonimbus are billowing storm clouds that stretch high up into the sky.

● Nimbostratus clouds are dark low masses signalling rain or snow.

● Altocumulus clouds are fluffy cloud waves. They signal weather changes.

Wild Weather

Follow this advice if you get caught in a thunderstorm:

Avoid sheltering under trees

Sometimes the weather is dramatic and powerful. For instance, 45,000 **thunderstorms** take place every day and most of them are capable of producing as much energy as an atom bomb.

Violent **hurricanes** and **tornadoes** are regular weather features in some parts of the world.

Thunderstorms

Thunderstorms occur when the air is warm and humid and rises upwards very quickly, forming giant towering **cumulonimbus** storm clouds. Inside the clouds, ice crystals and water droplets whirl around, colliding with each other and creating tiny **electrical charges** as they do so. Gradually the charges build up until giant sparks flash from cloud to cloud or down to the ground and back.

● Lightning finds the quickest path to the Earth, so it usually hits high buildings or trees. Tall buildings are fitted with copper strips called lightning conductors that carry the electric charge safely to the ground.

● You can tell how far away a storm is by counting the seconds between a lightning flash and a thunderclap. The storm is one kilometre away for every three seconds you count.

● Lightning travels down to the ground and then back up again along the same path. The journey is so fast that there only appears to be one flash.

● Lightning heats up the air in its path. The air expands rapidly, making the booming noise of thunder. Lightning and thunder occur at the same time, but you hear the thunder afterwards because sound travels more slowly than light.

Strange but true

● Cumulonimbus clouds may measure 18 km from base to top, twice the height of Mount Everest!

● The ancient Chinese believed that storms were caused by dragons fighting in the sky.

● It is said that a tornado in 1946 uncovered buried gold and showered it over a Russian town.

● American Roy Sullivan has been struck by lightning a record seven times.

● Sheet lightning does not look like a long fork. Instead it looks like a momentary glow in the sky. It is caused by lightning flashing within a cloud.

If you are in a car, stay inside it. You will be safe

 If you get stuck out in the open, crouch down or run for shelter

 Once you are indoors, you will be safe

Tornadoes

Tornadoes are found mainly on the plains of North America, when small pockets of air rise quickly and create towering fast-spinning funnels of wind that leapfrog across the land. They suck up anything in their path.

● There are about 640 tornadoes a year in North America, mostly in the plains states of Texas, Oklahoma, Kansas, and Nebraska. People who live in these areas have storm shelters in their homes to protect them if a tornado passes overhead.

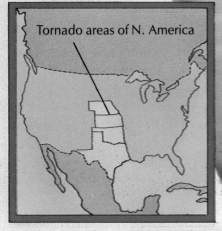

Tornado areas of N. America

● Tornado winds can spin at up to 640 km/h. They have been known to lift heavy trains into the air.

● A waterspout is a tornado over the sea, a swirling air column that sucks up seawater. If a waterspout moves onto land, it drops its load. This has been known to cause surprise showers of fish and crabs!

Hurricanes

Hurricanes are powerful tropical storms that occur in late summer and early autumn. They begin over warm seas near the Equator, when warm air rises over a wide area and forms huge pillars of cloud full of water vapour.

Cold air rushes in beneath the warm air and a giant spinning wheel of whirling cloud begins to move over the sea surface.

● Hurricanes bring thousands of tonnes of rain and strong winds of up to 320 km/h. They can do a great deal of damage if they reach a coastline.

● A hurricane can stretch over many kilometres, but in the middle there is always a clear, calm patch called the 'eye', usually measuring about 48 km across.

● Hurricanes are given individual names. The first hurricane of the season is given a name beginning with A. The next one gets a name beginning with B, and so on.

● Hurricanes are also referred to as typhoons, tropical cyclones and baguios. In some parts of Australia they are called 'willy willies'.

29

Climate and Seasons

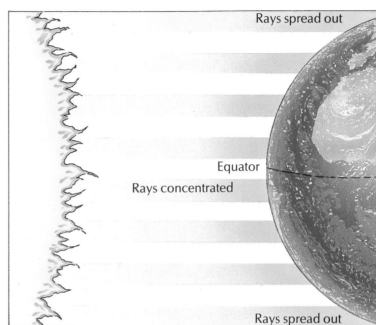
The **climate** of a place is the pattern of weather it has from year to year.

Climate varies across the world. For instance, some places are always very cold or very warm, whereas in other areas the temperature changes from season to season.

The **seasons** of spring, summer, autumn and winter come at different times to different places. **Seasonal weather** varies, too. For instance, during summer in Antarctica the temperature is still below freezing, whereas in southern Europe the Sun shines warmly.

Hot and cold spots

The **Sun's rays** hit the Earth in straight lines, but because of the planet's round shape they spread out more at the Poles than they do around the Equator.

When the rays spread out they provide less heat, so the further a place is from the Equator, the colder its climate tends to be.

Rays spread out

Equator
Rays concentrated

Rays spread out

Climate causes

Ocean currents, **distance from the sea**, **wind direction** and **mountains** are all factors capable of having an effect on the climate of a particular place.

● Places near the sea have a 'maritime' climate. The air temperature stays fairly steady all year round because it is influenced by sea temperature, which does not alter much.

● Big cities often have a climate that is warmer than the surrounding land. Concrete buildings absorb the Sun's heat during the day and radiate it at night, warming the city air.

● Places that are far from the sea have a 'continental' climate. The land heats up quickly but also cools down quickly, so there is a big temperature difference between summer and winter.

● The climate can vary within a very small area. For instance, in one garden there might be a cold shadowy corner alongside a warm sunny spot. Small areas like this are called microclimates.

Dallol, Ethiopia. The hottest place on Earth. Average temperature 34.4°C

 Sahara Desert. The sunniest place on Earth

 Siberia, Russia. Biggest temperature range. From −70°C to 37°C.

World climates

The world is divided into different **types of climate**. They are:

- **Polar** – Constantly cold; the land and sea are covered by thick ice sheets.

- **Temperate** – Changeable weather, with warm dry summers and mild winters.

- **Subtropical** – Warm, with alternate dry and rainy seasons.

- **Tropical** – Constant hot temperatures and no seasonal changes except for amount of rainfall.

Seasons

The **seasons** are caused by the **Earth's orbit**. For a few months each year half the Earth is tilted towards the Sun and gets strong heat rays, whilst the other half is tilted away and gets weak rays.

The position is gradually reversed through the year. When it is **summer** in one hemisphere it is **winter** in the other. In **autumn** and **spring** the two hemispheres are an equal distance from the rays.

Autumn in S. hemisphere

Spring in N. hemisphere

Summer in S. hemisphere
Winter in N. hemisphere

Summer in N. hemisphere
Winter in S. hemisphere

Autumn in N. hemisphere

Spring in S. hemisphere

- The land around the Equator gets heavy seasonal rains called monsoons, followed by a dry season. Farmers depend on the monsoon rains to grow their crops. If the rains do not arrive on time it can be disastrous for food production.

Strange but true

- Some Malayan houses are built on stilts to avoid the monsoon floods.

- From AD 1000 to AD 1200 the Earth's temperature rose. Some Arctic ice melted.

- From 1400 to 1850 the Earth had a mini ice age. Temperatures were 2 to 4°C lower than today.

- Some scientists think the climate is warming, but a few think it is cooling down.

Plant Life

There are more than 335,000 known **plant species**. They are vital to life on Earth because they produce the oxygen that animals need in order to survive.

Plants grow in most parts of the world. The type of **vegetation** that grows in a particular place depends on the **climate** and the type of **soil** there is to be found in the area.

Food-making

Many plants make their own **food**. In the process they create oxygen and use up **carbon dioxide**.

● Most plants contain a green substance called chlorophyll, which absorbs sunlight. The plants use this energy to make their own food.

● When a plant makes food it mixes carbon dioxide from the air with minerals and water from the soil. The process is called photosynthesis.

● During photosynthesis plants make oxygen and pass it into the air. Animals rely on this oxygen supply.

● When animals breathe they give out carbon dioxide. Plants rely on this supply for making their food.

Flowering plants

Many plants grow from **seeds**, and in order for a new plant seed to grow, a tiny **pollen grain** containing a male cell must join with a female cell inside an **ovule**. Some plants produce **flowers** and these contain pollen and ovules.

● Some flowers contain sweet nectar which insects feed on. When an insect visits a flower, tiny pollen grains brush onto its coat. It carries them to the next flower it visits and they join together with the ovules in the new flower.

● Some flowering plants, such as grasses, do not attract insects. Instead they rely on the wind to blow their pollen to other plants.

● After a plant is pollinated, it begins to grow seeds. The seeds eventually drop to the ground. If the weather and the soil conditions are right, they grow into new plants.

Strange but true

● The desert baobab tree can store up to 1000 litres of water in its trunk.

● The oldest living tree is a Californian bristlecone pine named 'Methuselah'. It is about 4600 years old.

● Bamboo can grow up to 91 cm a day.

● There were no grasses in the age of the dinosaurs – only ferns, conifers and cycad plants.

Rubber trees – the sap is used to make rubber.

 Conifers – the trunks are used to make paper.

 Cotton plants – the fluffy seeds are used to make cotton.

Plants around the world

Botanists divide the Earth into six different regions called **biomes**. Each biome is characterized by particular types of plants that grow there. The main biomes are shown below.

● Tropical rainforests cover about 6% of the Earth. They grow in a belt around the Equator. Because there is so much rain in these areas there is a rich variety of plants, more than in any other region in the world. Jungle trees are evergreen, which means they don't shed their leaves.

● In temperate regions there are forests of bushy-shaped broad-leaved trees. These are deciduous, which means they shed their leaves in autumn and grow new ones in spring.

● North of the temperate forests there is a huge belt of coniferous forest which covers ¼ of the Earth. Coniferous trees are good at surviving the cold well. They have tough waxy evergreen needles instead of broad leaves.

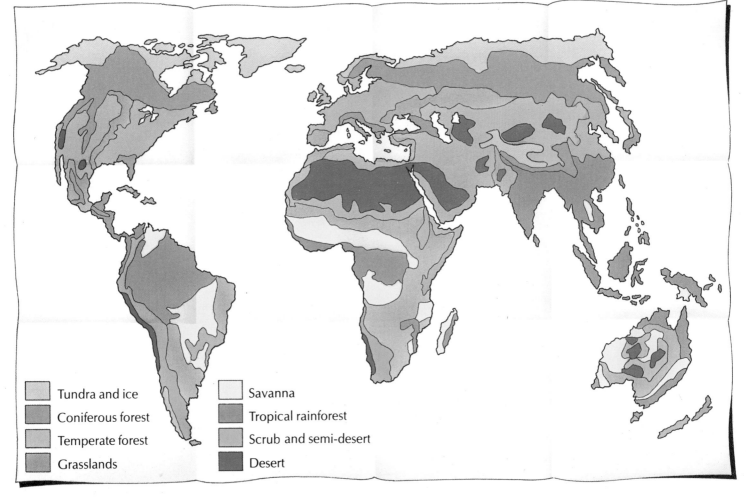

Tundra and ice
Coniferous forest
Temperate forest
Grasslands
Savanna
Tropical rainforest
Scrub and semi-desert
Desert

● North of the coniferous forests lies the tundra, an area where the ground is permanently frozen a few centimetres beneath the surface. There isn't enough soil for large trees to grow here. Instead there are carpets of moss and tiny flowers.

● Grasslands are areas where it is too dry for forests to grow but there is enough rain to stop the land being a desert. Carpets of tough grass grow here, weathering warm summers and cold winters. Grasslands near the Equator are called Savanna.

● A fifth of the Earth's surface is desert, where there is little or no rainfall. Plants which grow here must be able to survive in drought conditions. Many of them have waterproof leaves and thick rubbery flesh for storing moisture.

Rainforests

Bananas

Rainforests are dense jungles that grow in areas of **heavy rainfall** around the **Equator**. They are found in West Africa, Southeast Asia, South America and the islands of the western Pacific.

Rainforests of the world

Rainforests provide a home for the widest variety of animals and plants to be found anywhere in the world. For instance, in just one small area of the **Amazon** rainforest in South America there are likely to be hundreds of different kinds of trees and animals.

Rainforest layers

Different types of **animals** and **plants** are found living at different heights in rainforest trees.

- Extra-tall trees called emergents grow above the rest of the jungle at heights between 45 metres and 60 metres. Giant eagles nest in them.

- Lots of animals live in the canopy. This layer grows from about 30 metres to 45 metres high. It is rich in flowers and fruit.

- Rope-like plants called lianas grow up the tree trunks. Animals hang on to them to swing between branches.

- Small saplings and shrubs form the understorey layer, rising to about 10 metres high.

- On the ground there is a thin layer of rotting leaves and vegetation called 'leaf litter'. It provides a home for many insects and fungi.

- The trees spread their roots out near the surface to gather all the food and moisture they can. Some of them grow big flat buttress roots to support their weight.

Rainforest plants

- Rainforest trees flower at different times. Many of them have bright petals and sweet nectar to attract birds and insects to pollinate them (see p32).

- In some rainforests hummingbirds feed on the nectar from flowers. They hover in front of a flower, beating their wings so fast that they make a humming noise. They dip their beaks into each bloom and suck out the nectar with their tongues.

- Many different plants festoon themselves around the forest trees, dangling their roots in the air to pick up moisture.

Rainforest animals

Mammals, **birds**, **fish**, **insects**, **amphibians** and **reptiles** can all be found in the rainforests.

Jaguar

- Rainforest mammals include tree-living cats such as jaguars and margays.

- Jungle reptiles include lizards and snakes of all sorts and sizes.

Anaconda

- Jungle insects include ants, butterflies, termites and beetles of all different kinds.

- Some jungle leaves collect pools of water that attract many kinds of tree frog. Most tree frogs have suckers on their hands and feet to anchor them securely to branches.

Tree frog

- Bright macaws, parrots and toucans are just a few of the birds that nest in the jungle canopy.

Macaw

- Monkeys of all kinds swing from the jungle trees. Most South American monkeys have prehensile tails which they can use as an extra hand to grab onto things.

- Rainforests have rivers teeming with fish. The Amazon river is home to the ferocious piranha.

Piranha

Strange but true

- The goliath beetle is found in African jungles. It grows up to 14 cm long and when it flies it sounds like a small aircraft.

- Amazon army ants sometimes travel in groups up to 20 million strong. They destroy and eat everything in their path.

- Gibbon monkeys look acrobatic, but in fact many of them suffer from broken limbs through falling.

Jungle people

The **people** who live in rainforests are usually grouped in small **tribes**.

- Most rainforest people survive by hunting for meat and gathering plants. They have a great knowledge of the rainforests and know exactly where to find food supplies.

- The traditional livelihoods of the rainforest Indians are increasingly threatened by forest clearing and mining projects. International efforts are being made to help them survive.

Deserts

Deserts are places where less than 25 cm of rain falls per year. Food and water are difficult to find in these inhospitable regions.

There are lots of different types of **desert landscape**, ranging from sand dunes to rocky plains and mountains.

Deserts occur for several reasons. Some deserts are so far from the sea that by the time wind reaches them all the moisture in the air has gone.

Some deserts are dry because they are near mountains. All the moisture in the air falls as rain and snow on the mountain tops, before it reaches the desert on the other side.

Deserts of the world

The world's main **desert areas** are shown below:

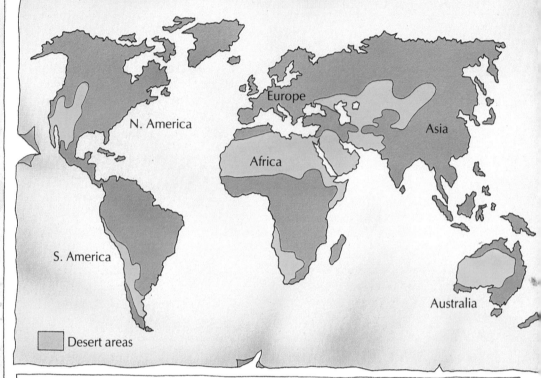

Europe

N. America

Asia

Africa

S. America

Australia

Desert areas

Desert plants

Desert plants are adapted to drought:

● They gather water through their roots, which either spread out near the surface to soak up dew or grow deep down to moist soil layers.

● Some cacti have pleated skins that stretch so they can store water.

● The biggest cactus is the saguaro, found in the Sonoran Desert in south-west USA. It can grow 15 metres high.

● Many desert plants only flower and seed themselves when rains come. The plant seeds then lie in the ground for years until the next rain shower comes along.

Desert flower

Saguaro cactus

● Desert plants often have bright beautiful flowers that only appear for a short time after rain has fallen. They don't live long, so they must attract pollinating insects quickly. That is why their petals are so colourful.

• North American deserts have rocky plains, deep ravines, salt lakes and canyons. The hottest place is Death Valley, California, where temperatures can reach over 56°C.

• The North African Sahara is the world's biggest desert, covering an area almost the size of the USA. Most of it is rocky. Only about a tenth of it is covered in sand dunes.

• A belt of desert stretches down the west coast of South America. It includes the Atacama Desert in Chile, the driest place in the world. Droughts there last for hundreds of years.

• Most of the centre of Australia is a barren desert plain called the 'Outback', dotted with rocky outcrops such as the famous Ayers Rock.

Ayers Rock

• The Arabian Desert is partly a sea of sand with dunes up to 240 m high. Bedouin tribes travel the desert, camping in tents wherever they stop.

• The Gobi Desert in Central Asia has hot summers and severe winters. The people who live there are nomads. They spend their lives travelling the barren, rocky land in search of grazing for their yak herds.

Yak and tribesman

• The Kalahari Desert in Southern Africa is on a huge plateau. In the middle there is a sea of red sand dunes. The Kalahari bushmen hunt and gather food from this wilderness.

Kalahari bushman

Desert animals

Desert animals usually shelter during the heat of the day and come out when the temperature drops in the evening. They get the moisture they need from eating plants or other creatures.

• Most desert spiders do not build webs. Instead they hunt for food. The camel spider is one of the largest desert specimens. It spans up to 15 cm.

• Camels can survive for many days without water. Their nostrils can close up to keep out the dust.

• Desert reptiles include all sorts of snakes and lizards. They stay in the shade when they can.

Strange but true

• Prehistoric paintings show the Sahara as fertile land.

• The first white explorers of the Australian Outback took a boat with them. They were looking for a fabled lake.

• In Saudi Arabia there are solar-powered pay phones in the desert.

• Desert ostriches sometimes eat sand, probably to help their digestion.

Polar Regions

The Arctic and the **Antarctic** are the coldest regions in the world.

The Arctic is the area within the **Arctic Circle**, an imaginary line going around the North Pole. The **Arctic Ocean** is in the middle, mostly covered by ice. Around the edge there is a belt of **tundra** (see p33).

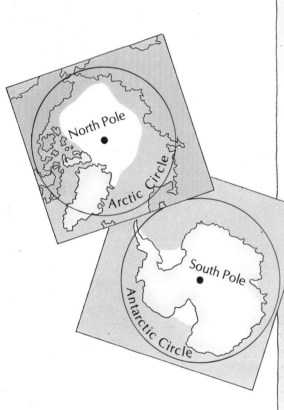

Antarctica is a continent surrounding the South Pole and includes the Antarctic Sea. It covers over 9% of the Earth's surface. Most of the Antarctic land is covered by a thick sheet of ice. Wildlife is found only around the coasts and on outlying islands, where the temperature is warmer than it is inland.

The Arctic

For most of the year the Arctic **tundra** is covered in snow. In the brief summer months the snow melts, but it cannot drain away because under the land surface there is a permanently frozen layer of earth called **permafrost**. Instead the water gathers in lakes, pools and bogs.

- Sometimes the wind whips up the Arctic snow and causes 'white outs' which are rather like sandstorms in the desert. White outs can start suddenly and last for days.

- Most Arctic animals are to be found on the tundra. They arrive in summer and migrate south or hibernate underground in winter.

- Tundra plants are small. They grow near the ground to avoid the biting winds and cold temperatures. Some of them have hairy stems that help to keep them warm.

The Antarctic

Antarctica is the **coldest** and **windiest** place on Earth. Its ice sheets hold a large amount of the Earth's permanent ice. In Antarctica:

- The tops of high mountains only just peek above the ice, which is up to 4 km thick in parts.

- The world's biggest icebergs, up to 100 km wide, break off from the coastal ice shelf and drift far out to sea. This process of breaking off is called 'calving'.

- Some areas of coastal land are exposed in summer. Algae and lichen grow here, but there are hardly any other plants.

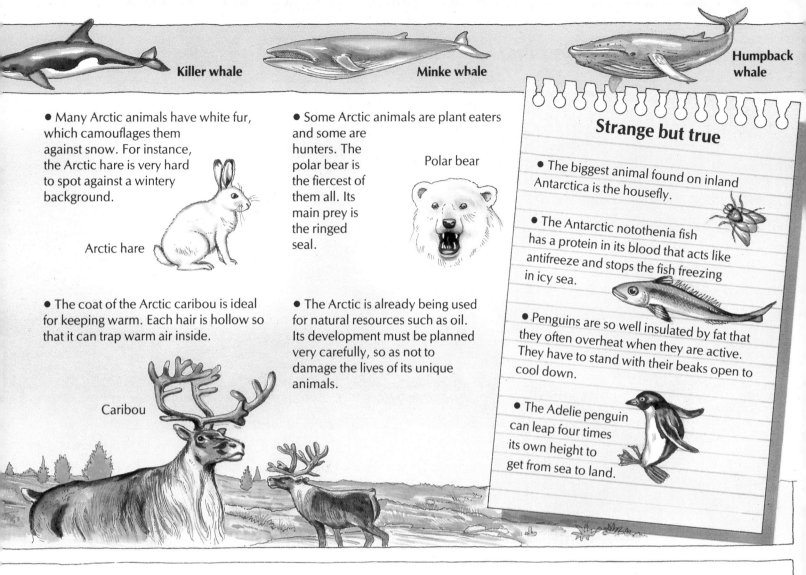

Killer whale

Minke whale

Humpback whale

- Many Arctic animals have white fur, which camouflages them against snow. For instance, the Arctic hare is very hard to spot against a wintery background.

Arctic hare

- Some Arctic animals are plant eaters and some are hunters. The polar bear is the fiercest of them all. Its main prey is the ringed seal.

Polar bear

- The coat of the Arctic caribou is ideal for keeping warm. Each hair is hollow so that it can trap warm air inside.

- The Arctic is already being used for natural resources such as oil. Its development must be planned very carefully, so as not to damage the lives of its unique animals.

Caribou

Strange but true

- The biggest animal found on inland Antarctica is the housefly.

- The Antarctic notothenia fish has a protein in its blood that acts like antifreeze and stops the fish freezing in icy sea.

- Penguins are so well insulated by fat that they often overheat when they are active. They have to stand with their beaks open to cool down.

- The Adelie penguin can leap four times its own height to get from sea to land.

Life in the Antarctic

- Tiny mites are found in parts of the Antarctic where no other creatures could survive. The mites can live at temperatures below −60°C.

Mite

- Nearly all the birds that visit the Antarctic coast are seabirds.

- Twelve species of whale visit the area, including the mighty blue whale, the biggest animal on Earth.

- Many Antarctic animals feed on tiny floating animals and plants called plankton. Plankton animals, called zooplankton, gather in shoals off the coast.

- The Antarctic may be rich in oil and minerals deep beneath the surface. Conservationists are trying to limit drilling and mining because of the damage it would do to the environment.

Blue whale

Albatross

Petrel

Emperor penguin

Skua

- Six species of seal live around the coast. They spend most of their time in the water but they go on land to breed.

Elephant seal

Saving the Earth

The Earth's rivers, seas and soil are threatened by **pollution**. It even affects the air we breathe. Scientists have realized that pollution is getting worse and that the whole planet will be seriously harmed unless something is done quickly to limit the damage.

Climate alert

Carbon dioxide (CO2) in the atmosphere traps some of the Sun's heat. The level of carbon dioxide has been rising so much through pollution that the Earth's **climate** may warm up as a result. Global warming is increased by:

● Dirty fumes from car exhausts, factories and power stations.

● Burning or cutting down forests. The burning releases fumes and the destruction of plants means that less CO_2 is taken out of the atmosphere.

● CFCs, which are chemicals used in some aerosols, fridges and air-conditioning systems. They destroy the ozone layer which protects us from harmful ultra-violet rays (see p.25).

Forest alert

It is estimated that **1 sq km of rainforest** is destroyed every 2.5 minutes. If this continues, the rainforests will disappear by the year 2050. The destruction of the rainforest is caused by:

● People clearing vast areas to graze their cattle herds.

● Flooding caused by hydro-electric dams being built across rivers.

● Chopping down hardwood trees to make products such as mahogany furniture.

Strange but true

● The USA uses 29% of the world's petrol and 33% of the world's electricity.

● Some Chinese farmers use flocks of ducks instead of pesticides to kill harmful insects.

● The industrial complex of Cubatao in Brazil is known as the Valley of Death because its pollution has destroyed the trees and rivers nearby.

Water alert

The world's **rivers** and **oceans** are gradually becoming more polluted. The pollution is caused by:

● Factories discharging polluted waste straight into rivers and seas.

● Oil leaking into the sea from ships and oil terminals.

● Artificial fertilizer and pesticide chemicals washed into the water supply by rainfall.

Buy environment-friendly products.

Make sure your family uses unleaded petrol.

Climate action

People are trying to reduce global warming by:

- Fitting industrial chimneys with filters that clean up waste fumes.

- Fitting catalytic converters to cars to clean up exhaust fumes.

- Recycling as many products as possible, such as glass, aluminium cans and paper.

- Developing new fuels to replace petrol.

- Phasing out the use of CFCs.

- Trying to stop the destruction of the world's forests.

Forest action

People are trying to save the rainforests by:

- Passing international laws to limit their destruction.

- Offering financial help through governments to countries where there are rainforests, to persuade them to stop cutting down the trees.

- Refusing to buy rainforest hardwood products such as mahogany.

Water action

People are trying to cut down water pollution by:

- Making it illegal for factories to dump untreated waste and for farmers to use dangerous chemicals.

- Finding more effective ways of getting rid of oil slicks.

Earth Facts and Lists

The Earth in Space

● The average distance between the Earth and the Moon is 384,365 km.

● Light from the Sun takes about 8 minutes to reach the Earth.

● The Earth's nearest star, apart from the Sun, is Proxima Centauri.

● It would take more than four light years to reach Proxima Centauri from Earth.

● The average speed of the Earth in orbit is 29.8 km per second.

● The Earth's density is 5.517 times the density of water.

● The Earth tilts on its axis at an angle of 23.5°.

● The light we see from the Moon at night does not really come from the Moon itself. What we see is light from the Sun shining onto the Moon's surface.

The Earth from birth

● If history up to AD 1 was squashed into a scale of one year, with the Earth's birth on 1 January, the first life on Earth wouldn't begin until the end of March.

● The first dinosaurs would appear in the middle of December.

● The first people would emerge only a few hours before the end of the year.

The Earth's surface

● The Earth's total surface area is 510,100,000 sq km.

● The total land area of the Earth is 148,800,000 sq km.

● If you were to jog round the Earth without stopping it would take you about 6 months.

Largest countries

The ten largest countries:

Country	Size
Russia	17,075,400 sq km
Canada	9,976,139 sq km
China	9,561,000 sq km
USA	9,363,123 sq km
Brazil	8,511,965 sq km
Australia	7,682,300 sq km
India	3,287,590 sq km
Argentina	2,776,889 sq km
Sudan	2,505,813 sq km
Algeria	2,381,741 sq km

Islands

The world's largest islands and their areas:

Island	Area
Greenland	2,176,000 sq km
New Guinea	792,500 sq km
Borneo	725,450 sq km
Madagascar	590,000 sq km
Baffin Island	476,065 sq km
Sumatra	473,600 sq km
Honshu	228,000 sq km
Great Britain	218,041 sq km
Victoria Island	212,197 sq km
Ellesmere Island	196,236 sq km

Peninsulas

A peninsula is a piece of land with water on three sides. These are the world's largest:

Peninsula	Area
Arabia	3,250,000 sq km
Southern India	2,072,000 sq km
Alaska	1,500,000 sq km
Labrador	1,300,000 sq km
Scandinavia	800,000 sq km
Iberian Peninsula	584,000 sq km

Volcanoes

Here are the ten most active volcanoes:

Volcano	Height	Country
Antofalla	6450 m	Argentina
Guallatiri	6060 m	Argentina/Chile
Cotopaxi	5897 m	Ecuador
Sangay	5320 m	Ecuador
Kluchevskaya	4850 m	Russia
Wrangell	4269 m	Alaska
Mauna Loa	4171 m	Hawaii, USA
Galeras	4083 m	Ecuador
Cameroun	4070 m	Cameroon
Acatenango	3959 m	Guatemala

● Toba in north-central Sumatra has the largest volcanic crater, with an area of 1775 sq km.

● When Laki in Iceland erupted in 1783, its lava flow stretched 65 km, the longest ever recorded.

● There are over 500 active volcanoes in the world.

● About 20 per cent of all volcanoes are underwater.

● Lava from an erupting volcano may be as hot as 1200°C.

● When Mount Tolbachik in Russia erupted, lava poured out at more than 100 metres per second.

● One eruption from Mauna Loa (in Hawaii) lasted 1½ years.

● The loudest noise ever known was produced by a volcanic eruption at Krakatoa, near Java, in 1883. The sound was heard in Australia, 5000 km away.

● The highest volcano, Cerro Aconcagua (6960 metres), is in the Andes. It is now extinct.

● Lava can take years to cool down.

Mountains

● About 25 per cent of all land is more than 900 metres above sea level.

● The further up a mountain you go, the colder the air becomes. The temperature drops by 2°C for every 300 metres you climb.

● Tibet is the highest country in the world. Its average height above sea level is 4500 metres.

● Some of the oldest mountains in the world are the Highlands in Scotland. They are estimated to be about 400 million years old.

Highest mountains

Here are the seven continents and their highest mountains:

Continent	Mountain	Height
Africa	Kilimanjaro	5895 m
Antarctica	Vinson Massif	5140 m
Asia	Everest	8848 m
Australia	Kosciusko	2228 m
North America	McKinley	6194 m
South America	Aconcagua	6960 m
Europe	Elbrus	5633 m

Longest ranges

Here are some of the longest mountain ranges:

Mountain range	Length	Country
Andes	7240 km	South America
Rockies	6030 km	North America
Himalayas	3860 km	Asia
Great Dividing Range	3620 km	Australia
Trans-Antarctic	3540 km	Antarctica

Glaciers

These are the longest glaciers:

Glacier	Length	Country
Lambert Fisher Ice Passage	515 km	Antarctica
Novaya Zemlya	418 km	Russia
Arctic Institute Ice Passage	362 km	Antarctica
Nimrod/ Lennox/ King Ice Passage	289 km	Antarctica
Denman Glacier	241 km	Antarctica
Beardmore Glacier	225 km	Antarctica
Recovery Glacier	225 km	Antarctica
Petermanns Gletscher	200 km	Greenland
Unnamed Glacier	193 km	Antarctica

Rivers and Lakes

● The highest lakes are in the Himalayan mountains, but the highest navigable lake is Lake Titicaca in the Andes, which is 3811 metres above sea level.

● The deepest lake is Lake Baykal in Russia. At its deepest point it is almost 2 km deep.

● Fresh water from the River Amazon can be found up to 180 km out to sea.

● The muddiest river is the Hwang He, or Yellow River, in China.

● The largest swamp is in the basin of the Pripyat River in Belarus. It covers an area of 46,950 sq km.

Lakes

Some of the largest lakes in the world:

Lake	Area	Country
Caspian Sea	371,800 sq km	Europe/Iran
Superior	82,350 sq km	Canada/USA
Victoria	69,500 sq km	E. Africa
Huron	59,600 sq km	Canada/USA
Michigan	58,000 sq km	USA
Aral Sea	40,100 sq km	Kazakhstan/Uzbekistan
Tanganyika	32,900 sq km	Africa
Great Bear	31,800 sq km	Canada
Baykal	30,500 sq km	Russia
Malawi	29,600 sq km	E. Africa

Rivers

Here are the ten longest rivers:

River	Length	Location
Nile	6695 km	Africa
Amazon	6570 km	South America
Mississippi/ Missouri	6020 km	North America
Yenisey/Angara	5540 km	Russia
Yangtze	5530 km	Asia
Ob/Irytsh	5410 km	Asia
Huang He	4840 km	Asia
Zaire	4630 km	Africa
Parana	4500 km	South America
Amur	4416 km	Asia

Earthquakes

The strongest earthquakes recorded are:

Date	Country	Strength on Richter Scale
1906	Ecuador	8.6
1920	China	8.5
1957	Aleutian Islands	7.75
1960	Chile	8.3
1964	Alaska	8.4

Some of the most disastrous earthquakes:

Date	Country	Number of people killed
1556	China	830,000
1775	Portugal	60,000
1908	Italy	160,000
1976	China	700,000
1978	Iran	25,000
1988	Armenia	25,000

Earth Facts and Lists

Waterfalls

These are some of the largest waterfalls and the countries they are in:

Waterfall	Total height	Country
Angel	979 m	Venezuela
Tugela	947 m	South Africa
Utigard	800 m	Norway
Mongefossen	774 m	Norway
Yosemite	739 m	USA
Ostre Mardola Foss	656 m	Norway
Tyssestrengane	646 m	Norway
Cuquenan	610 m	Venezuela
Sutherland	580 m	New Zealand
Kjellfossen	561 m	Norway

Oceans

● The oceans make up 97 per cent of the Earth's water.

● Most of an iceberg is hidden underwater. Only 10 per cent of it floats above the surface.

● The greatest difference in tides is in the Bay of Fundy in Canada. The difference between low tide and high tide is about 16.5 metres.

● The highest underwater mountain is in the ocean between Samoa and New Zealand. Its summit is 8690 metres above the seabed.

● The White Sea, in Russia, has the lowest temperature, only –2°C.

● The Persian Gulf is the warmest sea. In the summer its temperature reaches 35.6°C.

● The most salty sea in the world is the Dead Sea, in the Middle East.

Coastlines

● The total length of all of Earth's coastlines is more than 500,000 km – the equivalent of over 12 times round the world.

● There are 40 countries that have no coastline at all.

● Hudson's Bay in Canada is the largest bay in the world.

Polar regions

● About 10 per cent of all land on Earth is covered in ice.

● Icebergs can float at about 2.5 km/h, with the help of a strong wind.

● The tallest iceberg ever seen measured 167.6 metres high. It was spotted near Greenland.

● On the tundra only one type of tree grows – the dwarf willow tree. It grows to a maximum height of 10 cm.

● About 75 per cent of all the fresh water on Earth is contained in frozen glaciers.

● People in Greenland live only on the coasts, because most of the country is covered in an ice sheet.

The ice sheet in Greenland:

● is 1.6 km thick.
● covers almost 1.5 million sq km.
● has an average temperature of −20°C.

The Antarctic ice sheet:

● is 3-4 km thick.
● covers 13 million sq.km.
● has temperatures as low as −70°C.

The Arctic Ocean:

● has about 12,000,000 sq km of floating ice.
● has an average depth of 1500 metres.
● has the coldest winter temperature of −34°C.

● There is no land at all at the North Pole, only ice on top of sea.

● There is six months of light followed by six months of darkness at the Poles.

Deserts

● About 120,000 sq km of new desert is formed a year because of human activity.

● Snow has been known to fall in the Sahara Desert.

Here are some of the world's largest deserts:

Desert	Country	Area
Sahara	North Africa	8,400,000 sq.km
Gobi	Mongolia	1,295,000 sq.km
Gibson	Western Australia	647,500 sq.km
Great Victoria	Western/ Southern Australia	647,500 sq.km
Rub al Khali	Southern Arabia	587,500 sq.km
Kalahari	Southern Africa	562,500 sq.km

● Only about 15 per cent of the world's desert areas are sandy.

● Sand dunes can be as high as 400 metres.

Here are some of the worst droughts in history:

Year	Country	Estimated number of people killed
1333-37	China	over 4 million
1769-70	India	3-10 million
1837-38	India	800,000
1865-66	India	10 million
1876-78	India	3.5 million
1876-79	China	9-13 million
1891-92	Russia	400,000
1892-94	China	1 million
1896-97	India	5 million
1899-1900	India	1 million

Weather

● Lightning travels at speeds of up to 1500 km per second as it strikes down. It moves even faster as it travels back up again.

● The air in the path of lightning can reach temperatures of 30,000°C.

● A tornado can travel at 50 km/h.

● The winds at the edge of a tornado spin fastest – more than 700 km/h.

● Each year more than 16 million thunderstorms occur.

Here are some of the worst recent natural disasters:

● 1906 – A typhoon killed 50,000 people in Hong Kong.

● 1955 – In the USA, 200 people were killed by a hurricane.

● 1962 – An avalanche in Peru killed 3000 people.

● 1970 – In Bangladesh a cyclone and tidal waves killed 1,000,000 people.

● 1975 – Lightning in Zimbabwe killed 21 people.

Here are some of the world's most rainy places:

● Cherrapunji in India has an annual rainfall of 11,430 mm.

● In Debundsehsa in the Cameroon 10,277 mm of rain falls each year.

● Quibdo in Colombia is only slightly drier with 8991 mm.

Plant life

● The largest tree in the world is a giant sequoia growing in California. It is 84 metres tall and measures 29 metres round the trunk.

● The fastest-growing tree is the eucalyptus. It can grow 10 metres a year.

● The world's oldest trees are the bristlecone pines of California. One of them is about 4600 years old.

● The largest flower comes from the rafflesia plant. The flower can weigh 6 kg and grow to a width of 91 cm.

Here are some of the most heavily forested countries:

Country	% of country's total area covered by forest
Surinam	92
Solomon Islands	91
Papua New Guinea	84
Guyana	83
French Guiana	82
Gabon	78
Finland	76
Cambodia	75
North Korea	74
Bhutan	70

● Rice is the only grass that can grow in water.

● The tallest type of grass is bamboo. It can grow up to about 30 metres high.

● The saguaro is the tallest kind of cactus. It can grow to about 16 metres high.

Here are five different types of cereal:

● Barley
● Maize
● Oats
● Rye
● Wheat

Here are five types of coniferous trees (i.e. they produce cones):

● Cedar
● Douglas fir
● Larch
● Pine
● Spruce

Forests

● Some medicines are made from forest trees. For instance, quinine, which is used to treat malaria, comes originally from a chemical found in the bark of the cinchona tree.

● Only 1 per cent of sunlight reaches the rainforest floor.

● The USA, Russia, China and Malaysia are among the top producers of hardwood.

Here are five types of deciduous trees (i.e. they lose their leaves in autumn):

● Ash   ● Maple
● Birch   ● Oak
● Chestnut

● Lianas are strong rope-like rainforest plants. They can grow to a width of 2 metres and are strong enough to swing on.

● The largest forest in the world covers parts of Scandinavia and northern Russia and has a total area of over 9 million sq km.

Saving the Earth

● Scientists estimate that the Earth's average temperature could rise by as much as 2-4°C by the year 2030.

● If the Earth's temperature does rise, the ice sheets could melt and flood many coastal regions.

● Over 4 million cars in Brazil are now running on gasohol instead of petrol. Gasohol is a fuel made from sugar cane.

INDEX

Indexes to other sections
are on pages 94, 142 and 190.

abyssal plain 20—1
Aconcagua 43
Africa
    area 9
    formation of continent 9
    lakes 43
    mountains 43
    rivers 43
    shape 9
    see also North Africa; South
    Africa; Southern Africa
aftershocks 14
air 4, 5, 25
    dryness 36
    polluted 40
    pressure 24
aircraft, air pressure 24
air masses 27
air roots 34
Alaska
    area 42
    earthquakes 43
    volcanoes 42
albatross 39
algae 6, 7
    in Antarctic 38
Algeria, size 42
Alps, earthquakes 14
Amazon, River 19, 43
    fish 35
    life 34
amber 7
amino acids 6
amphibians 6, 35
    rainforest 35
anacondas 35
ancient Chinese 28
Ancient Egypt, gods 24
Ancient Greeks, beliefs about the
    stars 5
Andes 43
    lakes 43
    mountains 17
anemometers 25
Angel Falls, Venezuela 19, 44
animals 6, 34, 37
    desert 37
    dinosaurs 7
    Polar regions 39
    rainforests 34, 35
    sensitive to earth tremors 15
Antarctica 38—9
    coldest place on Earth 30
    drilling and mining 39
    formation of continent 9
    glaciers 43
    ice sheet 44
    mountains 43
    plants 38
    shape 9
    southernmost land 8
    summer 30
    wildlife 38
    windiest place 24, 38
    see also Polar regions; South
    Pole
ants 35
Arabia
    area 42
    deserts 37, 44
Archeozoic Era 6
arches 22
Arctic 38—9
    animals 38, 39
    fossils 9

see also North Pole; Polar
    regions
Arctic Circle 38
Arctic hares 39
Arctic Ocean 20, 21, 44
Arctic Sea 38
Argentina
    size 42
    volcanoes 42
army ants 35
Asia
    area 8
    formation of continent 9
    mountains 43
    rainforests 34
    rivers 43
Atacama Desert, Chile 27, 37
Atlantic Ocean 20, 21
atmosphere 24
    layers 25
    pollution 40
Australasia, mountains 43
Australia
    desert 37, 44
    exploration 37
    formation of continent 9
    Great Barrier Reef 20
    hurricanes 29
    size 42
autumn 30, 31
avalanches 14
    Peru 45
axis of Earth 5
Ayers Rock, Australia 37

bacteria 6
Baffin Island, area 42
baguios 29
bamboo 32, 45
bananas 34
Bangladesh
    cyclones 45
    hailstones 27
    river deltas 19
baobab tree 32
Barbados, beaches 22
barrier reefs 20
Baykal, Lake 18, 43
bays 44
beaches 22
Beaufort Scale 24
Beaver Lake, USA 19
beavers, dams 19
bedding planes 23
Bedouin people 37
beetles 35
Bermuda Islands, beaches 22
Bhutan, forests 45
biomes 33
birds 6, 18, 35
    Antarctic 39
    flight 25
    marsh 23
    rainforest 34, 35
blowholes 22
blue whales 39
Borneo, area 42
Bosumtwi, Lake 19
Brachiosaurus 7
Brahmaputra, River 19
Brazil
    cars run on gasohol 45
    pollution 40
    size 42
Brunei, lowest mountain 17
Burma
    rubies 11
    sapphires 11
bushmen of Kalahari 37
butterflies 35

cactus 36, 45
    biggest 36
calving 38
Cambodia, forests 45
camels 37
Cameroon
    rainfall 45
    volcanoes 42
Canada
    Hudson's Bay 44
    lakes 18, 43
    size 44
    tides 44
carbon dioxide 32, 40
caribou 39
cars run on gasohol in Brazil 45
cashews 35
Caspian Sea 43
cave paintings 37
caves 22
cells 6
Cenozoic Era 6
cereals 45
CFCs 40, 41
chemicals leaching into water
    supply 40
Chile
    deserts 37
    driest place 27, 37
    earthquakes 43
    volcanoes 42
China
    drought 44
    earthquakes 15
    hardwood producer 45
    size 42
chlorophyll 32
cities, effect on climate 30
cliffs 22, 23
climate 30-1
    pollution 40, 41
    reduce pollution 41
    vegetation 32
    warming 31
    world 31
    see also weather
clouds 27, 28
cloves 35
coal 11
coastlines 22—3, 44
cockleshells 23
cocoa 35
coldest place on Earth 30
cold spots 30
Colombia
    emeralds 11
    rainfall 45
colours of the sky 24
Commonwealth Bay 24
coniferous trees 17, 32, 33, 45
continental climate 30
continental crust 10
continental shelf 20
continents 8, 9
coral atolls 20
coral reefs 20
corals 7
cotton plants 33
countries 42
crabs 29
currents 21
cycad plants 32
cyclones, Bangladesh 45

dams 19
darkness, Polar regions 44
daylight, Polar regions 44
Dead Sea 44
Death Valley, USA 37
deciduous trees 17, 33, 45
deltas 19

deserts 36, 36—7, 44
    animals 37
    biggest 37
    plants 33, 36
dew 27
Dhaulagiri, Mount 17
diamonds 10, 11
    Namibia 22
dinosaurs 7, 10, 11, 42
    biggest 6
    extinction 7
    food 32
Diplodocus 7
disasters
    avalanches 45
    cyclones 45
    droughts 44
    earthquakes 43
    hurricanes 29, 45
    lightning 45
    typhoons 45
dogs 15
domes 12
dragons 6, 28
driest place on Earth 27, 37
drilling, in Antarctic 39
droughts 44
    Chile 27, 37
    plants 33, 36
ducks as pesticides 40

Earth 4—5, 42—3
    age 6
    axis 42
    circumference 4
    crust 8—9, 10, 11
    density 42
    first life 6—7, 42
    flat 5
    formation 6
    inner core 10, 11
    land area 42
    life requirements 4—5
    mantle 10, 11
    movement of plates 8, 9, 12,
    14, 16, 20
    orbit round the Sun 5, 31, 42
    outer core 10, 11
    pollution 40
    saving 45
    size compared to Sun 4
    surface area 42
    temperature rise 31, 45
    weight 4, 5
earthquakes 8, 14—15, 43
    areas 14
    buildings 14
    measuring 15
    prediction 15
    shockwaves 10, 14
Ecuador
    earthquakes 43
    volcanoes 42
Elbrus, Mount 43
electricity 40
Ellesmore Island, area 42
ellipse of the Earth 5
emeralds 11
environment friendly products 41
epicentre of earthquake 14
Equator 4, 31, 33, 34
estuaries 19, 23
Ethiopia, hottest place on Earth 31
Europe
    formation of continent 9
    mountains 43
    size 9
    summer 30
evaporation of water 26, 27
Everest, Mount 8, 16, 17, 43
evergreen trees 33

evolution 7
exhaust fumes 40, 41
exosphere 25

fault lines 14
ferns 32
Finland, forests 45
fires 14
fish 6, 18, 21, 35
    Antarctic 39
    showers 29
flooding 40
flowers 32, 33, 34
    largest 45
focus of earthquake 14
fog 26
foreshocks 15
forests 45
    burning down 40
    clearing 35
    largest 45
    plants 33
    pollution 40
    reduce pollution 41
    see also trees
fossil fuels 11
fossils 6, 7
    Antarctica 9
French Guiana, forests 45
fringe reefs 20
fumarole 12
fumes 40, 41
fungi 34

Gabon, forests 45
Ganges, River 19
gas 11
gasohol, fuel for cars in Brazil 45
gemstones 10−11
geysers 12
Ghana, lakes 19
giant eagles 34
giants 6
Gibson Desert, area 44
glaciers 17, 43, 44
    melting 18
glacier valley 17
global warming 31, 40, 41
Gobi Desert 37, 44
    area 44
gold, in seawater 21
goliath beetle 35
Gondwanaland 9
gorges 17
granite 10
grasses 32, 45
grasslands 33
gravity, Moon's pull on Earth 20−1
Great Barrier Reef 20
Great Britain, area 42
Great Dividing Range 43
Great Victoria Desert, area 44
Greece
    earthquakes 43
    see also Ancient Greeks
Greenland
    area 8, 42
    fossils 7
    glaciers 43
    ice sheet 44
    people 44
Guadeloupe, rain 27
Guatemala, volcanoes 42
Guyana, forests 45

hailstones 26
    heaviest 27
hammerhead sharks 15
hardwood trees 40
Hawaii

rainiest place 26
    volcanoes 42
Hawaiian Islands, beaches 22
heat and power 11
hemispheres 4
    seasons 31
Herculaneum 13
Himalayas 16−17, 43
    earthquakes 14
    lakes 43
    mountains 17
Hong Kong, typhoon 45
Honshu, area 42
hot spots 30, 31
hot springs 12
hottest place on Earth 31
hottest place in USA 37
housefly 39
Hudson's Bay, Canada 44
hummingbirds 34
humpback whales 39
hurricanes 28, 29
    names 29
    USA 45

Iberian Peninsula, area 42
icebergs 38, 44
    biggest 21
ice crystals 26, 28
Iceland
    geysers 12, 13
    volcanic island 13
    volcanoes 42
ice sheets 38, 44
    melting 45
    thickness 38
igneous rocks 10
    gems 11
India
    droughts 44
    formation of continent 9
    rainfall 45
    river deltas 19
    size 42
Indian Ocean 20, 21
Indo-Pacific, seashells 23
insects 32, 34, 35
    rainforest 35
Iran
    earthquakes 43
    lakes 43
iron 11
islands 42
    formed by volcanic eruption 13
Italy
    earthquakes 43
    volcanoes 13

jaguars 35
Japan, seashells 22−3
jellyfish 6, 7
jungle people 35
Jupiter 4

K2 17
Kalahari Desert 37, 44
    area 44
Kangchenjunga, Mount 17
Kashmir, sapphires 11
Kilimanjaro, Mount 43
killer whales 39
Kosciusko, Mount 43
Krakatoa 13, 42

Labrador, area 43
lakes 18−19, 43
    biggest 18
    deepest 18, 43
    highest 43
Laurasia 9
lava 12, 43

beaches 22
    crushed volcanic stone 12−13
leaf litter 34
lianas 34, 45
lichen, in Antarctic 38
life on earth 4, 6, 42
light 4
lightning 28
    conductors 28
    speed 28
    strikes record 28
    Zimbabwe 45
    see also thunderstorms
light waves 24
limestone 10
limpets 23
liquid droplets 26
lizards 35
    desert 37
lobsters 21
loudest noise 42
lugworms 23

macaws 35
McKinley, Mount 43
Madagascar, area 42
magma 10,
magnesium 11
mahogany 40, 41
Makalu, Mount 17
Malaya, houses on stilts 31
Malaysia, hardwood producer 45
mammals 6, 35
    rainforest 35
manganese 21
mangrove trees 23
marble 10
margays 35
maritime climate 30
marram grasses 23
Mars 4
    volcano crater 13
marshes 23
Mauna Loa 42
meanders 19
medicines, from forest trees 45
Mercalli Scale 15
Mercury 4
mesosphere 25
Mesozoic Era 6
metamorphic rocks 10
Mexico, earthquakes 43
microclimates 30
Middle East, Dead Sea 44
mining
    in Antarctic 39
    in rainforests 35
minke whales 39
Mississippi, River 19, 43
mites, Antarctic 39
molten rocks 10, 11, 12
Mongolia, deserts 44
monkeys 35
monsoons 31
Moon 5
    distance from Earth 42
    gravity 20−1
    light 42
moss 33
mountains 16−17, 43
    air pressure 24
    areas 16
    climate 30
    highest point of land 8
    ranges 16
mudskipper fish 22

Namibia, diamonds 22
Naples 13
neap tide 21
nectar 32, 34

Neptune 4
New Guinea, area 42
New Zealand
    geysers 12
    waterfalls 44
nickel 11
Nile, River 18, 19, 43
noise, loudest 42
nomads 37
North Africa, deserts 37, 44
North America
    area 9
    deserts 37
    formation of continent 9
    mountains 43
    movement away from Europe 9
    rivers 43
North Korea, forests 45
North Pole 4, 44
    northernmost land 8
    snow 26
    see also Arctic; Polar regions
Norway, waterfalls 44

obsidian 10
ocean crust 10
ocean currents, climate 30
Oceania, area 8
oceanic ridge 21
oceans 8, 20−1, 26, 44
    pollution 40
    trenches 20
oil 11
    in Arctic 39
    leaking into sea 40
ostriches 37
Outback, Australia 37
ovules 32
oxbow lakes 19
oxygen 6, 32
oysters 21
ozone layer 25, 40

Pacific Ocean 20
    earthquakes 14
    rainforests of western islands 34
Pacific Ring of Fire 12
Paleozoic Era 6
Pangaea 8, 9
Panthalassa 9
Papua New Guinea, forests 45
parrots 35
penguins 39
peninsulas 42
peppers 35
permafrost 38
Persian Gulf 44
Peru, avalanches 45
petrels 39
petrol 40
photosynthesis 32
pigeons 14
piranhas 35
planets 4, 6
plankton 39
plants 4, 6, 45
    desert 36
    first on Earth 6−7
    fossils 7
    mountains 17
    rainforest 34
    salt tolerant 23
    species 32
plates of the Earth's crust 8, 9, 12, 14, 16, 20
Pluto 4
Polar bears 39
Polar regions 38−9, 44
    climate 31
pollen 32
pollination 32, 34

pollution 40
polyps 20
Pompeii 13
Portugal, earthquakes 43
Pripyat, River 43
prism 24
Proterozoic Era 6
Proxima Centauri 32
pumice 10

radon 15
rainbows 27
rainfall 26−7, 45
   in deserts 36
   heaviest 26
   monsoons 31
rainforests 17, 33, 34−5, 45
   destruction 40
   layers 34
rapids 18
recycling 40−1
reefs 20
reptiles 6, 35
   desert 37
   rainforest 35
rice 32, 45
Richter Scale 15
rivers 17, 18−19, 26, 43
   damming 40
   pollution 40
   shortest 19
   terraces 19
   valleys 17
Rockies 43
rocks 10
Roe, River 19
Rub al Khali Desert, area 44
rubber trees 33
rubies 10, 11
Russia
   biggest temperature range 31
   droughts 44
   earthquakes 43
   forests 45
   glaciers 43
   hardwood producer 45
   lakes 18, 43
   size 42
   volcanoes 42

Sahara Desert 37
   area 44
   snow 44
   sunniest place on Earth 31
saltiness of water 44
salt marshes 23
Salto Angel Falls, Venezuela 19,
   43
San Andreas Fault, USA 14
sand 44
   black 22
dunes 23, 36−7
sandstone 10
sapphires 11
Saturn 4
Saudi Arabia see Arabia
Savanna, plants 33
saving the Earth 40−1
Scandinavia
   area 42
   forests 45
Scotland, mountains 43
scrub 33
sea fog 26
sea level 22
seals 39
seamounts 21
seas 20
   pollution 40
   underwater communities 21
sea shells 22−3

seasons 30, 31
sea water
   gold content 21
   plants 23
   salty 44
   temperature 20, 44
seaweed 21, 23
sedimentary rocks 10
seeds 32
seismographs 15
shale 10
sheet lightning 28
shellfish 21
shockwaves during earthquakes
   10, 14
silt 18
skuas 39
sky 24
slate 10
snakes 15, 35
   desert 37
snow 26, 38
   in the desert 44
   on mountains 17
snow line 17
soil
   pollution 40
   vegetation 32
solar energy, in desert 37
Solar System 4, 6
Solomon Islands, forests 45
source of the river 18
South Africa
   diamonds 10
   waterfalls 44
South America
   area 9
   deserts 37
   formation of continent 9
   monkeys 35
   mountains 4
   rainforests 34
   rivers 43
   shape 9
Southeast Asia, rainforests 34
Southern Africa, deserts 37, 44
Southern India, area 42
South Pole 4
   snow 26
   see also Antarctica
spaceships 25
spectrum 24
sperm whales 38
spiders, desert 37
spring 30, 31
spring tide 20
Sri Lanka, seashells 2
stacks 22
stars
   beliefs of ancient Greeks 5
   nearest to Earth 42
Stegosaurus 6
storms 28−9
stratosphere 25
submarine canyons 20
subtropical climate 31
Sudan, size 42
sugars 6
Sumatra
   area 42
   volcanoes 42
summer 30, 31
Sun 4, 26
   ancient beliefs 5
   Earth's orbit 5
   gravity 20−1
   rays 30
   rises and sets 24
   Solar System 4
   speed of light 42
   sunlight 4, 24

sunniest place on Earth 31
Superior, Lake, area 18, 43
Surinam, forests 45
Surtsey 13
swamps
   coastal 23
   largest 43

temperate climate 31
temperate forest 33
temperature
   Antarctic 38, 39
   atmosphere 24
   biggest range on Earth 31
   in Earth's core 10
   on mountains 17
   rise 31
   sea water 20, 44
tephra 12
termites 35
thermals 25
thermosphere 25
thunder claps 28
thunderstorms 28, 45
   safety measures 28−9
   see also lightning
Tibet, mountains 43
tides 20−1, 44
Titicaca, Lake 43
Tolbachik, Mount 42
tornadoes 29
   speed 45
toucans 35
Trans-Antarctic Range 43
tree frogs 35
tree line 17
trees
   coniferous 17, 32, 45
   deciduous 17, 45
   destruction 40
   fastest growing 45
   largest 45
   oldest 32, 45
   rainforests 34
   source of medicine 45
   on the tundra 44
   see also forests
tributaries 18
tropical climate 31
tropical cyclones 29
tropical rainforest 33
troposphere 25
tsunami 14
tundra 33, 38, 44
   plants 33, 38
typhoons 29
   Hong Kong 45
Tyrannosaurus 7

underground springs 18
underwater hotel 21
underwater mountains 44
underwater volcanoes 42
unleaded petrol 41
Uranus 4
USA
   cactus 36
   deserts 37
   earthquake−proof buildings 14
   earthquakes 14
   electricity consumption 40
   energy use 40
   geysers 12
   hardwood producer 45
   hurricanes 45
   lakes 18, 43
   largest tree 45
   oldest trees 45
   petrol consumption 40
   sapphires 11
   size 42

tornadoes 29
waterfalls 44

valleys 17
vegetation 32
Venezuela, waterfalls 19, 44
Venice, Italy 22
Venus 4
Vesuvius 13
Victoria, Lake 43
Victoria Island, area 42
Vinson Massif 43
volcanic bombs 12
volcanic islands 13
volcanoes 12−13, 16, 21, 42
   shapes 13
   types of eruption 13

warming of climate 31, 40, 41
Washington, Mount 24
waste pollution 40
water 4
   currents 21
   cycle 26−7
   droplets 26, 28
   evaporation 26, 27
   hot springs 12
   legislation on cleanliness 41
   pollution 40
   reduce pollution 41
   temperature 44
   vapour 26
   see also rainfall
waterfalls 19, 44
waterspouts 29
waves
   biggest 21
   caused by earthquakes 14
waves of energy 14
weather 26−7, 28−9, 45
   see also climate
West Africa, rainforests 34
West Indies, sea shells 23
West Wind Drift 21
whales 38−9
white outs 38
White Sea 44
willy willies 29
windiest place on Earth 24, 38
winds 21, 24, 25
   direction 30
   strength 24−5
   see also tornadoes
winter 30, 31
worms 6, 7, 23

Yangtze, River 19, 43
Yellow River, China 43
Yellowstone Park, USA 12
   Beaver Lake 19

Zimbabwe, lightning 45
zooplankton 39

48

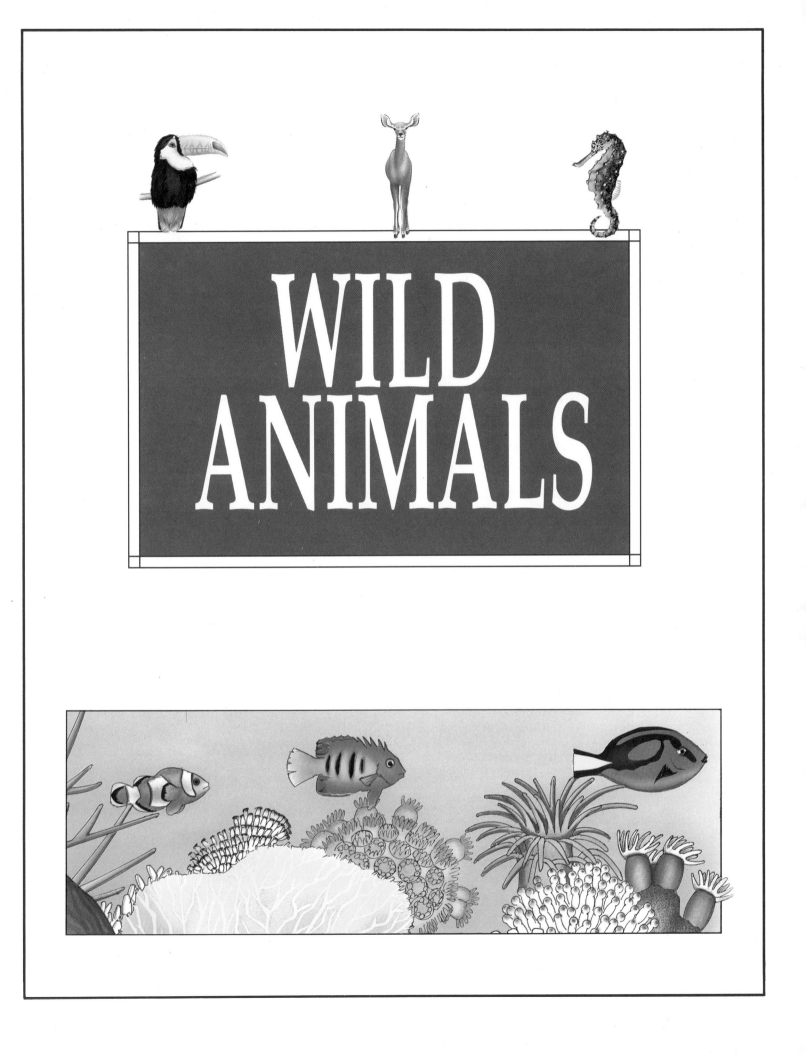

WILD ANIMALS

Part Two

WILD ANIMALS

The Animal Kingdom   52
Mammals   54
Insects   56
Fish   58
Reptiles and Amphibians   60
Birds   62
Grassland Animals   64
Rainforest Animals   66
Desert Animals   68
Northern Forest Animals   70
Mountain Animals   72
Polar Animals   74
Undersea Animals   76
Wildlife in the Home   78
Animal Babies   80
Camouflage   82
Strange Animals   84
Endangered Animals   86
Saving Animals   88
Wild Animals Facts and Lists   90
Index   94

Introduction

There are over a million different kinds of animals living on the Earth today. In this Part, you can find out how scientists divide animals into groups like mammals, reptiles, fish and birds.

Did you know that the present day is sometimes called the 'Age of the insects' because they outnumber all the other groups? There are probably many unknown types of insect still to be discovered.

The places where animals live can affect what they look like. For instance, one type of desert mammal called a fennec fox has especially big ears that help to keep it cool in the very hot sun. An unusual shark called a wobbegong has skin that looks like seaweed, so that it can lie unseen on the seabed.

Not all animals live in places like deserts or oceans. Find out how your home could be a good hunting ground and nesting place too.

There are four basic ways that animals reproduce, or make new generations. Tiny bacteria can reproduce every half-hour or so, but large creatures like elephants and whales take over a year.

About 5000 animal species may disappear because of what humans are doing. Discover what can be done to stop this happening.

The Animal Kingdom

Coelenterates – jellyfish, corals, sea anemones

Animals are creatures that breathe in **oxygen**. They have to **eat** plants or other animals in order to survive.

Animals have been on the Earth in one form or another for about 700 million years. The first animals were tiny single-celled creatures.

Single-celled creatures

Today, over a million different kinds of animals live on Earth. Scientists divide them into **related groups**.

Animal groups

Here are the main **animal groups:**

- Mammals (see p54) include such different examples as bats, whales, cats, kangaroos and humans. Many large creatures belong to this group.

- Reptiles (see p60) include snakes, lizards turtles and crocodiles. About 250 million years ago, reptiles dominated the Earth as dinosaurs.

- Amphibians (see p60) have bodies that are adapted to live on land or in water. This group includes frogs, toads, newts and salamanders.

Strange but true

- The present day is sometimes called the 'Age of the Insects'. Insects vastly outnumber all the other animal groups.

- Because grass gives so little nourishment, cows must graze all day to get enough for their needs.

- Some scientists think that apes and humans are descended from a type of rodent, rather like a rat.

Animal food

Animals eat different kinds of **food**, depending on their size, the type of stomach they have and the food available.

- Animals that eat only plants are called herbivores.

Herbivorous zebra

- Animals that eat both meat and plants are called omnivores.

- Animals that eat only meat are called carnivores.

Carnivorous lion

- Predators help to strengthen the animal population. They tend to catch and kill the weakest members of an animal group. The strongest ones are left alive. These are more likely to breed healthy offspring.

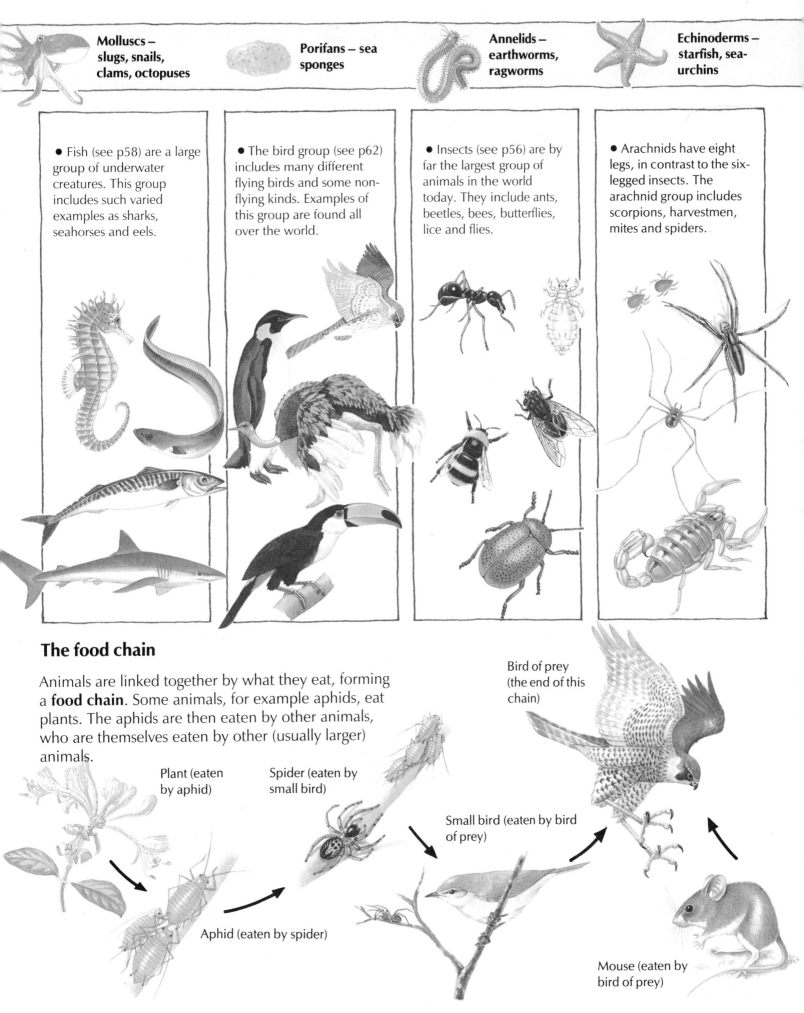

Molluscs – slugs, snails, clams, octopuses

Porifans – sea sponges

Annelids – earthworms, ragworms

Echinoderms – starfish, sea-urchins

● Fish (see p58) are a large group of underwater creatures. This group includes such varied examples as sharks, seahorses and eels.

● The bird group (see p62) includes many different flying birds and some non-flying kinds. Examples of this group are found all over the world.

● Insects (see p56) are by far the largest group of animals in the world today. They include ants, beetles, bees, butterflies, lice and flies.

● Arachnids have eight legs, in contrast to the six-legged insects. The arachnid group includes scorpions, harvestmen, mites and spiders.

The food chain

Animals are linked together by what they eat, forming a **food chain**. Some animals, for example aphids, eat plants. The aphids are then eaten by other animals, who are themselves eaten by other (usually larger) animals.

Plant (eaten by aphid)

Spider (eaten by small bird)

Bird of prey (the end of this chain)

Small bird (eaten by bird of prey)

Aphid (eaten by spider)

Mouse (eaten by bird of prey)

Mammals

Mammals are a very successful group of animals found all over the world. There are about **4500 species** in all.

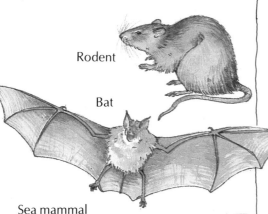

Rodent

Bat

Sea mammal

The mammal family includes **bats**, **rodents** (small gnawing creatures such as rats and mice) and some sea animals such as **whales** and **dolphins**. It also includes the **primates**. Human beings are part of the primate group, along with lemurs, monkeys and apes.

Primates

Mammal facts

Mammals have:

• Hairy bodies, to help them keep warm. Some mammals have thick fur; some only have a fine fur.

• Skulls and backbones. Animals with backbones are called vertebrates.

• A constant body temperature.

• The ability to suckle their young, which means that they can feed babies with milk from their body.

Different kinds of mammal

Zoologists split mammals into three **scientific groups**. Each group gives birth to babies in a different way.

• Monotremes lay eggs and hatch their young. There are only two types of monotremes: the duck-billed platypus from Australia and the spiny anteaters or echidnas from Australia and New Guinea.

Duck-billed platypus

• Placental mammal babies are born alive and well-developed. When a placental baby is growing inside its mother it lives inside a kind of protective sac. Its blood supply is linked to its mother's.

A human embryo.

• Marsupial mammal babies are born very tiny and undeveloped. Most marsupial babies finish growing inside pouches on their mother's body. Kangaroos are marsupials.

Baby in pouch

Giant panda (China)

Javan rhino (Java)

 Mountain gorilla (Congo, Uganda)

Amazing mammals

Mammals are lots of different shapes and sizes. That is partly because they have developed to survive in many different kinds of places. Here are some **mammal record-breakers:**

● The world's noisiest land animals are South American howler monkeys. When the male monkeys call, their screams can be heard from 16 km away.

● The world's largest land mammal is the African elephant. Adult bull elephants grow over 3 metres tall and weigh about 5.7 tonnes.

● Cheetahs are the world's fastest animals on land. They can run up to 70km/h over 400 m.

● The giraffe is the tallest mammal in the world. It can grow over 5 metres. It has a long neck so that it can reach leaves high up in the trees.

Primates

Primates are the most well-developed mammals. They have:

● Complex brains, which means that they are able to think better than most other creatures in the animal kingdom.

● The ability to stand upright for long periods.

● More highly-developed hands than any other animal group. They can use their hands for all kinds of complicated skills.

● Eyes set side by side in the front of the head, which means that they can see more clearly than most other creatures.

Strange but true

● Many mammals sleep for long periods. Lions sleep up to 20 hours a day.

● Gorillas sleep in nests which they build in treetops.

● Lions and tigers have been successfully crossed to make a new animal – the 'tigon'.

● Blue whale babies weigh up to 7 tonnes at birth.

Insects

Insects are the biggest animal group. There are vast numbers of them, and there are probably many unknown types of insect still to be discovered.

Insects are found all over the world, even on frozen lands and in scorching deserts where other animals find it hard to survive.

Most insects live on their own for most of their lives, but some insects, such as bees, live in **organized communities** with many companions of the same type.

Insect parts

Insects do not all look the same, but they all have some characteristics in common. **All insects** have:

- A protective outer covering called an 'exoskeleton'. Insects are 'invertebrates', which means that they do not have backbones. They do not have internal skeletons.

- A head which carries the eyes, antennae and feeding parts.

- An abdomen, made up of a series of segments. Vital organs such as the heart are inside.

- A thorax, which carries legs and sometimes wings.

Head

Thorax

Abdomen

- Three pairs of jointed legs.

- Cold blood, which means that they cannot control their own body temperature. They rely on the temperature of their surroundings to keep them alive.

Eye

- Many insects have compound eyes, made of hundreds of tiny lenses.

Strange but true

- Some butterflies have scented wings, to attract a mate.

- Some insects produce tiny lights on their bodies to attract mates.

- Crickets have ears positioned on their knees.

- Prehistoric dragonflies had wingspans up to 76cm across, wider than many modern birds.

Growing up

Some insects go through a complete change of body and appearance called **metamorphosis**. There are four stages:

1. The female insect lays lots of tiny eggs, sometimes on the underside of a leaf.

2. The eggs hatch into larvae. Caterpillars, grubs and maggots are all forms of insect larvae.

3. When the larva has grown enough it changes into a pupa (or chrysalis), inside a hard case called a cocoon, the insects' body dissolves and reforms into a new shape.

4. Once the change has occurred, the cocoon splits open and the adult insect comes out. Butterflies, moths, beetles, flies, ants and bees all go through metamorphosis.

Types of insect

The **insect world** is divided into groups. Here are some of them:

Honey bees

• Crickets and grasshoppers have strong hind legs for jumping. They can rub parts of the body together to make a 'singing' sound that attracts a mate.

Grasshopper

• Wasps and bees live in well-organized communities, where each insect has a particular job to do.

Dragonfly

• Dragonflies and damselflies have fierce jaws which they use to catch other flying insects such as flies.

• Bugs are insects with mouthparts made for sucking. Some bugs feed on plant juices; some feed on blood.

Blackfly bug

• Flies have only one pair of wings, but they also have tiny balancing organs at the back of their bodies. These help them to land upside-down.

• Some bugs live in or on water. You can often see them walking over the surfaces of ponds.

• Beetles are the biggest insect group. Their front wings are hard outer coverings for their back wings.

Stag beetle

Pond skater

• Butterflies and moths have tiny scales that cover their bodies. The scales are made up of thousands of tiny hairs.

57

Fish

Fish live in oceans, rivers, lakes and ponds. They are **cold-blooded**, which means that they cannot change their own body temperature.

There are about 20,000 different **species**, ranging from giant whale sharks about 12 metres long to dwarf gobies no bigger than a thumbnail.

Bony fish

Most fish belong to the **bony fish** group, which means that they have **bone skeletons** inside their bodies. Many of the fish we eat are of this kind.

- Bony fish have a gill slit on either side of the body. The slits are covered over with flaps of skin.

- Flat fish, such as plaice and sole, are bony. They lie on one side of their bodies.

Jawless fish

Lampreys and hagfish belong to the **jawless** fish group.

- Jawless fish have round sucking funnels for mouths. They have sharp teeth to hook onto their prey.

- Lampreys suck the blood of prey. Hagfish eat the flesh of their victims.

- Most bony fish have a little air-filled sac called a swim bladder inside their bodies. This bladder acts rather like water-wings; it keeps the fish floating in the water.

Fish facts

Most fish have:

- Backbones. All fish are vertebrates.

- A scaly skin, which stays moist and waterproof. Eels and lampreys are the only fish to have smooth skins.

- Gills, which are underneath slits or flaps of skin on either side of the head. When a fish opens its mouth water comes in and washes over the gills. They absorb oxygen from the water and pass it into the fish's body. Waste water goes out through the slits.

Strange but true

- Pufferfish can puff their bodies up to scare away enemies.

- Salmon live in the sea, but they return to breed in the river where they were born.

- There are probably about a trillion herring in the Atlantic Ocean (a million million million).

- A female cod can lay up to 9 million eggs.

Jawless fish mouth

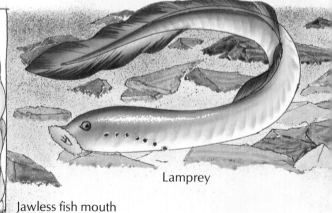

Lamprey

Cartilaginous fish

The **cartilaginous** fish family includes sharks, rays, skate and dogfish. They have:

● Skeletons made of tough, gristly cartilage instead of bones.

● No swim bladders. This makes them heavier than water. They must keep swimming all the time, or they will sink.

● Fins and a tail that help the fish to steer through the water.

● A streamlined shape, which is smooth and curved. This makes it easier for the fish to slip smoothly through the water.

● Five gill slits on either side of the body. These are easy to see because they are not covered by skin flaps.

● A special sense called a 'lateral line', made of groups of cells which form a line along both sides of the body. The cells can feel changes of pressure in the water around them, caused by objects such as rocks and other fish.

Fish reproduction

Most female fish lay thousands of tiny **eggs** that float in the water. Many of the eggs are eaten by predators before they hatch.

● The male seahorse is unusual because it carries the eggs instead of the female. The female lays her eggs into a pouch on the male's body. When the babies hatch they stay in the pouch while they grow.

● Unlike most fish, tilapia look after their young. When its family is threatened this fish opens its mouth and its babies swim inside for safety.

● Skate and dogfish lay their eggs inside horny cases, which are known as mermaids' purses. Sometimes the old discarded cases can be found washed up on the beach.

59

Reptiles and Amphibians

Amphibians are a group of animals that spend part of their lives in water and part of their lives on land. **Frogs**, **toads**, **newts** and **salamanders** are all examples.

Amphibians

Reptiles live and breed mostly on land, although a few live in water. **Snakes**, **lizards**, **crocodiles** and **turtles** are all reptiles.

Reptiles

Amphibians

Amphibians have moist **slimy skin**. They always live near **fresh water** because they must return there in order to breed.

● There are swimming frogs, burrowing frogs, climbing frogs and even flying frogs that can glide from tree to tree.

● Like most amphibians, baby frogs metamorphose, which means that they change completely before they become adult (see p56). They grow from tiny tadpoles into frogs.

Spawn   Tadpole   Legs form   Frog

Reptiles

Reptiles are **cold-blooded**, which is why they need to live in warm climates. They have scaly, **waterproof skin** and most of them lay **eggs** with tough protective shells.

Lizards are reptiles with scaly bodies and four limbs:

● Some lizards have collars of skin which they puff out to make themselves look bigger when they are excited or scared.

● The largest, heaviest lizard is the komodo dragon from Indonesia. It can grow up to 3 metres long, and is a fierce hunter.

Frilled lizard

Komodo dragon

Tortoises, **terrapins** and **turtles** are reptiles with protective shells.

● Turtles live in seawater. They only come ashore to lay their eggs.

Hairy frog
(Central Africa)

Surinam toad
(S. America)

Horned Escuerzo
(S. America)

● Newts and salamanders are long, thin and lizard-like. There are many different types and colours.

Tiger salamander (N. America)

● There is a third small group of amphibians called caecilians. They are strange creatures that look more like earthworms. They spend their lives burrowing in sand and mud.

Mexican caecilian

Strange but true

● Snakes can see through their eyelids.

● Chameleon lizards can look in two directions at once.

● If a lizard's tail is broken off, it can usually grow a new one.

● Ancient Egyptians thought crocodiles were sacred. They mummified (preserved) thousands of them.

Snakes are limbless reptiles.

● Some snakes have poisonous fangs. When they bite, poison runs down into the wound through grooves in the fangs.

● The fanged cobra is amongst the most dangerous snakes in the world. It raises a hood of skin on its neck when it feels threatened.

● Some snakes kill their victims by coiling around them and squeezing them to death. These 'constricting' snakes are not poisonous but they are often very large. The anaconda and python are examples.

Poisonous fangs

Cobra

There are 120 species of **crocodiles** and **alligators**.

● The difference between the two is that when a crocodile's mouth is closed you can see its fourth tooth sticking out over the lower jaw.

Crocodiles

Birds

Birds are **warm-blooded** animals with **internal skeletons**. They all have **wings** and **feathers**, although not all birds can fly. There is a wide variety of birds. They live in many different habitats all over the world, from icy polar lands to hot tropical rainforests. Some birds live alone or in small groups. Others live in **colonies** numbering many thousands.

Bird facts

Most birds have bodies designed for flight. All **flying birds** have these physical features:

- A light, waterproof covering of feathers over most of the body. They help birds to fly and also keep body heat in, so the bird stays warm.

- A streamlined body shape. This helps birds to travel smoothly through the air by cutting down air resistance.

- Two wings covered with extra-strong flight feathers. The wings help to raise the bird into the air and the bird keeps itself aloft by flapping them.

- A horny pointed beak for feeding. Different birds have differently shaped beaks.

- Lightweight, partly hollow internal bones.

- Scaly legs and feet with three or four toes and sharp claws.

Strange but true

- The earliest known bird, called Archaeopteryx, lived 150 million years ago. Unlike modern birds it had teeth.

- Swifts spend almost all their lives in the air. They only land to breed.

- Flamingoes are pink because their bodies take on the pink colour of the shrimps they eat.

- The Andean sword-billed hummingbird has a beak longer than its body.

Eggs and nests

Bird species breed at certain times of the year, when the weather is mild and there is a good supply of food.

- Some male birds use complicated dances, special songs, or displays to attract females. For instance, the male peacock shows off its bright tail feathers to interest a mate.

Peacock male

- Eggs vary in colour and shape. For instance, some are speckled so that they are difficult to spot when they are lying in a nest.

Types of bird

Here are some different **bird groups:**

Osprey with fish

● Birds of prey (also called raptors) hunt other animals. They have curved talons for grasping prey, hooked beaks for tearing flesh and good eyesight to help them hunt. Eagles, owls and hawks are all birds of prey.

African ostrich

● Some bird species have lost the ability to fly. The world's largest bird, the African ostrich, is an example. It is too heavy to take off but it has powerful legs and can run as fast as 65 km/h.

Weaver bird's nest

● Most birds build nests where they lay eggs and hatch young. One of the most complicated examples is the carefully woven bell-shaped nest of the weaver bird, found in Africa and Australia.

Feathers

Bird feathers are made from **keratin**, a substance which is also found in hair and horn.

● Down the middle of a feather there is a stiff horny shaft called a quill.

● The flat part on either side of the quill is called the vane. It is made from tiny fibres called barbs. There are about 600 barbs on either side, each carrying smaller offshoots. All the barbs and offshoots are locked tightly together by hooks to make a smooth surface.

Quill

Vane

Barbs

● Water birds have long legs for wading. They often have webbed feet to help them paddle, and long bills or beaks for finding food in the water. Cormorants, ducks and flamingoes are examples of waterbirds.

A colony of flamingoes

Grassland Animals

Grasslands can support lots of animals because they eat different foods:

Wildebeest eat short grass

Grasslands are wide, open areas where grasses and shrubs grow. **Temperate grasslands** are found in cool parts of the world in the middle of large land masses, where rainfall is low. These areas are often used for cattle.

Tropical grassland is found mainly in Africa and South America. In Africa it is called **savanna**, and in South America it is called **pampas**. Here rain falls only in summer.

Tropical grassland provides a home for many wild animals.

Plant-eating animals

Most grassland animals are **grazers**, eating grass and other plants. Some grazers live together in **herds**, for safety. They move about looking for fresh pastures and water pools. Here are some examples of plant-eaters on the **African savanna**:

- Antelope live in most tropical grassland areas. Species include oryx, eland and gazelles. Although they are only 60 cm tall, gazelles can run at 90 km/h to escape danger.

- The African savanna has shrubs and trees as well as grass. These provide food for giraffes, elephants and rhinos.

- Zebras move in large herds, often accompanied by wildebeest. While some zebras graze, others stay on the lookout for lions, their main enemy. Zebras can hear and smell better than most other grazing creatures.

Strange but true

- Elephants spend 23 hours a day eating.

- Some antelope can leap 3 metres in the air from a standing start.

- Vultures sometimes eat so much they can't take off again.

- No two zebras have exactly the same pattern of stripes. Like human fingerprints, each zebra pattern is unique.

Meat-eaters

The main threat to the grassland plant-eaters are **meat-eaters** such as lions, leopards and hunting dogs.

- Lions live in groups called prides. They hunt and kill only when they are hungry. Antelope and zebras are their favourite food.

- African hunting dogs live in large, well-organized packs. They hunt together, separating weak or young animals from herds.

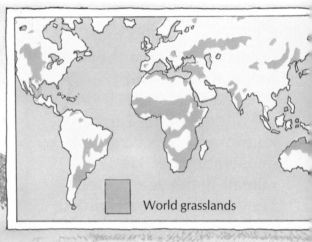
World grasslands

Scavengers

Scavengers are creatures who eat the leftovers from dead animal carcasses. When the grassland hunters have finished with their prey, the scavengers move in to pick the bones clean.

- Vultures are large birds found in many grassland areas of the world. They use their keen eyesight to spot dead animals far below them.

- Hyenas usually eat the remains of another animal's kill, but they will hunt if food is scarce. Their 'chuckling' hunting cry sounds rather like a human laugh.

- Although vultures and hyenas have a bad reputation, they provide a useful 'garbage disposal' service, because if carcasses are left to rot they attract flies and disease.

65

Rainforest Animals

Rainforests are hot, steamy jungles that grow in areas on either side of the Equator – an imaginary line that circles the middle of the Earth. Rainforest areas have **high temperatures** and **heavy rainfall** all the year round. They are the richest animal and plant habitats in the world.

Equator

Rainforest area

Strange but true

- The African jungle okapi's tongue is so long, it can be used to lick the creature's eyes.

- The African giant snail grows up to 39 cm long.

- The strongest-known animal poison comes from the arrow-poison frog.

- The Amazon 'Jesus Christ lizard' can run across water.

Rainforest birds

Many **birds** make their home in the rainforest trees.

- Each forest region has its own giant eagle species. These birds build huge twig platforms on top of the highest trees.

Hornbill

Toucan

- Brightly-coloured macaws, hornbills and toucans make their nests in holes in tree trunks.

Macaw

- There are lots of different hummingbird species in the Amazon region. They hover by flowers, drinking the sweet nectar with their long beaks. They beat their wings between 50 and 80 times a minute.

Hummingbird

Rainforest insects

There are many, many thousands of different insect species in the rainforests.

- Ants can be found everywhere in the rainforests. Huge columns of fierce army ants travel through the forest areas of Central America, destroying everything in their path.

- Giant butterflies flit amongst the trees. Many of them are brightly-coloured. This is a signal that they taste horrible.

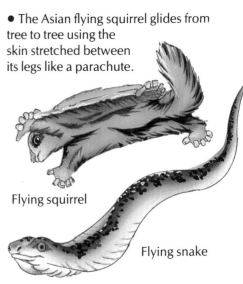

Gliders

- The Asian flying squirrel glides from tree to tree using the skin stretched between its legs like a parachute.

Flying squirrel

Flying snake

- When the flying snake launches itself, it flattens its body into a broad ribbon shape so that it can glide through the air.

Animals in the trees

Most rainforest **mammals** live up in the tree branches.

- The Amazon sloth hangs motionless and upside down for days on end. It has a shaggy coat and long claws for gripping branches.

Sloth

Margay

- There are lots of different jungle monkeys. Some of them have prehensile tails, which can be used like a hand to grip on to things.

- The Amazon margay and the ocelot are types of rainforest cat. Both are expert tree climbers.

Ocelot

Reptiles

Rainforests make ideal homes for warmth-loving **reptiles**.

- The world's biggest insect, the Goliath beetle, lives in African rainforests.

- The bushmaster snake lives amongst tree branches. It has heat-sensitive patches on its head, so it can find possible victims by sensing their body heat. Its bite can kill humans.

- The world's heaviest snake is the anaconda, found in South America and Trinidad. It can weigh up to 150 kg, and strangles its prey by coiling around it. It feeds mainly on birds, deer and rodents.

Desert Animals

About one eighth of the Earth's surface is **desert**. A desert is an area where less than 25 cm of rain falls on average each year.

Some deserts are very cold in winter. Others are hot all the year round, with high temperatures during the day and cooler temperatures at night.

Most desert animals tend to come out at night, staying out of the daytime heat by sheltering under rocks or in their underground burrows.

The major problem of desert survival is **lack of water**. Many animals are cleverly adapted to cope with the drought.

Strange but true

- Crocodile tracks have been found in the middle of the Sahara Desert.

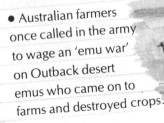

- Prehistoric rock paintings in the Sahara show giraffes, antelope and elephants. None of these animals live in the region today.

- Australian farmers once called in the army to wage an 'emu war' on Outback desert emus who came on to farms and destroyed crops.

Snakes and lizards

Snakes and **lizards** are cold-blooded (see p60) and need the Sun's heat in order to survive. Deserts are ideal homes for them.

- There are many different kinds of American rattlesnake, most of them highly poisonous. When a rattlesnake is angry, it makes a warning rattle by shaking scales positioned on the end of its tail.

Rattlesnake

- Sidewinder snakes have developed an efficient way of travelling over soft sand. They use their bodies to lever themselves along, leaving trails of wavy lines behind them on the sand.

Sidewinder snake

Amphibians

- The American spadefoot toad burrows underground during hot weather. It can stay buried for up to 11 months because its waterproof coat keeps moisture in its body. When rain arrives, the toads come out to breed.

Insects and spiders

There are many different **desert insects** and **spiders**.

- When it rains, the eggs of bugs, beetles and butterflies hatch, after lying dormant for many months.

- A Namib Desert darkling beetle collects water from sea fog that rolls in from the nearby Atlantic. The fog condenses on the beetle's body and runs into its mouth.

- Most desert spiders do not use webs to trap prey. Instead they wait for creatures to get too close to them.

Darkling beetle

Red-kneed tarantula (Mexico)

Bighorn sheep (USA): can store water in its stomach

 Desert tortoise (USA): keeps cool by licking its head and neck **Moloch lizard (Australia): can condense water from the air onto its skin**

Desert mammals

Desert mammals usually stay out of the daytime heat, in order to conserve water. Many of the smaller mammals never drink, getting all the moisture they need from seeds, shoots, or other creatures.

● The Saharan fennec fox has especially big ears that help to keep it cool. Blood vessels run near the skin surface of the ears, giving off heat as air blows across them.

Saharan fennec fox

Kangaroo rat

● The most common desert mammals are rodents. The kangaroo rat is an example. It stores plant seeds deep in its burrow, leaving them to collect moisture from the soil. This way, the rat gets a ready supply of water.

● Camels can survive for many days without regular water or food. They have wide, hairy feet to stop them sinking in the sand, and their nostrils can close up to keep out dust.

Dromedary camel

Desert birds

Most **desert birds** shelter from the daytime heat beneath rocks or plants.

● The saguaro cactus is found in the Sonoran desert in south-west USA. It can grow up to 15 metres high, and provides a home for several desert birds. Gila woodpeckers peck out nest holes in the rubbery cactus flesh. Tiny elf owls nest in vacant holes and cactus wrens nest in forks.

● The emu is found in Australian desert regions. It is the world's second largest bird (after the ostrich). It grows up to 1.7 metres high, and although it cannot fly it can run up to 64 km/h over short distances.

Gila woodpecker

Cactus wren

Elf owl

● Roadrunners are found in Mexico and Arizona. They are famous for their speed. They can run up to 37 km/h to catch snakes and lizards.

Roadrunner

Northern Forest Animals

In northern parts of the world there are areas of cool forest which provide a home for all sorts of different creatures.

There are two types of cool forest. In warmer areas the trees are mainly deciduous, which means they shed their leaves in winter. In cold areas the trees are mainly coniferous, which means they have long-lasting needles instead of leaves.

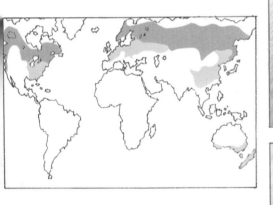

Coniferous forest

Deciduous forest

Many forest creatures are very shy and will hide if they hear strange noises. A good time to spot forest wildlife is at dusk or very early in the morning, when the animals tend to feed.

Deciduous woods

Deciduous trees have widely-spread branches. The gaps between their leaves allow plenty of sunlight through to the forest floor, where lots of plants grow and provide food for animals.

● Foxes live in burrows called 'earths'. They survive well in the forest because they will eat most things and they have very few enemies. During the daytime they lie low. During the night they hunt for birds, rodents and rabbits.

● The wood mouse is one of the most common forest rodents. It has long front teeth for gnawing through wood and nutshells.

Coniferous forests

Trees in coniferous forests are densely packed together. Very little light penetrates to the poor soil beneath, so there are few small plants. There is less animal life than in deciduous forests because there is less to eat.

● Red deer are common in northern forests. Male deer (stags) have long antlers covered in soft velvet. Each year, the antlers drop off and a new pair grows.

● Martens have long bodies and short legs. There are several different species, including the pine marten.

70

Woodlouse

Centipede

Pill millipede

Snail

Bark beetle

- Lots of different insect-eating birds find food amongst the trees.

- Badgers are timid night time creatures. They can see well in the dark and have a strong sense of smell, so it is difficult to watch them without disturbing them.

- Caterpillars and insects feed off the tree leaves, while bark beetles bore into the trunks.

- Wild rabbits live in large groups in complicated tunnel networks called 'warrens'.

- Woodpeckers have strong beaks for drilling nest holes in tree trunks. They can sometimes be heard hammering on wood.

- A squirrel can leap 4 or 5 metres from branch to branch quite effortlessly, using its powerful hind legs to launch itself into the air. It uses its outstretched tail like a rudder, to steer its flight.

Strange but true

- The woodpecker has an extra-strong shock-resistant skull.

- Wood ants squirt powerful formic acid at their enemies.

- Male stags must not be approached when they call during the mating season, as they are liable to attack anyone nearby, mistaking them for a rival.

- Squirrels sometimes wrap their bushy tails around themselves to keep warm.

Mountain Animals

Some animals are adapted to survive the harsh weather conditions often found in **mountains**.

The higher you go, the colder and wetter the climate becomes. Mountain animals tend to have **thick furry coats** or **extra layers of fat** to keep them warm.

Rocky Mountain goat

Mountain animals

● Yaks have long, thick coats to keep them warm in the Himalayan Mountains in Tibet. Sometimes they graze at heights above 4500 metres, making them the highest-living land animals.

Yak

● Llamas and vicuna belong to the camel family. They are farmed for wool and meat by the Quechua Indians high up in the Andean mountains of South America.

Llama

● The spectacled bear lives in the Andes Mountains. It gets its name from round facial markings.

Spectacled bear

● The Apollo butterfly lives high up in mountainous regions across the world. Spiders are found high up, too. However, it is usually too cold for reptiles and amphibians to survive.

Apollo butterfly

● Cougars (also called pumas or panthers) live in the mountain forests of America. They are very strong, powerful animals and can travel hundreds of kilometres a week in search of food.

Cougar

● Rocky Mountain goats are experts at climbing steep rocks. They have hoof pads which give them extra grip and allow them to climb up almost vertical surfaces. Their toes are shaped like pincers to help them get a firm footing.

● The chamois goat can climb very quickly. It has been known to climb over 1000 metres in 15 minutes.

Chamois

Strange but true

● The cougar can jump as high as 5 metres from a standing position.

● High in the mountains the level of oxygen in the air gets less, so some animals have larger hearts and lungs than normal, to compensate.

● A griffon vulture once crashed into an aircraft at the amazing height of 10,800 metres above ground level.

Red panda
(Himalayas)

Snow leopard
(Asia)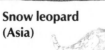

Marmot (N.
America,
Eurasia)

High flyers

Many mountain birds are **raptors**, or birds
of prey (see p63).

● The Andean condor is the world's
largest bird of prey, weighing as much as
12 kg. It has a wingspan of about 3
metres. Like its relatives the
vultures, it is a scavenger, which
means it feeds on animal
carcasses (see p65).

● The bobcat hunts
small animals in
the mountainous
regions of North
America and
Mexico. During the
breeding season it
makes eerie
screaming sounds.

Bobcat

Andean condor

Golden eagle

Coping in the cold

In the winter months, when the
weather is at its fiercest and food
is hard to find, some mountain
animals **hibernate**, which means
that they sleep deeply for a long
period of time. During hibernation:

● Body temperature drops.

Hibernating
mountain
hare

● The animal's heartbeat slows down,
so that it uses up less energy.

● The body's fat reserves are gradually
used up for nutrition.

● Eagles can fly very high. They glide on
warm air currents called thermals to help
lift them higher. Remains of Steppe eagles
have been found on Mount Everest at
heights of 7500 metres. It is thought that
some eagles even fly right over Mount Everest.

73

Polar Animals

At the far south of the Earth there is a large area of land called **Antarctica**. It is always frozen over with ice.

Most Antarctic animals are **seabirds** and **ocean creatures** such as seals and fish.

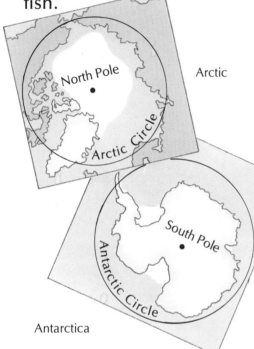

North Pole

Arctic

Arctic Circle

South Pole

Antarctic Circle

Antarctica

The **Arctic** is the area at the far north of the Earth. The Arctic Ocean is in the middle, covered by a huge floating sheet of ice.

Within the Arctic Circle there is barren land called **tundra**, where most of the Arctic animals live.

Arctic tundra animals

Most animals only come to the Arctic tundra during the short **summer months** and **migrate south** when winter comes. A few species brave the winter blizzards. Some of them burrow underground to wait for warmer temperatures in spring.

● Musk oxen are gentle creatures with warm, shaggy coats. They live in family groups which wander the tundra grazing on grasses. They stay on the tundra in winter.

● Lemmings are the commonest small tundra animals. They are part of the rodent family. They live in underground burrows during winter and come up to the surface to feed in summer.

● Polar bears are the fiercest Arctic animals. They stay all year round, hunting for seals. They can swim and dive well and they can sniff the scent of prey from several kilometres away. Male polar bears spend most of the time on their own. Female bears look after their cubs for a year or so.

● In summer, big herds of caribou (also called reindeer) travel up to the tundra from North America and Scandinavia.

Caribou

Musk oxen

Lemming

Polar bears

Arctic whales

● Bowheads are baleen whales. Instead of teeth they have curtains of bony strips. As a whale swims along, the strips sieve the water, collecting tiny shrimp-like krill to eat.

● The beluga is a toothed whale, so it doesn't rely on krill for its food. It feeds on fish at the floe-edge, which is the place where the Arctic pack-ice meets the sea.

Narwhal

● Male narwhals grow long spiralling tusks. They are sometimes nicknamed sea-unicorns.

Beluga

Bowhead

Arctic birds

Lots of **seabirds** migrate to the Arctic in summer.

● More than half a million seabird pairs nest in summer on the cliffs of Prince Leopold Island, in the Canadian Arctic.

Seabird

Antarctic animals

Since most of the Antarctic is covered in ice, there are very few land animals. But the oceans are rich in **fish**, **squid** and **krill**, providing plenty of food for other sea creatures. In the Antarctic Ocean region there are:

● Fish that produce a natural kind of anti-freeze to protect themselves from the extremely cold temperatures underwater.

Antarctic fish

● Blue whales, the world's biggest, heaviest living creatures. They can grow up to 30 metres long. They feed through baleen plates.

● Seven different types of Antarctic seal. They swim under the ice and saw through it with their teeth to make breathing holes that go up to the surface.

Crabeater seal

● Very few inland animals. The only ones are flies, mites, lice, fleas and tiny microbes. Mites are the most southerly-living animals on Earth.

Blue whale

Albatross

● Giant albatross seabirds, which come to the Antarctic coast to breed. They can live for up to 70 or 80 years.

● Several different types of penguin. The biggest one is the emperor penguin, which breeds in large colonies.

Emperor penguin with chick

Arctic seals

Seals sit on the Arctic ice-floes or swim in the ocean looking for fish to eat.

Ringed seal

Bearded seal

Strange but true

● The biggest Antarctic inland animal is a wingless fly measuring about 60 mm long.

● Antarctic squid can grow up to 20 metres long. Many of them are cannibals – they attack and eat other squid.

Undersea Animals

The **oceans** provide one of the largest wildlife habitats in the world. They cover about 70 per cent of the Earth's surface, and animals live in almost every part.

Ocean communities vary depending on the temperature and depth of the sea. Animals that live near the water surface are quite different from those that live deeper down.

Coral reefs and seaweed forests provide specialized habitats for particular kinds of creatures.

Ocean food

Ocean creatures have their own **food chain** (see p53):

● The food chain begins with tiny floating plants called phytoplankton. They float around in the seawater, near the surface. They are eaten by microscopic floating creatures called zooplankton.

Magnified zooplankton

● The zooplankton are eaten by small fish, which often travel around in groups called shoals.

● Baleen whales are at the beginning of the food chain even though they are large. They eat zooplankton (see p74).

● The small fish are eaten in their turn by larger fish, such as tuna.

● Some of the larger fish are eaten by humans.

Coral reefs

Coral reefs are made up of many thousands of individual animals called **polyps**. There are two kinds of corals: **hard** and **soft**.

A coral polyp

● A coral polyp is a cylinder-shaped animal with a ring of tentacles. It takes calcium carbonate from the water and makes it into limestone.

● Hard corals build up a hard wall of limestone around themselves. As the polyps grow and increase, a reef grows.

● Soft corals have a soft layer of tissue on the outside of a central rod.

76

Stingray: poisonous tail spine

Stonefish: poisonous spines

Blue-ringed octopus: deadly bite

Unusual fish

Here are some examples of **unusual ocean fish**:

● The sawfish is found in warm oceans. It has a long flattened snout with toothed edges. As the fish moves along, it swings its saw from side to side, stunning and wounding small fish which it then eats. It is harmless to humans.

Sawfish

Bridal burrfish

● The wobbegong is an unusual shark found off Australia, China and Japan. Its skin is nobbly and fringed like seaweed, so that it can lie unseen on the seabed.

Wobbegong

● The Atlantic trumpetfish is a clever hunter. Its body is long and thin, and it hovers upside down in long seaweed, swaying so that tasty shrimps and small fish mistake it for a plant.

Trumpetfish

● The bridal burrfish lives on coral reefs. It has a round body covered in sharp spikes. When it needs to defend itself, it inflates into a spiky ball that makes it look twice its original size.

The ocean depths

Many areas of the ocean are too **deep** for sunlight to reach. Some creatures have adapted to life in the darkness.

● Some deepsea fish carry their own lights around, to confuse their enemies or to attract prey. For instance, the viperfish has a luminous pattern along its body.

Viperfish

● The female deepsea anglerfish has tentacles on her body. At the tip of each tentacle there is a shining lure designed to look like food for smaller fish. The anglerfish lies on the seabed, waiting to gulp down any unsuspecting prey.

Anglerfish

Strange but true

● Corals attack each other with stinging cells, in order to gain more territory.

● Sailors have been known to mistake basking whales for islands and try to land on them.

● Some tiny male anglerfish live permanently attached to the larger female.

● Giant-sized worms, crabs and clams live near underwater volcanic areas.

Wildlife in the Home

In some parts of the world there are harmful house guests:

Sydney funnelweb spider (Australia): deadly bite

Ypu may not realize it, but you could be sharing your house with wild animals. Houses are good **hunting grounds** and **nesting places** for a variety of creatures, and they provide food stores, too.

Although modern houses tend to be too clean and dry for some pests, it is not unusual to find the occasional beetle, moth, woodlouse, fly or spider in your home.

Parasites

Parasites are creatures that depend completely on other animals to survive. They often feed on blood.

● Bed bugs grow to about 4 mm long. By day they hide in warm dark places such as mattresses. At night, they come out to feed on their victim, leaving tiny itchy bites.

Bed bug, magnified many times

● If you vacuum your bed mattress regularly, you won't be visited by bed bugs. However, if you have cats or dogs, you will sometimes get a flea.

● Fleas leave itchy swelling bites. Human fleas are not very common, but cat and dog fleas will occasionally bite people if there are no dogs or cats to feed on.

The eggs of the fleas survive in carpets when they fall off the animal host. After they hatch, they jump onto the nearest cat or dog.

Fleas are visible on an animal. They are very flat and dark. They are not easy to catch as they move very fast and away from the light.

Furniture and fabric eaters

Some small house creatures like to eat **wood** and **fabric**. They find a perfect supply of food in furniture, carpets, curtains and clothes.

● Furniture beetles lay their eggs in the crevices of damp wood. When the eggs hatch, the larvae (called woodworm) eat their way to the surface, making tiny tunnels.

● Clothes moths eat feathers, fur and wool. They live in damp, dark places such as cupboards and old chests and they lay their eggs on clothes or old carpeting.

● Woodlice like to eat damp paper. They breathe through gills on their legs. The gills must be kept wet, so woodlice live in damp places.

● Carpet beetles lay their eggs amongst carpet fluff. When the larvae hatch they are called 'woolly bears'. They eat feathers, dead insects, fur and wool.

● Bookworms are beetle larvae that live on paper. They like damp paper best.

Hunters

Some house creatures spend their time looking for smaller animals to capture and eat. These **hunters** help to keep the insect population down.

● A house spider's home is usually a sheet of webbing built in a shadowy corner. The spider lives in a silk tube built at the edge of the web. The threads in the web are sticky and trap flying insects, which make the web shake, and the spider then rushes out to kill them.

Garden spider

● False scorpions often live in house cellars, amongst piles of damp paper. Although they are small, they are fierce insect hunters.

False scorpion, magnified

Strange but true

● Fleas can jump up to 30 cm, twenty times their own body length.

● Bluebottle flies can smell meat from distances 7 km away.

● There are flour mites, prune mites, biscuit mites, chocolate mites and even cheese mites.

● House mice prefer chocolate, nuts, seeds and cereals to cheese.

Food stealers

Some creatures are out to steal **your food**. An estimated 15 per cent of all stored food ends up inside insects or rodents.

● Food mites are about the size of dust specks. They like to live on stale, damp food that is left at room temperature – inside a larder, for example.

● There are an estimated 3 million bacteria on one housefly. The fly will land on any food it can find, and is likely to leave some bacteria behind when it flies away.

Housefly, magnified

● House mice live in dark, secret places such as lofts and cellars. They like to eat bread and cereals, but they will occasionally eat more unusual items such as soap and candles!

● The tiny bed mite eats the scales that constantly fall from human skin. It is widespread but harmless.

Silverfish, magnified

● Silverfish are thin, silvery insects about 1 cm long. They live in crevices in bathrooms and kitchens, and come out at night to look for food scraps.

Animal Babies

All animal species produce **new generations**. Most species reproduce when the climate and food supply is right. For instance, many birds hatch new families in spring, when there is plenty of food to eat.

Within the animal kingdom there are many different kinds of **babies** and methods of **giving birth**.

Strange but true

● Grey tree frogs build nests of foam hanging over water. The tadpoles drop out of the foam when they hatch.

● The ichneumon fly injects its eggs into a caterpillar. The larvae hatch and eat their way out.

● Bacteria divide themselves once every 30 minutes or so.

Babies and parents

Some animals are good **parents**, protecting their babies and teaching them survival skills. However, the majority of creatures give no parental care at all.

● Most fish, amphibians and reptiles lay their eggs and then abandon them. Female fish lay their eggs in the water. Many cannot recognize their own eggs and they often eat them later.

Baby alligator

● The South American discus fish is a good parent. It makes sure that its newborn babies stay close to it for protection, by producing a tasty skin secretion which the babies eat.

● Crocodiles and alligators are caring parents. The female digs a pit, lays her eggs and then covers them with vegetation. When the babies hatch they squeal at the mother to dig them out.

Discus fish

● Mammal mothers feed and tend their young. For instance, most monkeys carry their babies with them wherever they go. The babies hold on to the mothers' fur.

80

Guinea pig:
nine weeks

Human:
nine months

Whale:
one year

Elephant:
twenty months

• The female midwife toad lays a string of eggs on land. The male then carries the string wrapped around his back legs. When they are ready to hatch he takes the eggs to the water.

Male midwife toad

• Young domestic fowl chicks must teach themselves to feed. They begin by pecking at everything on the ground, including their own toes! Gradually they learn which things are the best to eat.

• Some cuckoos do not look after their own chicks. Instead they lay a single egg in a smaller bird's nest. The cuckoo hatches and pushes the other chicks out. Then it takes all the food the unwitting parent brings.

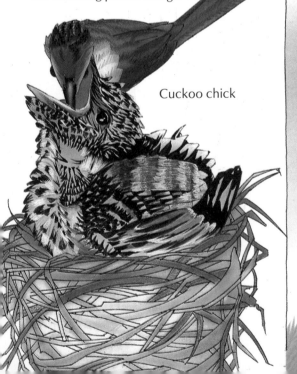

Cuckoo chick

Ways of reproducing

Here are the four basic ways that animals **reproduce**:

• The simplest forms of one-celled animals, such as amoebae, reproduce by splitting themselves in half to form two identical creatures. This is an example of asexual reproduction.

An amoeba splits in two.

A hydra buds to make a new hydra.

• Most animals have different male and female sexes. The male produces cells called sperm. The female produces egg cells called ova. The male sperm must join with the female egg before a new animal is produced. This method is called sexual reproduction.

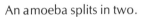

• Some simple animals, such as sea corals and freshwater hydra, produce new creatures by 'budding'. They grow a new branch which is a small version of the parent. Eventually the branch splits off to become a new individual.

Female egg

Male sperm

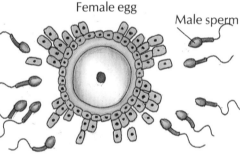

Hermaphrodite worm

• Earthworms and some snails are hermaphrodite. This means that each animal is both male and female, and can produce both sperm and eggs. However, hermaphrodites still have to pair with each other in order to reproduce new creatures.

Eggs and babies

An egg is **fertilized** by a sperm in sexual reproduction. Once this occurs, the egg starts to develop into a new animal.

• Some animals, including most mammals, develop inside their mother's body before they are born. For instance, a newborn foal looks like a miniature version of its parent, and can walk almost immediately.

• Creatures such as birds and many insects lay their eggs once they are fertilized. The babies then develop inside the egg.

Camouflage

Camouflage is a pattern or colouring that **disguises** an animal so that it can hide from enemies, or creep up unseen on prey.

Camouflaged animals blend in with their surroundings. For instance, young deer usually have white spot markings that make them harder to see in the dappled light of a forest.

Some animals, such as the zebra, have vivid skin patterns that blur their outlines and make them hard for predators to see.

Changing colour

Some animals can **change colour** to match different backgrounds. Here are some examples:

- The Arctic fox, snowshoe rabbit and ptarmigan live on the Arctic tundra all year round (see p74). In winter they turn white to blend in with the snow and in summer they change back to darker colours.

Ptarmigan's winter coat

Ptarmigan's summer coat

- The cuttlefish changes colour as it swims over different plants and rocks. It has sacs of colour pigment in its skin. They expand or contract to produce a wide variety of shades.

Cuttlefish

Master of disguise

The **chameleon** is one of the animal kingdom's masters of disguise. It can change colour very quickly.

- The chameleon has colour cells called chromatophores in its body. Brain signals make the cells smaller or larger to alter the reptile's skin colour.

Chromatophores

Nerves in the spine relay brain signals.

Tricking enemies

These animals fool their enemies by looking like **fiercer creatures**:

- Many butterflies have false eyes on their wings to make them look like a much larger animal.

- The hawkmoth caterpillar can disguise itself to look like a deadly viper. It puffs itself up to show a false snake's head.

- The king snake is coloured with red, yellow and black rings to make it look like the much deadlier coral snake.

Strange but true

- Sloths let green algae grow on their hair as camouflage.

- A chameleon's colour can alter depending on its mood. In general, the calmer it is the paler it is.

- A nightjar on its ground nest looks just like a branch. Unfortunately, its camouflage is so good that it sometimes gets stepped on.

Sea colour

Creatures that live in the open sea or in cool waters tend to be dull in colour, whilst those that live in warmer waters are often brightly coloured. Many have startling patterns, too.

- The sea dragon is camouflaged to mimic seaweed. It has skin extensions which look like the long strands of weed it swims through.

Sea dragon

Stonefish

- The poisonous stonefish lives in warm waters. It has a speckled, lumpy body that enables it to lurk unseen amongst the stones on the seabed, waiting to grab passing prey.

Insect hide-and-seek

Insects have many enemies, so they are amongst the most effectively camouflaged creatures in the animal kingdom. They use a variety of different tricks to hide from attackers.

- One species of leaf insect has a flattened body and wings to copy the flat leaves it feeds on. The disguise is so successful that the leaf insects sometimes try to eat each other!

- The Italian cricket can throw its voice, just like a ventriloquist, so its enemies never know where it is.

- Peppered moths living in polluted cities have turned dark brown. Members of the same species living in the countryside have stayed a speckled white colour.

83

Strange Animals

Some animals have unique **abilities** or **body parts** that no other species possess. These individual features have usually been developed as ways of helping an animal to survive in one way of another. For instance, many creatures have unusual **defence mechanisms** to surprise their enemies.

Some creatures have unique body parts that help them to feed or to survive in harsh conditions.

Other animals are so extraordinary that scientists are still baffled by the reasons for their behaviour.

Amazing animals

Here are some animals with **unusual skills**:

● The tarsier can turn its head right round to look behind it without moving its body.

Tarsier

● When the three-banded armadillo is threatened by enemies, it rolls itself into a very tight armoured ball.

Curled-up armadillo

● A gorilla called Koko was taught by humans to use sign language. She used this skill to signal that she wanted a cat as a pet.

Koko the gorilla

● The Texas horned lizard can squirt blood out of its eyes, possibly as a form of defence against enemies.

Texas horned lizard

Strange but true

● Guillemots can 'fly' underwater.

● Flies take off backwards.

● It takes an elephant calf six months to learn how to use its trunk.

● Crocodiles sometimes climb up trees.

Hatchet fish   Stonefish   Arrow crab

• Most lizards have a tail that can break off if the lizard needs to escape from the grip of a predator. The tail is usually capable of growing again, at least once.

• Giraffes have 45-centimetre long black tongues which they can use to clean their ears.

Curious connections

Here are some strange animal **similarities**:

• The African elephant's closest relative is the hyrax, which is the size of a rabbit.

• The giraffe has seven neckbones, exactly the same number as a human.

Hyrax

Bizarre birds

Here are some unusual patterns of **bird** behaviour:

• Once the female Emperor penguin has laid an egg, the male keeps it warm by balancing it on his feet under a flap of skin.

• Some birds, such as the reed warbler, can sing two tunes at once.

Reed warbler

Hummingbird

• The hummingbird is the only bird that can fly backwards.

Fascinating sea animals

The **underwater world** is full of strange surprises:

• The arawana lives in the flooded Amazon rainforest. It can jump up to 2 metres out of the water to feed on small birds or bats in the trees above.

• The African lungfish lives in mud at the bottom of dried-out swamps. It burrows into the ground and covers itself with mucus to keep moist.

• Dolphins, whales and porpoises talk to each other with clicking and whistling noises.

Endangered Animals

Cuban crocodile

About 5000 animal species are **endangered**. This means that their numbers are decreasing and that they may die out forever.

An animal species that has disappeared is called **extinct**. The population of some animal species has become so low that they are almost certain to become extinct within the next 20 years.

The endangered panda.

Some animals' lives are threatened because their homes and food are being destroyed by **pollution**, **farming** or **building**. Some are **hunted** for their fur and meat. Sadly, there is a huge illegal trade in 'luxury' **animal products** such as rare animal skins and furs.

Land mammals

Although there are organizations to protect endangered wildlife, many animals are still being **poached**, which means that they are killed illegally. Here are some examples:

• The rhinoceros is poached for its horn, which some people believe makes good medicine. Since 1960 the world rhino population has dropped by 85 per cent.

• For many years the African elephant was hunted for its ivory tusks, used for jewellery and ornaments. Now the world ivory trade is banned.

Ivory goods

• In Africa, some restaurants serve gorilla steaks. Gorillas are also hunted because they can damage crops. The most endangered species is the mountain gorilla.

• The musk deer is poached for its musk gland, which is used to make perfumes and is said to help treat snake bites.

Marine threat

Harmful chemicals and **oil** find their way into the oceans, making them hazardous for ocean life. Some creatures may escape the pollution, only to become victims of other life-threatening dangers:

• Some countries hunt whales for scientific reasons, but sometimes the carcasses are used illegally for food, despite strict hunting laws.

• Many dolphins and other sea creatures die when they are trapped in huge fishing nets.

Dolphin

Blue whale

Sea otter (Pacific coast)

Snow leopard (Asia)

Lemur (Madagascar)

Whooping crane (North America)

Birds in danger

About one fifth of all the world's endangered species are **birds**. **Oil pollution** causes a large number of bird deaths, but many are **trapped** or **shot** by humans. Protection laws are hard to enforce.

Rare hyacinthine macaws.

● Exotic birds are often captured illegally and sold worldwide as caged pets. Amongst the rarest species is the large hyacinthine macaw of the Brazilian rainforest.

A cormorant clogged with oil.

● An estimated 300,000 seabirds died when oil was spilt from a tanker off Alaska in 1989.

● Several well-known species of fish may eventually disappear because of overfishing. If shoals are caught more quickly than the fish can reproduce, the numbers decline.

Herring shoal

● Many turtles have been forced away from the beaches where they breed, as hotels and tourism take over. Sometimes turtles have been deliberately killed.

Loggerhead turtle

Strange but true

● In Japan you can buy a pair of real turtleshell glasses for about £1000.

● Rare African gorillas are sometimes shot so that their hands can be used to make ashtrays.

● When a mother river dugong is killed, the tears of her young are bottled and sold as good luck potion.

Saving Animals

All over the world, groups of people are working to **protect** endangered animals and to limit fur, skin and ivory hunting.

Areas of land called **reserves** have been set aside to provide safe homes for rare animals. There are also underwater nature reserves, where scuba diving and fishing are limited.

Sometimes rare species are kept in **zoos**, where they can safely breed new generations. Occasionally some of these animals are released back into the wild to build up the species once more.

Project tiger

Until recently, the **tiger** was one of the most threatened animal species in the world. In 1972 the Indian government and the World Wide Fund for Nature launched **Operation Tiger:**

● Tiger reserves were set up across India and Asia to provide safe areas where hunting is banned. Here the animals can breed without disturbance.

● Thanks to the Operation Tiger project, the number of tigers in India alone has more than doubled to over 4000 since the opening of the reserve areas. The tiger is no longer top of the endangered species list, and numbers are continuing to grow.

Tiger reserves in India

● Thousands of people pay to visit the reserves every year. The money helps to maintain the land on the reserves and goes towards funding important research.

Bengal tiger

Strange but true

● The rare kakapo parrot lays one egg every four years.

● The coelacanth fish was thought to be extinct for 70 million years, until one was found alive in 1938.

● Insecticide pollution has been traced in the bodies of Antarctic penguins, thousands of kilometres from civilization.

● The natural habitat of the panda is gradually being destroyed in south-western China. Wildlife groups are working to create reserves for them along the lines of the Operation Tiger project in India.

Zoo work

- The Arabian oryx became extinct in the wild 20 years ago. Surviving oryx were reared in Arizona, USA, and the species is now back in the wild.

Arabian oryx

- Several endangered monkey species have been bred in zoos. However, it is not always safe to release them back into the wild because their jungle homes are still being destroyed.

- The rare Chatham Island black robin was saved from extinction by New Zealand wildlife experts, who used tom tits to foster the robin chicks.

Chatham Island robin

Extinct animals

An animal is officially **extinct** if it has not been seen for over 50 years. Here are some animals forced into extinction by humans.

- The dodo bird once lived on Mauritius. It was killed off in the seventeenth century when humans arrived on the island.

Dodo bird

- The great auk was hunted to extinction in the North Atlantic. It disappeared in the 1500s.

Great auk

- The South African quagga looked like a zebra. It was hunted for food until it died out.

What you can do

Here are some things **you** can do to help protect wildlife:

- Do not buy endangered animal skins or ivory products.

- Never steal birds' eggs from nests.

- Join your local conservation group, to help conserve the wildlife that lives near you.

WWF

World Wide Fund for Nature badge

Wild Animals Facts and Lists

Wild cats

Wild cats are found in all the continents of the world. This table shows where some wild cats live:

	Asia	Africa	India	China	South America	North America	Europe
Cheetah	●						
Hyena	●	●	●	●			
Jaguar					●		
Leopard	●	●	●	●			
Lion			●	●			
Lynx	●		●	●		●	●
Ocelot					●		
Puma					●		
Tiger			●	●			

Endangered and extinct animals

● Scientists believe that up to a third of all known plant and animal species may be extinct by the year 2500.

● Dinosaurs became extinct about 65 million years ago.

● The passenger pigeon from America was killed for food and became extinct in 1899.

Here are some more endangered animals:

Arabian oryx	Sand lizards
Cranes	Spiny anteaters
Crocodiles	Tasmanian wolves
Giant tortoises	The platypus
Golden cats	Tigers
Indian lions	Tragopan pheasants
Lynx	Wallabies
Rhinoceroses	Whales

The last dodo died in 1681

Pets and wild animals

Some wild animals are now often kept as pets:

The European tortoise
The Australasian cockatiel
The Australian budgerigar
African and Asian waxbills
African and Asian gerbils
South American cavies, or guinea pigs
Asian and North European hamsters
(All present-day golden hamsters in capitivity are descended from a litter found in Syria in 1930.)

Flightless birds

Here are some examples of birds that cannot fly, even though they have wings:

Emus	Wattlebirds
Cassowaries	Ostriches
Penguins	Kakapo parrots

Burrowing animals

These animals live in burrows:

Mongooses	Congo eels
Aardwolves	Moles
Hyenas	Rabbits
Burrowing clams	Wombats
Fiddler crabs	

The foods animals eat

Here are some examples of animals that eat meat only (carnivores):

Anacondas	Polar bears
Crocodiles	Praying mantis
Eagles	Tigers
Komodo dragons	Lions

Here are some animals that eat plants and meat (omnivores):

Baboons	Cockroaches
Badgers	Common snapper
Bush babies	Earwigs
Bustards	Harvestmen spiders

These animals eat carrion (the remains of dead animals):

Carrion Beetles	Hyenas
Golden Eagles	Vultures

Pests

● Pests are creatures that destroy crops or other plants.

● Aphids are insects that carry plant diseases and damage plants by eating them.

● Quelea birds may damage whole fields of grain, partly because of the huge numbers that feed together.

● Locusts are a large kind of grasshopper. Some types of locust are among the world's most destructive pests, flying in huge swarms and eating any plant they land on.

● Weevils are a large family of insects. They have long 'snouts' with which they make holes in fruit, nuts or seed. The Granary Weevil and the Rice Weevil are the most destructive pests of grain in the world.

● Colorado beetles are found in parts of the USA and in Europe. They are a serious pest to potato crops and have been known to destroy entire crops by eating them.

Plant eaters

These animals eat mainly plants:
Bears (except polar bears)
Green turtles
Iguanas
Emus

These animals eat only plants:
Gorillas
Rhinoceroses
Zebras
Antelopes
Elephants

Animal communication

Animals communicate with each other so that they can find food, or to attract a mate. This is how some animals communicate:

● Silk moths use their scent to attract a partner.

● Glow-worms have a green light that attracts other glow-worms.

- Mayflies swarm together and 'dance' over the water.

- Honey bees do an elaborate dance that directs the other bees to food.

- Ants leave trails to mark the route from their nest so they can return.

- Blue whales make sounds that can be heard by other whales up to 850 kilometres away.

- Squirrelfish make noises that can be heard even out of the water.

- Sticklebacks swim in a zig-zag pattern to attract females.

Changing shape

Here are some examples of animals that go through metamorphosis (change of shape) at different stages in their life:

Earwigs
Grasshoppers
Dragonflies
Butterflies
Moths
Flies

Migration

Some animals migrate (travel from one place to another) at certain times of the year to breed or find food. These are some examples:

- The North American monarch butterfly travels as far as California and Mexico for the winter months.

- Salmon hatch in rivers and migrate to the sea, returning to their birthplace to breed.

- Eels migrate up to 5600 kilometres to reach their breeding grounds.

- Tuna fish travel long distances to reach the Mediterranean where they breed.

- Many birds migrate, but the Arctic tern travels furthest. It flies from the Arctic to the Antarctic, and back again, a trip of 32,000 kilometres.

Camouflage

Here are some examples of animals that can change colour quickly as a way of hiding from their enemies or prey:

Chameleons
Grouper fish
Flatfish
Octopuses
Tree frogs
Blossom spiders

Night-time animals

Nocturnal animals come out at night to feed or hunt, and rest during the day. These animals are nocturnal:

Many frogs and toads
Coral snakes
The Kakapo parrot
Owls
Nightjars
Opossums

Regrowing limbs

Here are some animals that can regrow parts of their bodies if damaged:

- Starfish can grow new 'arms'.

- Slow-worms can regrow broken-off tails.

- Lizards can grow new tails.

Whales

There are 90 species of whales, dolphins and porpoises. Here are some whales and their sizes:

Blue whale	30 metres
Gray whale	15 metres
Sperm whale	13 metres
Killer whale	6 metres
Pygmy sperm whale	4 metres
Narwhal	4 metres

Hibernation

- To hibernate means to go into a deep sleep through the winter.

- Newts, hedgehogs, bats and dormice hibernate over the winter.

- Only two kinds of birds hibernate, and they are both nightjars.

Desert creatures

This is how some desert animals survive:

- Camels store fat in their humps and water in their stomachs.

- The addax antelope does not need to drink very often.

- Jerboas burrow deep underground to keep away from the heat.

- Rhinoceroses bath in muddy water which then dries on them, protecting them from the Sun.

Biggest sea creatures

These are some of the largest creatures to be found in the sea, apart from whales:

Ribbon worm	54 metres
Whale shark	18 metres
Giant squid	17 metres
White shark	12 metres
Giant spider crab	3.65 metres
Starfish	1.37 metres
American lobster	1 metre

Dangerous animals

- One golden poison-dart frog could kill up to 1500 people with its poison.

- The mosquito carries diseases such as malaria, elephantiasis and yellow fever. Malaria kills over a million people a year.

- The great white shark is the most feared man-eating shark.

Wild Animals Facts and Lists

Reptiles

This table shows the average sizes of some reptiles:

Anaconda	9 metres
Reticulated python	9 metres
Saltwater crocodile	8 metres
King cobra	5.48 metres
Boa constrictor	4.26 metres
Mamba	2.13 metres
Leatherback turtle	2 metres
Grass snake	1 metre
Thread snake	114 mm
Gecko lizard	17 mm

This is how long it takes some reptile eggs to hatch:

Grass lizard	42 days
Marine turtle	55 days
Alligator	61 days
Python	61 days
Tortoise	105 days

Amazing eyes

● The giant squid has the largest eyes of any animal. They can be 39 cm across, which is 16 times wider than a human eye.

● A peregrine falcon can spot its prey from more than 8 km away.

● The golden eagle can spot its prey from over 3 km away.

Giant invertebrates

● The bird-eating spider from South America has a body as big as a child's hand.

● The African giant snail measures over 390 mm when fully grown.

● The Borneo dragonfly has a wingspan of 190 mm.

Birds

● There are about 100 billion birds in the world.

● There are 9000 species of birds.

● The North American ostrich is the tallest bird, at 2.74 metres.

Fast fliers

Spine-tailed swift	170 km/h
Pigeon	96 km/h
Hawk moth	53 km/h
Monarch butterfly	32 km/h
Honeybee	17 km/h

Beaks

The shape of birds' beaks gives a clue to the food they eat and how they eat it:

Hooked bills	eating flesh
Baggy beaks	scooping fish
Spear beaks	spearing fish
	spearing worms
Parrotbills	cracking seeds
Pointed beaks	spearing insects
	eating seeds
Crossbills	removing seeds from fir cone scales
Chisel beaks	boring nest holes and feeding
Tiny beaks	catching insects in the open mouth while flying

Wing shapes

Hovering birds	small, broad wings
Gliding birds	long, thin wings
Diving birds	wings fold back
Circling birds	long, wide wings
Dodging, diving birds	short, wide wings

Animal nests

Nests are made by many animals in lots of different ways:

● Swans make floating nests of reeds and sticks.

● Sticklebacks make nests using sand and weed.

● Swallows make nests using grasses woven or stuck together with mud and spit.

● Queen bumblebees often use old underground voles' nests in which they make a wax egg chamber.

● Siamese fighting fish make nests out of bubbles, which they hold together like shampoo froth.

● Eagles make the biggest nests. A bald eagle nest found in Florida, USA, in 1968 was 2.9 metres wide and 6 metres deep.

Treetop colonies

These birds make treetop nests in groups:

Crows
Herons
Storks
Pelicans
Weaver birds

Eggs

Here are the biggest and smallest bird egg sizes:

Ostrich	177 mm
Helena's hummingbird	12.7 mm

● After an egg has been laid, the time it takes to hatch is called its 'incubation time'.

Egg incubation times:

Finch	12 days
Thrush	14 days
Wren	16 days
Falcon	28 days
Ostrich	42 days
Hawk	44 days
Emperor penguin	63 days
Royal albatross	79 days

Animal sizes

These are the heights of some animals:

Giraffe	5.79 metres
African elephant	3.02 metres
Ostrich	2.74 metres
Brown bear	2.43 metres

Weights

Animal weights, from smallest to largest:

Bee hummingbird	1.4 grams
Mouse	22.4 grams
Goliath beetle	85 grams
Rat	455 grams
Marmoset	0.68 kg
Ringtail monkey	2.72 kg
Otter	5.89 kg
Armadillo	6.12 kg
Ocelot	19.27 kg
Porpoise	46.72 kg
Cheetah	57.83 kg
Alligator	57.83 kg
Llama	170 kg
Polar bear	324 kg
Moose	362 kg
Pilot whale	680 kg
Walrus	1625 kg
African elephant	7112 kg
Sperm whale	37,593 kg
Blue whale	155,963 kg

Animal pregnancies

This is how long some babies take to grow inside their mothers before they are born:

Opossum	13 days
House mouse	19 days
Chimpanzee	237 days
Camel	406 days
Giraffe	410 days
Rhinoceros	560 days
Indian elephant	624 days

Animal speeds

● The sleepiest mammals are armadillos, sloths and opossums. They spend 80 per cent of their lives sleeping or dozing.

● The sleepiest mammals are armadillos, sloths and oppposums. They spend 80 per cent of their lives sleeping or dozing.

Animal lifespans

This is how long some animals live:

Mayfly	1 day
Mouse	2-3 yrs
Rattlesnake	18 yrs
Lion	25 yrs
Hippopotamus	40 yrs
Ostrich	50 yrs
African elephant	60 yrs
Dolphin	65 yrs
Rhinoceros	70 yrs
Tortoise	100 yrs

Animal skins

● Snakes and lizards have scaly skins. The rough scales underneath help a snake to move along. The skin is watertight, enabling snakes and lizards to live in or out of the water.

● Tortoises have developed their scaly skin into an armoured shell.

● Furry or feathered skins keep some animals warm in winter.

● Birds lose some of their feathers in the summer to keep cool.

● Birds such as penguins oil their feathers from an oil gland in their skin to waterproof themselves.

Animal feet

● Swans and ducks have webbed feet which they use as paddles when swimming.

● The blue-footed booby uses its webbed feet to incubate its eggs during breeding.

● Lizards, newts, gorillas and lemurs are examples of animals that have five toes on each foot. Toes are used for climbing and gripping.

● The elephant's foot is also five-toed, but is round and massive to support its weight.

History of how life began

The development of animals and plants has taken millions of years. The facts below shows this evolution as if it had happened in a year.

● January 1: the Earth forms.

● March 29: bacteria and other simple life forms appear.

● November 27: the first fish develop in the sea.

● December 15: the first dinosaurs appear.

● December 28: various mammals develop.

● December 31: the first ape-men appear. Modern humans develop just hours before the end of the year.

WILD ANIMALS
INDEX
Indexes to other sections
are on pages 46, 142 and 190.

aardwolves 90
abdomens of insects 56
addax antelopes 91
African elephants 55, 64, 93
African gerbils 90
African ostriches 63
African waxbills 90
albatrosses 75, 92
alligators 93
    babies 80
    crocodiles, difference 61
    hatching time 92
American lobsters 91
amoebae 81
amphibians 52, 60-1
    babies 80
    deserts 68
anacondas 61, 92
    food 90
    rainforests 67
    size 67
Andean condors 73
Andean sword-billed
    hummingbirds 62
anglerfish 77
animal products 86
annelids 53
Antarctic animals 75
Antarctic squids 75
anteaters 54
antelopes 64-5, 90-1
antennae 56
antlers 70
ants 66
    communication 91
    northern forests 70-1
ape-men 93
apes 52
aphids 53, 90
Apollo butterflies 72
Arabian oryx 89, 90
arachnids 53
arawanas 85
Archaeopteryx 62
Arctic animals 74-5
Arctic foxes 75, 82
Arctic hares 75
Arctic tundra 82
Arctic wolverines 74
armadillos 84, 93
arrow crabs 85
arrow-poison frogs 66
asexual reproduction 81
Asian gerbils 90
Asian waxbills 90
Australasian cockatiels 90
Australian budgerigars 90

babies 80-81
    amphibians 80, 81
    birds 80
    fish 80
    mammals 80
    reptiles 80
baboons 90
backbone
    fish 58
    insects 56
    mammals 54
bacteria 79, 80, 93
badgers 71, 90
bald eagles 92
baleen whales 74, 76
barbs 63
bark beetles 71

basking whales 77
bats 54, 91
beaks 62, 66
    shapes 92
bearded seals 75
bears 93
    food 90
    mountains 72
    polar 74
bed bugs 78
bed mites 79
bee hummingbirds 93
bees 56, 57
    communication 91
    nests 93
beetles 57, 93
    carrion eaters 90
    deserts 67
    home wildlife 78
    northern forests 71
    pests 78-9, 90
    rainforests 67
beluga whales 74
Bengal tigers 88
bighorn sheep 69
bird-eating spiders 92
birds 62-3, 93
    babies 81
    body parts 62-3
    camouflage 82
    deserts 69
    endangered animals 87,
    88-90
    eyes 92
    flightless 90
    hibernation 91
    incubation times 92
    migration 91
    nests 92
    night-time animals 91
    northern forests 71
    pets 90
    rainforests 66
    saving animals 88-9
    scavengers 65
    strange animals 84-5
birds of prey 53, 63, 73
birth 80
blackfly bugs 57
black widow spiders 79
blood temperatures
    cold 56, 58, 60, 68
    warm 54, 60
blossum spiders 91
bluebottle flies 79
blue-footed boobies 93
blue-ringed octopuses 77
blue whales 55, 91
    endangered animals 86
    polar animals 75
    weight 93
boa constrictors 92
bobcats 73
body shape 59, 62
bone skeletons 58
bony fish 58
bookworms 78
Borneo dragonflies 92
bowhead whales 74
bridal burrfish 77
brown bears 93
budding reproduction 81
budgerigars 90
buffaloes 88
bugs 57, 68, 78
bumblebees 92
burrowers 90
bush babies 90
bushmaster snakes 67
bustards 90

butterflies 56-7, 92
    camouflage 83
    deserts 68
    migration 91
    mountains 72
    rainforests 66

cactus wrens 69
caecilians 61
camels 69, 91, 93
camouflage 82-3, 91
cannibals 75
carcasses 65
caribou 74
carnivores 52, 90
carrion eaters 90
cartilaginous fish 59
cassowaries 90
caterpillars 80
    camouflage 83
    metamorphosis 56
    northern forests 71
cats 90
cavies 90
centipedes 71
chameleons 61, 82, 83, 91
chamois goat 72
Chatham Island black
    robins 89
cheetahs 55, 90, 93
chemicals, harmful 86
chicks 81
chimpanzees 90, 93
chinchillas 72
chromatophores 82
chrysalises 56
clams 53, 77, 90
claws 62
cobras 61, 92
cockatiels 90
cockroaches 90
cocoons 56
cod 58
coelacanths 88
coelenterates 52
cold-blooded animals 56, 58,
    60, 68
colonies 62
Colorado beetles, 90
colour changing 82
communication 90-1
compound eyes 56
coniferous forests 70
conservation 88-9
coral snakes 91
corals 52, 76-7
cormorants 63, 87
cougars 72
cows 52
crabeater seals 75
crabs 85, 90
    size 91
    undersea animals 77
cranes 87, 90
crickets 56, 57, 83
crocodiles 60, 61
    babies 80
    deserts 68
    endangered species 86, 90
    food 90
    size 92
    strange abilities 84
crows 92
Cuban crocodiles 86
cuckoos 81
cuttlefish 82

damselflies 57
dangerous animals 91
darkling beetles 68

deciduous forests 70
deepsea fish 77
deer
    camouflage 82
    endangered species 86
    northern forests 70
defence mechanisms 84-5
desert animals 68, 91
desert tortoises 69
dinosaurs 52, 90, 93
discus fish 80
diseases 57, 90
disguises 82
dodos 89, 90
dogfish 59
dogs 65
dolphins 54
    communication 85
    endangered species 86
    life span 93
dormice 91
dragonflies 56, 57, 91, 92
dromedary camel 69
duck-billed platypuses 54
ducks 63, 93
dugongs 87
dwarf gobies 58

eagles 63
    food 90
    mountains 73
    nests 92
    rainforests 66
earth, history of 93
earthworms 53, 81
earwigs 90, 91
echinoderms 53
eels 58, 90, 91
eggs
    amphibians 60
    birds 62
    conservation 89
    desert animals 68
    fish 59
    hatching periods 92
    home wildlife 78
    incubation times 92
    insects 56
    mammals 54
    reproduction 80-1
    reptiles 60
    sizes 92
elands 64
elephants 55, 84
    endangered species 86
    food 90
    grasslands 64, 65
    pregnancy length 81
elf owls 69
emperor penguins 75, 85, 92
emus 68, 69, 90
endangered species 86-90
European tortoises 90
evolution 93
exoskeleton, insects 56
extinction 86, 88-90
eyes
    amazing types 92
    insects 56
    mammals 55

fabric eaters 78
falcons 92
fangs 61
farming 86
feathers 62-63, 93
feet 93
fennec foxes 69
fertilization 81
finches 92

fins 59
fish 53, 58-9
    babies 80
    body parts 58-9
    camouflage 82, 83, 91
    communication 90-1
    deepsea 77
    endangered animals 87
    extinct 88
    food chains 76
    history 93
    migration 91
    nests 92
    polar animals 75
    reproduction 59
    strange animals 85
    undersea animals 76-7
flamingoes 62, 63
flatfish 83, 91
fleas 75, 78, 91
flies 57, 91
    body parts 56
    home wildlife 79
    polar animals 75
    strange abilities 84
flightless birds 63, 90
flying birds 62
flying snakes 67
flying squirrels 67
foals 81
food 53, 64-5, 90
food chains 53, 76
food stealers 79
forest animals 70
forests 70-71
fowls 81
foxes
    camouflage 82
    northern forests 70
    polar animals 75
fresh water amphibians 60
frilled lizards 60
frogs 52, 60, 84
    camouflage 91
    dangerous animals 91
funnelweb spiders 78
fur 93
    endangered animals 86
    mammals 54
    mountain animals 72
furniture beetles 78
furniture eaters 78

gannets 63
gazelles 64
gecko lizards 92
generations, new 80-1
gerbils 90
giant albatrosses 75
giant butterflies 66
giant eagles 66
giant invertebrates 92
giant pandas 55
giant snails 66, 92
giant spider crabs 91
giant squids 91, 92
giant tortoises 90
giant whale sharks 58
gila woodpeckers 69
gills 58, 78
giraffes 55, 85
    grasslands 64-5
    size 93
gliders 67
glow-worms 90
goats 72
golden cats 90
golden eagles 73, 90, 92
golden hamsters 80, 90
golden lion marmosets 54, 67

golden poison-dart frogs 91
goliath beetles 67, 93
gorillas 55
    endangered species 86, 87
    feet 93
    food 90
    strange animals 84
grasshoppers 57, 91
grassland animals 64-5
grass lizards 92
grass snakes 92
gray whales 91
grazers 64
great auks 89
greenflies 56
green turtles 88, 91
grey tree frogs 80
griffon vultures 72
ground squirrels 68
grouper fish 91
grubs 56
guillemots 84
guinea pigs 81, 90

hagfish 58
hairy frogs 61
hamsters 80, 90
hares 73, 75
harmful insects 78-9
harvestmen spiders 90
hatchet fish 85
hawk moths 83, 92
hawks 63, 92
hedgehogs 91
Helena's hummingbirds 92
herbivores 52, 90
herds 64
hermaphrodites 81
herons 92
herrings 58, 87
hibernation 73, 91
hippopotamuses 93
history 93
home wildlife 78-9
honey bees 91, 92
hornbills 66
horned escuerzo 61
housefiles 79
house mice 79, 93
humans 52, 54, 81, 93
hummingbirds 62
    egg size 92
    rainforests 66
    strange abilities 85
hunters 79
hunting animals 86
hunting dogs 65
hunting grounds 78
hyacinthine macaws 87
hydras 81
hyenas 65, 90
hyraxes 85

ichneumon flies 80
iguanas 90, 91
Indian elephants 93
Indian leaf butterflies 83
Indian lions 90
insecticides 88
insects 53
    body parts 56
    camouflage 83
    communication 90-1
    dangerous animals 91
    deserts 68
    giant invertebrates 92
    harmful 78-9
    home wildlife 69
    metamorphosis 91
    nests 92

northern forests 71
    pests 90
    rainforests 66, 67
    reproduction 81
invertebrates 5
Italian crickets 83
ivory 86, 89

jaguars 90
Javan rhinos 55, 66
jawless fish 58
jellyfish 52
jerboas 91
Jesus Christ lizards 66

kakapo parrots 88, 90, 91
kangaroo rats 69
kangaroos 54
keratin in feathers 63
kestrels 89
killer whales 91
king cobras 92
king snakes 83
Koko, gorillas 84
Komodo dragons 60, 90
krills 74-5

lampreys 58
larvae 56, 78, 80
lateral lines 59
leatherback turtles 92
lemmings 74
lemurs 87, 93
leopards
    endangered species 87
    grasslands 65
    mountains 73
lice 75
life spans 93
limbs, regrowth 91
lionfish 76
lions 55, 90
    carnivores 52
    grasslands 65
    life span 93
lizards 60-1
    deserts 68, 69
    hatching time 92
    limb regrowth 91
    size 92
    skin 93
    unusual skills 84, 85
llamas 72, 93
lobsters 91
locusts 90
loggerhead turtles 87
lungfish 85
lynxes 90

macaws 66, 87
maggots 56
malaria 56
male tree frogs 84
mambas 92
mammals 52, 54-5, 90-1, 93
    babies 80-1
    burrowers 90
    deserts 69, 91
    endangered species 90
    feet 93
    food 90
    grasslands 64, 65
    life-spans 93
    mountain regions 72-3
    northern forests 70, 71
    pets 90
    polar animals 74, 75
    pregnancy length 93
    rainforests 67
    record-breakers 55

sizes 93
    speeds 93
    weights 93
margays 67
marine turtles 92
marmosets 54, 67, 93
marmots 73
marsupials 54
martens 70
Mauritius kestrels 89
mayflies 91, 93
meat-eaters 65
metamorphosis 56, 60, 91
Mexican caecilians 61
mice 53, 70, 79, 93
microbes 75
midwife toads 81
migration 74, 91
millipedes 71
mites 75, 79
moles 90
molluscs 53
moloch lizards 69
monarch butterflies 91, 92
mongooses 90
monkeys 55
    endangered species 89
    rainforests 67
    weight 93
monotremes 54
mooses 93
mosquitoes 56, 91
moths 56, 57
    camouflage 83
    communication 90
    home wildlife 78
    metamorphosis 91
mountain animals 72-73
mountain gorillas 55
mountain hares 73
mountain pygmy possums 89
mud puppies 60
musk deer 86
musk oxen 74

narwhals 74, 91
nerves 82
nesting places 78
nests 63, 81, 92
new generations 80
newts 60, 61, 91, 93
nightjars 83, 91
night-time animals 91
nocturnal animals 91
northern forest animals 70

ocean wildlife 74-7
ocelots 67, 90, 93
octopuses 53, 91
oil damage 86, 87
oil protection 93
okapis 66
omnivores 52, 90
one-celled animals 81
Operation Tiger 88
opossums 90, 91, 93
orang-utans 67
organized communities 56
oryxes 64
    Arabian 89, 90
ospreys 63
ostriches 90, 92, 93
otters 87, 93
ova 81
owls 63, 69, 91
oxygen 52, 58, 72

pampas 64
pandas 55
    conservation 88

endangered species 86
  mountains 73
panthers 72
parasites 78
parents 80
parrots 63, 88
passenger pigeons 92
peacocks 62
pelicans 92
penguins 90, 92-3
  polar animals 75
  pollution 88
  unusual skills 85
peppered moths 83
peregrine falcons 62, 92
pests 78-9, 90
pets 90
phytoplankton 76
pigeons 92
pill millipedes 71
pilot whales 93
pine martens 70
placental babies 54
plaice 58
plant eaters 64, 90
plants 93
platypuses 90
poaching 86
poisonous fish 76-7, 83
poisonous snakes 60, 68
polar animals 74-5
polar bears 74
  food 90
  weight 93
pollution 86-7
  insecticides 88
polyps 76
pond skaters 57
porifans 53
porpoises 85, 91, 93
praying mantises 90
predators 52, 82, 85
pregnancies, lengths 80-1, 93
prey 63
primates 54, 55
products, animal 86
protection 88-9
ptarmigans 82
pufferfish 58
pumas 72, 90
pupas 56
pygmy possums 89
pygmy sperm whales 91
pythons 61, 92

quaggas 89
queen bumblebees 92
queleas 90

rabbits
  burrowers 90
  camouflage 82
  northern forests 71
ragworms 53
rainforest animals 66-7
raptors 63, 73
rats 69, 93
rattlesnakes 68, 93
rays 59
red deer 70
red-kneed tarantulas 68
red pandas 73
reed warblers 85
regrowth of limbs 91
reindeer 74
reproduction 80-81
reptiles 52, 60-61
  babies 80
  camouflage 82
  endangered animals 90

mountains 72
rainforests 67
size 92
reticulated pythons 92
reserves 88
rhinoceroses 55
  deserts 91
  endangered 66, 86, 90
  food 90
  grasslands 64
  life span 93
ribbon worms 91
ringed seals 75
ringtail monkeys 93
roadrunners 69
Rocky Mountain goats 72
rodents 52
  deserts 69
  home wildlife 79
  mammals 54
  northern forests 70
  polar animals 74
royal albatrosses 92

saguaro cactus 69
Sahara desert life 68
salamanders 60-1
salmon 58, 91
saltwater crocodiles 92
sand lizards 90
savanna life 64
saving animals 88-9
sawfish 77
scavengers 65, 73
scientific groups 54
scorpions 79
sea anemones 52
sea animals 91
seabirds 74-5, 87
sea corals 81
sea dragons 83
seahorses 59
seals 75
sea otters 87
sea sponges 53
sea urchins 53
seaweed 76
sexual reproduction 81
shape change 56, 60, 91
sharks 59, 77, 91
sheep 69
shoals 78
shrimps 62
Siamese fighting fish 92
sidewinder snakes 68
silk 79
single-celled creatures 52
skates 59
skeletons 56, 62
skin 60, 93
  camouflage 82
  saving animals 89
sloths 67, 83, 93
slow-worms 91
slugs 53
snails 53
  giant invertebrates 92
  northern forests 70
  rainforests 66
  reproduction 81
snakes 60-1, 91
  camouflage 83
  deserts 68
  rainforests 67
  sizes 92
  skin 93
snappers 90
snow leopards 73, 87
snowshoe rabbits 82
soles 58

Sonoran desert life 69
South American cavies 90
spadefoot toads 68
spawn 60
species 58
spectacled bears 72
speed records 92, 93
sperm 81
sperm whales 91, 93
spiders 53, 90
  camouflage 91
  deserts 91
  giant invertebrates 92
  home wildlife 78, 79
  mountains 72
spine-tailed swifts 92
spiny anteaters 90
squids 75, 91
  large eyes feature 92
squirrelfish 91
squirrels 68, 71
stag beetles 57
stags 70-71
starfish 53, 91
steppe eagles 73
stick insects 83
sticklebacks 91, 92
stingrays 77
stonefish 85
  camouflage 83
  poisonous animals 77
storks 92
strange animals 84-5
suckling 54
Surinam toads 61
survival 84-5
swallows 92
swans 92, 93
swifts 62
swim bladders 58

tadpoles 60, 80
talons 63
tarantulas 68
tarsiers 84
Tasmanian wolves 90
teeth 74
temperatures
  deserts 68
  rainforests 66
tentacles 76, 77
termites 79
terrapins 60
Texas horned lizards 84
thermals 73
thoraxes, insects 56
thread snakes 92
three-banded armadillos 84
thrushes 92
tigers 55
  conservation 88
  food 90
tigons 55
tilapias 59
toads 60
  babies 81
  desert 68
tortoises 60
  deserts 69
  endangered species 90
  European 90
  hatching time 92
  life span 93
  pets 90
  skin 93
toucans 66
Tragopan pheasants 90
tree frogs 84, 91
trees 70
treetop colonies 92

tropical grasslands 64
trumpetfish 77
tsetse flies 56
tuna 91
  food chains 76
tundras 74
turtles 60
  endangered species 87, 88
  food 90
  hatching time 92

undersea animals 76-7
unusual skills 84

vertebrates 54
vicunas 72
viperfish 77
voles 92
vultures 64, 65, 90

wallabies 90
walruses 93
warblers 85
warrens 71
wasps 57
water, deserts 68
water birds 63
wattlebirds 90
waxbills 90
weaver birds 63, 92
webs 79
weevils 90
weights 93
whales 54, 91
  babies 81
  endangered species 86, 90
  polar animals 74-5
  strange abilities 85
  weights 93
whale sharks 91
white sharks 91
whooping cranes 87
wild cats 90
wildebeest 64
wildlife
  home 78-9
  ocean 76-7
wingless flies 75
wings
  birds 62, 73
  insects 57, 66
  shapes 92
wobbegongs 77
wolverines 74
wombats 74
wood ants 71
woodcocks 82
wood eaters 78
woodlice 71, 78
wood mice 70
woodpeckers 63, 69, 71
woodworms 78
'woolly bears' 78
worms 91
  communication 90
  reproduction 81
  undersea animals 77
wrens 69, 92

yaks 72

zebras 52
  camouflage 82
  food 90
  grasslands 64, 65
zooplankton 76
zoos 88

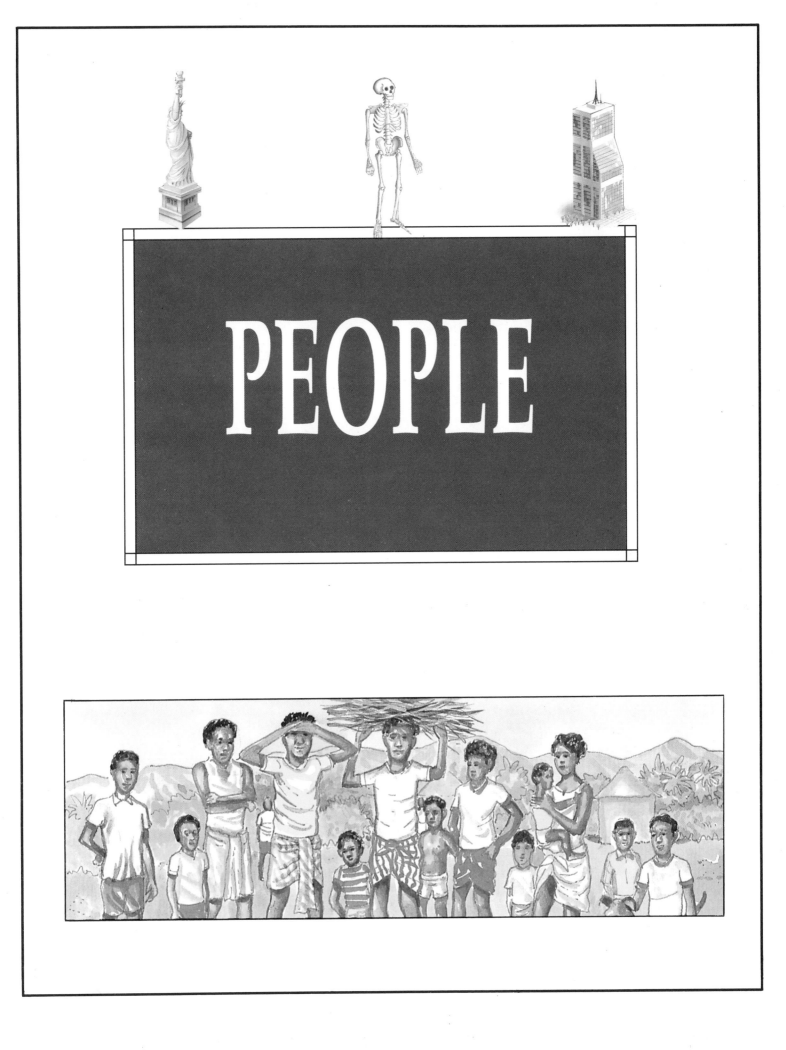

PEOPLE

Part Three

PEOPLE

The First People	100
People of the World	102
The Human Body	104
Body Controls	106
New Life	108
Living Together	110
Talking to Each Other	112
Food	114
Clothes	116
Homes	118
Religion	120
Government	122
The Arts	124
Famous People	126
Inventions	128
Sports and Games	130
Limits and Records	132
Conflict and Crime	134
The Future	136
People Facts and Lists	138
Index	142

Introduction

In this Part, you can discover how your body works, how people live around the world, and some important things that people have done in the past.

Human beings are remarkable creatures, and the human body is an amazing collection of different parts, including thousands of kilometres of internal tubing. Did you know that on average, a person eats 50 tonnes of food and drinks 50,000 litres of liquid in a lifetime?

Human beings are the only creatures that wear clothes, because people's bodies don't have any fur or feathers to protect them.

Did you know that some nomadic people live in tents, so that they can move around looking for work or pasture for their animals?

People believe in many different gods and religions, and have done for thousands of years. Early humans thought that their gods made things like thunderstorms happen.

Find out about people who have become famous in history for their daring deeds, or for helping others, or for things that they have created.

Life on Earth has changed more during the last hundred years than at any other time since people lived on the planet.

The First People

Pebble tools: Homo habilis (2.5 million years ago)

The first recognizable **human beings** probably appeared about 2 million years ago, although groups of human-like creatures existed before then. People looking similar to ourselves have lived on Earth for only about 100,000 years – which is just a fraction of time in the history of the Earth.

The first humans

Scientists studying **fossils** of bones and other remains have managed to piece together some idea of what the **first humans** were like.

Australopithecines

● 3.5 million years ago, Australopithecines lived in Africa. They had ape-like faces but walked upright and probably used sticks and pieces of bone as tools.

Neanderthal skull

Modern skull

● Two million years ago, creatures called Homo habilis (handy man) lived in Africa. They had larger brains than Australopithecines. They sharpened stones to make tools, built shelters and worked together to hunt animals.

Homo habilis

● Homo erectus (upright man) appeared 1.6 million years ago, first in Africa then also spreading to Asia. These people were taller than Homo habilis, with larger brains. They used many different stone tools and discovered how to use fire for cooking and keeping warm.

Homo erectus

A Neanderthal man

● About 200,000 to 100,000 years ago Homo sapiens (thinking man) appeared. People today belong to this group. The Neanderthal people were an early kind of Homo sapiens. They lived in caves in Europe until 40,000 years ago, wore animal skins and made carvings of animals.

Strange but true

● The axes in use today are very like some of the earliest hunting weapons.

● About 30,000 years ago, some humans in Central Europe built huts from mammoth bones covered over with animal skins.

● Early humans may have learned to cook meat by accidentally dropping it onto a fire.

● The human being's nearest animal relatives are thought to be gorillas, chimpanzees and orang-utans.

The first modern people

The Neanderthal people gradually died out, but by this time other types of **Homo sapiens** had developed and spread around the world. These are some of the things the **first modern humans** did:

• Decorated tools with pictures of animals and painted hunting scenes on the walls of their cave homes.

• Made jewellery from shells and animal teeth, and clothes from skins sewn together with needles made of bone.

• Buried their dead, painting the bodies red and putting tools and weapons in the graves. This may have been part of a religious ceremony, showing belief in life after death.

The first farmers

At first, people lived as **nomads**, which means they wandered around in small groups or tribes searching for good hunting grounds. About 10,000 years ago an important change took place. People living in the Middle East began to settle down and farm. These **first farmers** learned how to:

• Sow seeds and grow crops.

• Capture wild goats and sheep and breed them to provide people with milk, meat and skins.

• Build houses of mud and straw that dried hard in the sun.

• Bake bread in ovens. Early bread was flat and hard.

Towns and trading

When people settled in groups or communities, they sometimes produced more goods than they needed for themselves. So they began to **trade** their extra goods for other things made by people nearby. Gradually, towns grew in size and became busy **trading centres**.

• People living in settled farming communities had more time to develop skills such as pottery, weaving and tool-making.

• Eventually, some people became craftworkers, specializing in making certain goods to sell.

• Before money was invented, people bartered (swapped) their goods. People with spare wheat, for example, might swap it with someone else for pottery or wool.

Weaving at a loom

101

People of the World

For thousands of years the **number of people** living on Earth increased very slowly. Early peoples lived **shorter lives** than most people do today. Very little was known about **medicine**, so many people died from illness or injury before they reached old age.

Today, in many countries people are better housed and fed and there are **medical services** to take care of illness, so people live longer. As a result, the number of people in the world has grown rapidly.

BC and AD

The letters BC after a number mean the years before the birth of Christ. AD (written before the number) stands for the Latin words anno domini (year of Our Lord) and means a date after the birth of Christ.

● BC numbers count backwards, so (for example) 1000 BC is further back in time than 500 BC.

How cities have grown

These are the populations of some of the world's largest **cities**, now and in the past:

The population explosion

About 155 people are born every minute of every day. This recent rise in population is often called the **population explosion**. If this rate of growth continues, the world population will · have trebled by the end of the next century.

● World population grew much more slowly in the past. It took about 11,500 years for it to grow from 10 million to 500 million. Since 1800 it has grown very quickly.

This diagram shows how the population has increased over the last thousand years.

POPULATION–BILLIONS

1000 /1100 /1200 /1300 /1400 /1500 /1600 /1700 /1830 /1930 /1961 /1975 /1987 /2000 AD

These are some **population figures** from the past:

● In 8000 BC there were probably only about 6 million people in the world. Most lived in Asia and Africa.

● By AD 1, people had spread to most parts of the world. The population had grown to about 255 million.

● By 1600 the world population had doubled to about 500 million.

● In 1987 the world population rose to 5 billion, ten times as many people as in 1600. About three-quarters of the world's people today live in Asia and Europe.

● At its present rate of growth, the world population doubles about every 40 years.

Rome

Jericho

● 27,000 BC: The city of Dolní Vestonice (in modern Slovakia) contained about 100 people.

● 7800 BC: Jericho (now in occupied Jordan) contained about 27,000 people.

● As early as 133 BC, Rome was a huge city with a million inhabitants.

Great Britain: 75 years

USA: 76 years

Ethiopia: 52 years

Strange but true

- The Chinese population is increasing at 35,000 a day – over 12 million a year!

- At present, one person in three is under 15 years of age. Fewer than one person in ten is over 64 years of age.

- It is estimated that the average length of life in AD 400 was about 33 years for a man and 27 for a woman.

- In these countries most people live in towns or cities: UK 91%, Australia 85%, USA and Japan 76%. In these countries, most people live in the country and work as farmers: India 72%, Kenya 80% and Burkina (Africa) 91%.

Population problems

The rapid rise in population has created many **problems**:

- Shortage of food. To feed everyone, we will have to produce more food and share it out more fairly.

- Pollution due to the increased use of fuels. Supplies of oil, coal and gas are also running low and cannot be replaced.

- Destruction of wildlife habitats for housing, industry and farming.

- Widespread poverty and hunger, especially in Africa and Asia.

- Shortage of housing.

- Unemployment.

Countries

At present, the world is divided into about 170 **independent countries**. This number keeps changing, as countries join together or become separate.

- An independent country is one that has its own government, makes its own laws and has its own flag.

Vatican City

- The smallest independent country is the Vatican City in Rome. It is an area of 0.4 sq km governed by the Roman Catholic Church.

- The country with the highest population is China, with over 1 billion people living there.

London

- London did not have one milliion inhabitants until 1800. Now it has over 6 million.

Tokyo

- Some modern cities:
  1985: Mexico City, 8.8 million
  1989: Tokyo, Japan, 8.2 million
  1988: New York, 7.3 million
  1989: Shanghai, China, 7.2 million

The Human Body

The **human body** is made up of many different parts, including billions of **cells**, thousands of kilometres of **tubing** and hundreds of **muscles** and **bones**. Each of the many different parts of the body has its own special job, but all the parts have to work together to keep the body alive.

Cells

Everything in the body is made up of tiny living units called **cells**. A fully grown body has about **50 billion cells**.

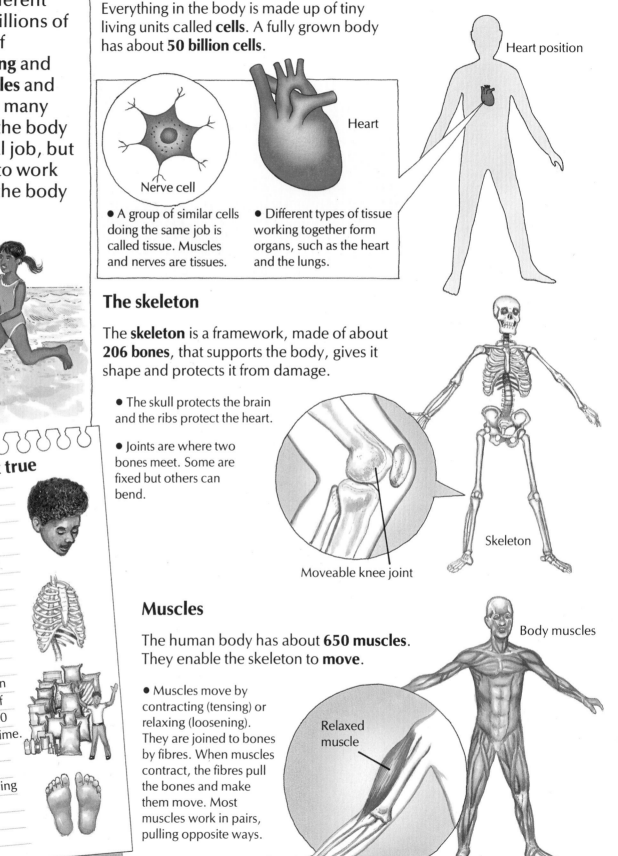

Nerve cell

Heart

Heart position

Heart

Skeleton

Moveable knee joint

Relaxed muscle

Body muscles

- A group of similar cells doing the same job is called tissue. Muscles and nerves are tissues.

- Different types of tissue working together form organs, such as the heart and the lungs.

The skeleton

The **skeleton** is a framework, made of about **206 bones**, that supports the body, gives it shape and protects it from damage.

- The skull protects the brain and the ribs protect the heart.

- Joints are where two bones meet. Some are fixed but others can bend.

Muscles

The human body has about **650 muscles**. They enable the skeleton to **move**.

- Muscles move by contracting (tensing) or relaxing (loosening). They are joined to bones by fibres. When muscles contract, the fibres pull the bones and make them move. Most muscles work in pairs, pulling opposite ways.

Strange but true

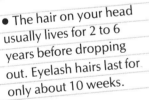

- The hair on your head usually lives for 2 to 6 years before dropping out. Eyelash hairs last for only about 10 weeks.

- Most people have 12 pairs of rib bones, but some have 13.

- On average, a human being eats 50 tonnes of food and drinks 50,000 litres of liquid in a lifetime.

- Each person walks about 25,000 km during a lifetime.

The blood system

Blood carries **oxygen gas** and dissolved food particles called **nutrients** to all the cells in the body, so that they can make **energy**.

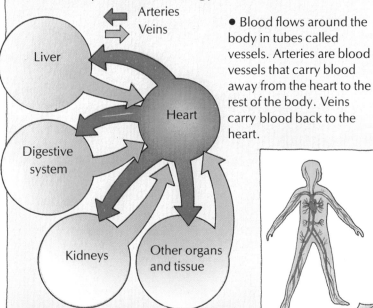

Arteries
Veins

Liver

Heart

Digestive system

Kidneys

Other organs and tissue

● Blood flows around the body in tubes called vessels. Arteries are blood vessels that carry blood away from the heart to the rest of the body. Veins carry blood back to the heart.

The lungs

Oxygen passes into the blood through the lung walls when we breathe in. Waste **carbon dioxide** gas is passed back into the lungs from the blood.

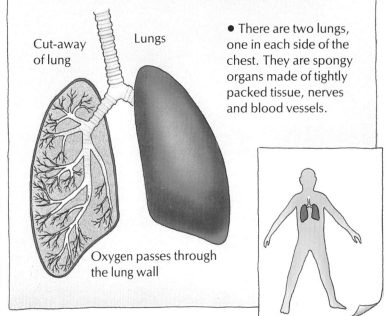

Cut-away of lung

Lungs

● There are two lungs, one in each side of the chest. They are spongy organs made of tightly packed tissue, nerves and blood vessels.

Oxygen passes through the lung wall

The digestive system

Everything a human being eats has to be broken down by the body before **nutrients** from the food can be taken into the blood and turned into energy.

This process takes place in the **digestive system**, a series of connected parts that make up a passage beginning at the mouth and ending at the anus.

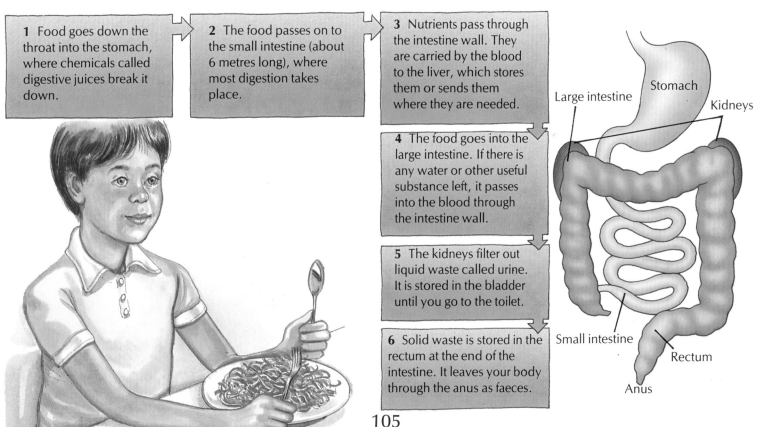

1 Food goes down the throat into the stomach, where chemicals called digestive juices break it down.

2 The food passes on to the small intestine (about 6 metres long), where most digestion takes place.

3 Nutrients pass through the intestine wall. They are carried by the blood to the liver, which stores them or sends them where they are needed.

4 The food goes into the large intestine. If there is any water or other useful substance left, it passes into the blood through the intestine wall.

5 The kidneys filter out liquid waste called urine. It is stored in the bladder until you go to the toilet.

6 Solid waste is stored in the rectum at the end of the intestine. It leaves your body through the anus as faeces.

Large intestine

Stomach

Kidneys

Small intestine

Rectum

Anus

105

Body Controls

 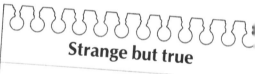

The human body has a very efficient system for **sensing** the world around it. It can feel, see, hear, smell and taste things and deal with all this information better than any computer. It has to do this to survive.

All the information the body receives is processed by the **brain**, which is thought to be more highly developed in humans than in any other animal species.

Brain power

The **brain** is the body's **control centre**. It keeps the body running smoothly, thinks and makes decisions, stores memories and produces feelings such as happiness, anger and sorrow.

● The body is continually sending messages to the brain telling it what is happening. The brain sends messages back telling the body parts what to do. The messages pass along nerves that run throughout the body.

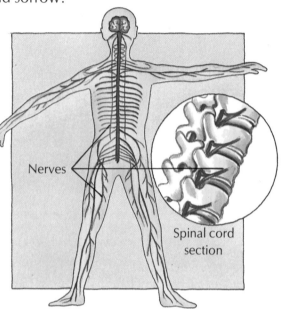

Nerves

Spinal cord section

● Nerves work rather like telephone wires, carrying information in the form of tiny electrical signals.

● The spinal cord is a large bundle of nerves that runs from the brain down the back, inside the bones that make up the spine. Smaller nerves run from the spinal cord to the rest of the body. Messages travel up and down the spinal cord.

● The brain gets messages about the world outside the body from the senses. People have five main senses – sight, hearing, smell, taste and touch. The sense organs are the body parts that sense things. They are the eyes, ears, nose, tongue and skin.

Strange but true

● An adult's brain weighs about 1.4 kg. It is roughly the size and shape of a cauliflower.

● The body's fastest messages pass along the nerves at 400 km/h.

● Very few women are colour-blind, but on average 1 in 12 men cannot see some colours properly.

● One brain cell may be connected to as many as 25,000 other brain cells.

Seeing

The **eye** has a special lining called the **retina**. This contains cells that are sensitive to light. Messages from these cells pass along **nerves** to the **brain**, which works out what the eyes are looking at.

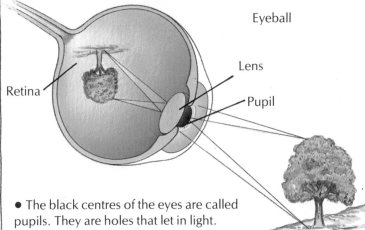

Eyeball

Lens

Pupil

Retina

● The black centres of the eyes are called pupils. They are holes that let in light.

● Behind the pupil is a lens. It focuses light rays into an upside-down picture on the retina inside the back of the eyeball. The brain turns the image the right way up.

Hearing

The part of the ear you can see is called the **outer ear**. This collects and funnels sounds into the **inner ear**. Inside the inner ear:

● The sounds make the eardrum vibrate, or shake. The vibrations pass on through two small bones called the hammer and the anvil, and then through a group of three tiny bones called the stirrup.

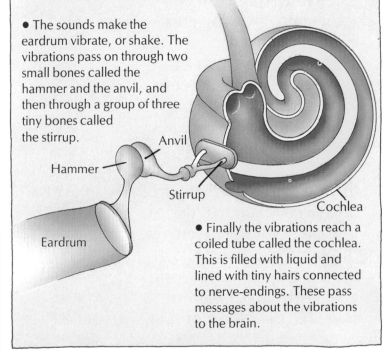

Anvil

Hammer

Stirrup

Cochlea

Eardrum

● Finally the vibrations reach a coiled tube called the cochlea. This is filled with liquid and lined with tiny hairs connected to nerve-endings. These pass messages about the vibrations to the brain.

Smelling and tasting

Inside the back of the **nose** there are nerve-endings that pick up **smells** and send messages about them to the brain. On the **tongue**, special groups of cells called **tastebuds** pick up and send messages about **taste**.

● Tiny smell molecules travel through the air and enter the nasal cavity behind your nose.

Magnified tastebud

Nasal cavity

● Tastebuds can pick up four basic kinds of taste – bitter, sweet, sour and salty.

Touching

Your **skin** is full of nerve-endings that supply the brain with information about **touch**. There are lots of different nerve-endings to pick up information about different kinds of touch sensations.

● A piece of skin the size of a small coin has at least 35 nerve-endings in it, as well as over 3 million cells, 1 metre of blood vessels and many tiny bundles of cells called glands, which produce sweat and oil.

107

New Life

All new life begins with just one **cell**. To make this first cell, a male **sperm** must enter a female **egg** called an **ovum**. The cell then starts growing and dividing to make new cells. These divide in turn to make the millions of cells found in the human body. The creation of new life is called **reproduction**.

People grow and change throughout their lives, from birth to old age. No two human beings are exactly the same in looks or in personality, but everyone goes through the same stages of development.

How babies are born

The moment when a sperm enters an egg is called **conception** or **fertilization**.

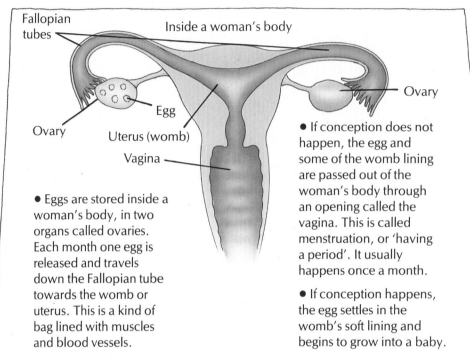

Inside a woman's body

Fallopian tubes

Ovary

Egg

Ovary

Uterus (womb)

Vagina

● Eggs are stored inside a woman's body, in two organs called ovaries. Each month one egg is released and travels down the Fallopian tube towards the womb or uterus. This is a kind of bag lined with muscles and blood vessels.

● If conception does not happen, the egg and some of the womb lining are passed out of the woman's body through an opening called the vagina. This is called menstruation, or 'having a period'. It usually happens once a month.

● If conception happens, the egg settles in the womb's soft lining and begins to grow into a baby.

Strange but true

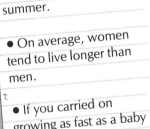

● Children tend to grow faster in spring and summer.

● On average, women tend to live longer than men.

● If you carried on growing as fast as a baby does in the womb, you would be 16 metres tall by the time you were 10 years old!

● The most babies born to a mother at one birth is 10.

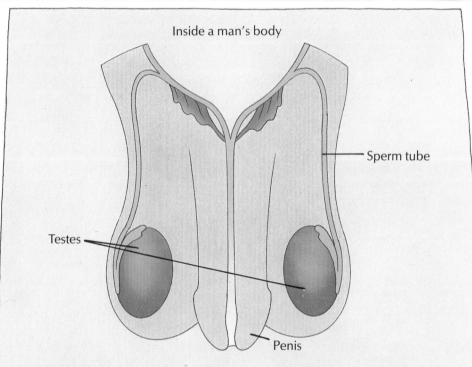

Inside a man's body

Sperm tube

Testes

Penis

● Sperm are made in a man's testes, two organs near to the penis. Millions of microscopic sperm are put into the woman's vagina by the man's penis during sexual intercourse, or making love. They swim up towards the Fallopian tubes, but only one enters the egg.

Iron: as much as in a 2.5 cm-long nail

Carbon: as much as in 9000 pencils

Water: two-thirds of the body is water. Adults contain about 45 litres.

How babies grow

From **conception** to **birth** takes about 38 weeks. Here are some of the stages along the way:

● 6 weeks: the baby is very small, about 2.4 cm long. It has begun to develop a nervous system, a heart, digestive tract and sense organs. It has buds that will develop into arms and legs.

● 12 weeks: the baby is between 6.25 cm and 7.5 cm long. It is inside a fluid-filled bag called the amniotic sac, connected to its mother by an umbilical cord. The cord is attached to a placenta that transfers blood and oxygen between mother and baby.

● 28 weeks: the baby is between 30 and 36 cm long and weighs about 900 grams. A creamy-coloured wax has now developed over its body, to stop the fluid in the amniotic sac from making its skin dry out.

● Around 38 weeks: the baby is ready to be born. It is 50 cm long and weighs 3 to 5 kg.

Umbilical cord

Placenta

About 6 weeks

About 12 weeks

About 28 weeks

About 38 weeks

From child to adult

The period of time when children are growing into adults is called **adolescence**. The early part of adolescence, when bodies change, is called **puberty**. The changes take place at any time between the ages of 10 and 15. Here are some of them:

● Girls start to menstruate (have periods). Their breasts start to grow bigger, their hips get broader and they grow more body hair.

● Boys start making sperm in their testes. They grow facial hair and their voices 'break' or deepen. Their shoulders and chests get broader.

Growing older

Once people are fully grown their bodies very slowly start to **wear out** and **slow down**.

● When women get older, eggs stop being released from their ovaries. They cannot have babies any more because menstruation stops. This time is called the menopause. For most women it happens some time during their late 40s or early 50s.

● In old age, bones become more fragile, skin stretches and wrinkles, and hair often goes white and gets thinner. Muscles become weaker and some people cannot hear or see as well as they once could.

Living Together

Most people live in small groups called **families** that contain **parents**, **children** and (sometimes) other **relatives**. One important purpose of the family is to look after its members. The aged and sick can be looked after by younger members of the family, and babies and young children can be cared for until they are old enough to look after themselves.

Not all families are the same. Here you can find out about some of the ways people live around the world.

Families

There are different **kinds of families**. Nuclear families are the most common kind, but there are many other family patterns.

- Nuclear family: a mother, father and a child or children living together.

- Extended family: a large group of grandparents, parents, children and other relatives all living together.

- Single-parent family: a child or children living with one parent only.

- Commune: a large group of people living together as a family, but not necessarily related.

- Clan or tribe: a large group made up of families that are related to each other.

Strange but true

- The custom of giving wedding rings dates back to Ancient Roman times.

- An American man called Glynn Wolfe has been married a total of 27 times!

- Viking families always sent their children away to live with other people.

- 6516 couples were married in the same mass ceremony in South Korea in 1988.

Marriage

Marriage is an agreement made by a man and woman to live together. The **wedding** or **marriage** **ceremony** is important in many religions (see p120). It is usually a time for **celebration.**

• In societies such as Australia, Canada, Europe and the USA, most people are free to choose who they want to marry.

• In most societies, people have one marriage partner at a time. This is called monogamy.

• In a few societies, men can have more than one wife at a time. This is called polygamy.

• A common-law marriage is when a couple live together as husband and wife but do not go through a legal or religious marriage ceremony.

• Some married couples decide that they are not happy living together. In many societies they can end the marriage by getting divorced.

• In some places, such as India and the Middle East, parents choose marriage partners for their children.

Having babies

Different societies around the world have special **customs** for the birth of a baby:

• The Mbuti pygmies of the African rainforests tie a piece of jungle vine around a new baby's waist. They attach a small piece of wood to the vine to pass on the strength of the forest to the baby.

• The Ainu hunters of northern Japan make a tiny cut in a new baby's thigh. They dress the cut with fungi to pass on the magical power of sacred trees.

• The Nootka tribe, from the north-west coast of North America, believe that twins are magical. If a family has twins, the parents and children are kept apart from the rest of the tribe for four years, so their magical properties will develop.

• In many societies births are followed by a religious festival. In Christian countries babies are christened. They have the sign of the cross made on their foreheads with holy water.

Although many creatures communicate with each other using sounds, only humans have developed **spoken language** to tell each other about their ideas and feelings.

There are about 5000 languages in the world today, but many of them are spoken only by small groups of people. Most languages have variations or **dialects** – different forms of a language that are spoken only in particular areas.

People have tried to invent a new language that everyone in the world could share. The most successful so far is **Esperanto**, which more than 100 million people have learned since its invention in 1887.

Learning a language

Most young children learn the **language** spoken by their **family** very easily, almost without knowing they are doing so.

- Babies learn by listening to the voices they hear around them and by copying sounds and words.

- By the time they are two years old, most children can use several hundred words.

- Children who are brought up hearing two languages all the time soon learn to speak both. Someone who speaks two languages is called bilingual.

Languages

Languages are divided into groups, called **families**. All the languages in a family developed from one earlier language.

- 48% (almost half the world's people) speak a language from the Indo-European family. This includes all the major languages of Europe as well as some from Iran and India.

- 23% (nearly a quarter of the world's people) speak one of the Chinese family of languages.

mat (Russian)

meter (Greek)

madre (Spanish)

mutter (Germany)

mère (French)

mother (English)

- Here are some words for 'mother' in Indo-European languages. They all come from the word *mata*, which is 'mother' in the ancient Sanskrit language.

Changing languages

Languages change all the time. Words may be **borrowed** from other languages, or **invented** to name a new idea or object.

- These English words were borrowed: *Mosquito* (Spanish), *Tea* (Chinese), *Sugar* (Arabic), *Shampoo* (Hindi), *Ski* (Norwegian), *Robot* (Czech), *Ketchup* (Malay), *Anorak* (Eskimo).

- Many English words have been invented. For example, the word *television* was invented using *tele* (a Greek word meaning 'far') and *vision* (from the Latin word for 'to see').

Writing things down

Writing developed much later than spoken language. Here are some facts about **written languages**:

Hieroglyph examples

Greek alphabet

αβγδεζηθικλμνξοπρσςτυφφχψω
ΑΒΓΔΕΖΗΘΙΚΛΜΝΞΟΠΡΣΤΥΦ
ΧΨΩ 1234567890 .,:;

Arabic alphabet

ابتثجححخدذرزسشصضطظععغفقكلمنهوىلا
١٢٣٤٥٦٧٨٩٠

Chinese symbols

生 拿 個
火。燈
你

- The first written languages used picture symbols to represent whole words.

- The earliest-known picture symbols were used in the Iranian region in about 3500 BC. The Ancient Egyptians began using picture symbols called hieroglyphics in about 3000 BC.

- Most modern languages are written in alphabets. The words are spelled out with letters which represent different sounds.

- The Phoenicians, who lived along the Mediterranean, developed the first alphabet in about 1000 BC.

- Chinese is the only major modern language that has no alphabet. Instead it has around 50,000 picture symbols.

- Some Chinese words are made from one symbol. Others are made up of various symbols mixed together.

Speaking without words

Movements made by the face, head, arms, hands and body can signal thoughts and feelings almost as clearly as spoken words. These signals are called **body language**.

- When people are nervous they often fidget with their hands.

- The distance between people who are talking to each other is important. If one person stands too close, the other one may feel threatened and move away.

- Body language varies from place to place. For example, in some countries looking a person straight in the eye means that you are honest and truthful. In other countries it is regarded as bad manners.

Strange but true

O

- O is the oldest letter in our alphabet. It has not changed since 1300 BC.

- The islands of New Guinea together have about 500 languages, about 10% of the world's total.

- The greatest number of languages spoken by one person is 28.

- The most complicated written character in Chinese is made up of 64 brushstrokes and means 'talkative'!

Exam

Food

Without food, people cannot survive. Food gives the body **energy** to make it work.

To stay healthy, you need a **balanced diet**: a good mixture of the different kinds of food available. Sadly, many people in the world today do not have enough food to eat.

Meal with animal products

Vegetarian meal

All food comes from plants or animals. Humans are **omnivorous**, which means they are able to eat both meat and plants. However, some people choose to be **vegetarian**, which means they do not eat meat.

Plant food

Plants that grow well in a particular part of the world provide the **staple diet**, or main food, of that area. Here are some staple foods and the places where they are eaten:

- Wheat: North America and Europe. It is used to make bread, pasta and breakfast cereals.

- Maize: Eastern and Southern Africa. It is also eaten in South and Central America as tortillas and North America as cornflakes.

- Yams, manioc and sweet potatoes: Plant tubers eaten in tropical countries. Tubers are swollen plant stems.

- Rice: China, India and South-East Asia. It is grown in flooded areas called paddy fields.

Fruits and vegetables

These **plant foods** help to make a healthy diet:

- Fruit contains a plant's seeds. Many fruits are sweet and juicy.

- Vegetables come from different plant parts. Here are some examples:

ROOTS: carrots, beetroot and parsnips

LEAVES: lettuce and spinach

STALKS: celery and asparagus

BUDS: cabbage and sprouts

SEEDS: peas, beans and sweetcorn

FLOWERS: cauliflower

China: birds'
nest soup

Middle East: camel
hump and sheep's eyes

Central and South
America: alligator

What food contains

Food contains **nutrients**, which the body needs to keep it healthy. Here are the main nutrients, what they do, and a list of some of the foods in which they are found:

Nutrients	What They Do	Where Found
Proteins	Help the body cells to grow and repair injuries	Meat, fish, cheese, eggs, beans
Carbohydrates	Provide energy	Bread, potatoes, pasta, rice, flour, sugar
Fats	Build body cells and provide energy	Milk, cheese, oils, butter, oily fish, nuts
Vitamins	Keep the body healthy	There are about 20 vitamins, found in many different foods. Vitamin C, for example, is found in fruit and vegetables
Minerals	Many minerals are found in food, including calcium (builds teeth and bone) and iron (keeps blood healthy)	Cheese, milk (calcium) Liver, brown bread (iron)

Cooking food

The first humans ate their food raw. Then, about 500,000 years ago, people learned how to use fire for **cooking**. This is what cooking does:

● Breaks down tough food so that you can eat and digest it more easily. Cooking different foods together creates new tastes.

● Helps to preserve food from going rotten. It also destroys some nutrients, so vegetables and fruit are sometimes better for you if eaten raw.

Strange but true

● The longest sausage ever made was 21 km long – enough to reach to the top of the world's tallest building 44 times.

● Kebabs (meat cooked on skewers) were invented by Turkish soldiers who spiked meat onto their swords to roast in a fire.

● The first plates were simply large pieces of bread that you ate along with the meal.

Clothes

Human beings are the only creatures that wear **clothes**. People need clothes because, unlike most other animals, they have no **fur or feathers** to protect them.

The earliest people wore simple clothes made of **animal skins** to protect their bodies. Over the years people began to use clothes for decoration as well as for comfort.

Clothes can tell you something about a person, for instance, which part of the world they come from, or what work they do.

Making clothes

Over thousands of years, humans have developed **tools** for making clothes and have learnt how to make and use lots of different **fabrics** (materials).

- The first needles were made of bone. They were used about 40,000 years ago.

- The first sewing thread was made from narrow strips of leather.

What clothes tell you

Clothes can sometimes tell you what **work** people do or what **group** they belong to. Here are some examples of this:

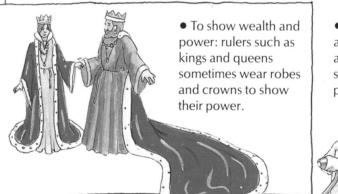

- To show wealth and power: rulers such as kings and queens sometimes wear robes and crowns to show their power.

- For protection at work: astronauts, firefighters and surgeons all wear special clothing to protect their bodies.

- To show membership of a group: sports teams wear uniforms; fans wear the team's colours.

- To show authority: police, soldiers, pilots, ships' officers and many others wear uniforms that people can identify.

North America: native Indian headdress

Hawaii: grass skirt and flowers

Africa: tribal celebration dress

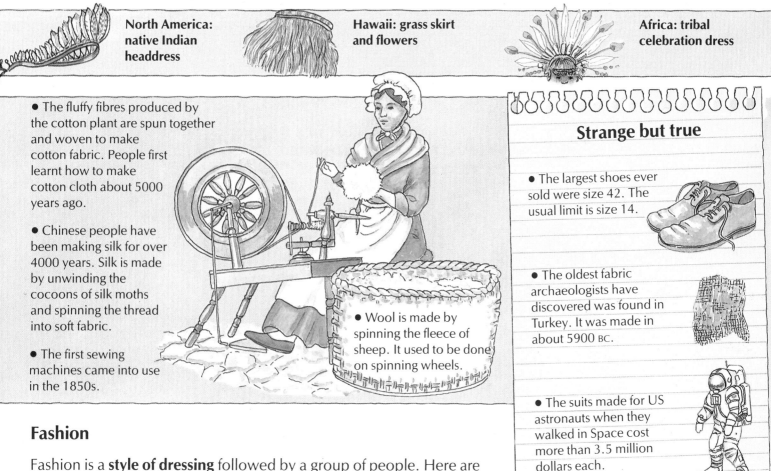

- The fluffy fibres produced by the cotton plant are spun together and woven to make cotton fabric. People first learnt how to make cotton cloth about 5000 years ago.

- Chinese people have been making silk for over 4000 years. Silk is made by unwinding the cocoons of silk moths and spinning the thread into soft fabric.

- The first sewing machines came into use in the 1850s.

- Wool is made by spinning the fleece of sheep. It used to be done on spinning wheels.

Strange but true

- The largest shoes ever sold were size 42. The usual limit is size 14.

- The oldest fabric archaeologists have discovered was found in Turkey. It was made in about 5900 BC.

- The suits made for US astronauts when they walked in Space cost more than 3.5 million dollars each.

Fashion

Fashion is a **style of dressing** followed by a group of people. Here are some of the ways European men and women have dressed in the past:

- About 600 years ago, men and women wore long robes.

- About 500 years ago, many men wore doublets (jackets with a padded chest) and hose (leggings).

- Long trousers for men did not appear until about 1830. Women did not wear trousers regularly until about 1940.

- Today, many boys and girls wear the same kinds of clothes. Trousers, t-shirts and trainers are popular in many countries.

1300

1500

1850

1990

Climate

Clothes are designed to keep people warm or keep them cool, according to the **climate**.

- In the freezing Arctic areas of Canada and Greenland people wear layers of thick padded clothing to keep warm.

- In many hot countries, people wear long cool robes to protect them from the Sun.

Homes

People need **homes** where they can eat, sleep and shelter from the weather. Most houses are made of materials that are easy to find in the place where they are built. They are usually designed to suit the **climate** of their area.

In some countries people build their own homes. In other countries, architects design houses and builders construct them.

Shapes and sizes

Here are some traditional house styles from around the world, built to suit the **climate** and local **materials**.

● Iceland: turf roofs are used to keep the heat in.

● Arctic: Inuit people build temporary houses made of blocks of snow, called igloos.

Homes on the move

Nomads are people who have no fixed home. They move around looking for work or pastures for their animals.

Strange but true

● The world's largest palace has 1788 rooms. It was built for the Sultan of Brunei.

● Lavatories were not installed in most houses until the mid 1800s.

● The world's tallest apartment block is the Metropolitan Tower in New York. People live in the top 48 storeys, with 30 office floors below.

● South America: the Quechua Indians build homes of mud bricks with thick pampas grass on the roof.

● Around the Mediterranean: many houses are painted white to reflect sunshine. Some have window shutters to keep the inside cool.

● Switzerland: houses have long sloping roofs so that snow can slide off them in winter.

● Asia: in marshy areas, people live in houses built on stilts to protect them from floods and wild animals.

● Big cities: land is scarce and expensive so buildings are built high into the air with lots of families living in each building.

● In the last century, North American settlers lived in covered wagons as they travelled across the country to the West.

● In the Sahara Desert nomadic people live in tents made from cloth of woven goat hair. The sides can be rolled up to let cool breezes in.

● In Iran the Turkoman people live in circular tents made of wood and felt.

● In Siberia some nomadic people live in tents made of walrus skin.

Houses in the past

Here are some **ancient** house styles:

Dugout hut

Roman villa

● Prehistoric dugout hut (Europe: about 3000 BC).

● Roman villa built around a courtyard (Europe: about 2000 years ago).

● Half-timbered houses (parts of Northern Europe: 500 years ago).

Half-timbered houses

Religion

Religions are beliefs that are found all over the world. They have **rules of behaviour** that their followers obey, and a **god** or **gods** that they worship. There are usually special **religious ceremonies** and **places of worship**.

Religion began thousands of years ago. Early humans explained natural events such as thunderstorms by saying that gods made them happen. People also made gods of the Sun, Moon and Earth. They prayed to them for good hunting or crops.

Today, millions of people follow one or other of the major world religions.

World religions

These are the major **world religions**:

● Christianity: founded by Jesus Christ, whose birth nearly 2000 years ago marks the beginning of the Christian calendar. Christians believe there is one God, and that Jesus Christ was God on Earth in human form. Their holy book is the Bible.

● Hinduism: developed in India at least 2500 years ago. There are many gods, with Brahma as the most important. Hindus believe in reincarnation, which means that people are reborn many times. In each new life they are rewarded or punished for their deeds in an earlier life.

● Shinto: a Japanese religion whose followers believe that spirits are present in all living things. They worship at holy places called shrines.

An Anglican (Christian) Bishop

Strange but true

● Archaeologists think that some caves in Europe were used as places of worship more than 14,000 years ago.

● The world's largest temple is Angkor Wat in Cambodia. It is over 1000 years old.

● The largest recorded gathering of people was at a Hindu religious festival in India in 1989. It was attended by about 15 million people.

Holy objects

In all religions, **holy places** and **sacred objects** are an important part of worship.

● Copies of the Torah, the Jewish Holy Law, are written in Hebrew on parchment scrolls and kept in a casket called the Ark.

Jewish religious service

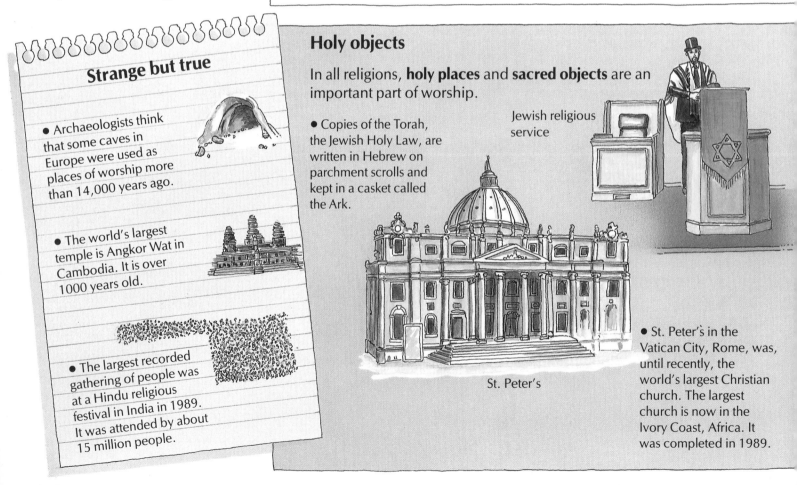

St. Peter's

● St. Peter's in the Vatican City, Rome, was, until recently, the world's largest Christian church. The largest church is now in the Ivory Coast, Africa. It was completed in 1989.

A Buddhist priest

Odin

● Buddhism: founded in India about 2500 years ago by Siddhartha Gautama, who was given the title 'Buddha'. He said that people could escape suffering and find perfect peace ('nirvana') by following his teachings.

● Islam: the religion of Muslims - people who follow the teaching of Muhammad. It was founded nearly 1400 years ago in the Middle East when the prophet Muhammad received messages from Allah (God). They were written down to form the Koran, the Islamic sacred book.

● Judaism: the religion of Jewish people, founded more than 4000 years ago. Jews believe in one God who has chosen them to pass on his Commandments (laws) to the world. They believe a Messiah (saviour) will come from God to bring peace to the world.

Ancient religions

● The Viking people of Scandinavia had many gods. The most important, Odin, rode an eight-legged horse. The gods lived in a paradise called Valhalla.

● Aztec people, who lived in Mexico about 800 years ago, worshipped many gods. They made human sacrifices by killing people and tearing out their hearts.

The Ka'bah in Mecca

● Statues of the Buddha decorate Buddhist temples and shrines.

Statue of Zeus

● The Ka'bah in Mecca, Saudi Arabia, contains a sacred black stone. It is the most holy shrine of Islam. Many thousands of Muslims visit it each year.

● The Ancient Greeks believed in many gods and goddesses, who lived on Mount Olympus. Zeus was the chief god.

● Ancestor worship still survives in parts of Africa and China. People believe the dead look after the living, so they perform ceremonies to their ancestors in the hope they will bring good luck.

Government

To live together in peace, people need to agree on certain rules or **laws**. Each country of the world has a **government** that makes decisions about how a country should be run, and makes the laws for its people. The kind of government varies from one country to another.

Governments collect **taxes**, which is money taken from the wages that people earn. These taxes are used to pay for such things as schools, hospitals and roads.

Democracy

Most Western countries are **democracies**. Democracy means:

● 'Rule by the people'. People vote to choose representatives who take part in the government of the country.

● There is a choice of political parties to elect (vote for).

● There are basic human rights, such as the freedom to criticize the government.

Communism

There have been **communist** governments in what was the USSR, and in China, Cuba and parts of Africa. Under communism:

● People can vote, but only for officials of the Communist Party.

● All factories, farms and shops are owned by the State.

● There is no freedom of speech; no-one is allowed to criticize the government or its leaders.

Dictatorship

In a **dictatorship**, one person holds all the power. The people are not allowed to take any part in government or to criticize the leader.

● The Ancient Romans sometimes passed all power to one man – a dictator – in times of war. This ensured that they had a strong leader in a time of trouble. After the war, his power was supposed to end.

● Modern dictators include Hitler (Germany), Stalin (USSR), Mao Tse-tung (China), Ceausescu (Romania) and Saddam Hussein (Iraq).

Strange but true

● English medieval monks practised a form of communal government. They owned all their possessions jointly.

● New Zealand was the first country to allow women to vote. This happened in 1893.

● The world's largest election was held in India in 1989. Over 304 million people voted and 3½ million staff were needed to collect the votes.

1774: the American Revolution. America won independence from Britain

1789: the French Revolution. The king was overthrown and a republic set up

1917: the Russian Revolution. A communist government was set up

Government by parliament

The word **parliament** comes from an old French word meaning 'to talk'. Parliament is where politicians elected by the people meet to discuss problems and govern the country. The **British parliamentary system** is the oldest in the world:

● The British parliament is divided into the House of Commons and the House of Lords. Members of the House of Lords are not elected.

● King Edward I of England held a parliament in 1295. All later parliaments are based on it.

● Many other countries have parliaments based on the British system.

Houses of Parliament, London

● In Britain the monarch (king or queen) heads the country but is not directly involved in government. Monarchs inherit their titles and are not elected.

Government of the USA

The United States of America is a **republic** (a country without a king or queen). It is led by an elected **president**.

● Each state of the USA has its own local government. The national government in Washington controls all the state governments.

The White House, Washington, home of the President of the USA

● People vote in elections for the political party they want to govern the country. The leader of the winning party becomes the president.

● There are three branches of government: the Executive, Congress and the Supreme Court. In this way, power is divided and each branch is able to check the actions of the other two.

● Congress is divided into an upper and lower house – the Senate and the House of Representatives.

The Arts

Human beings express their thoughts and feelings through **art**, by writing stories and plays, drawing, playing music, painting pictures and making sculptures.

Cave painting

Some arts are very ancient. Prehistoric cave paintings and carvings, Ancient Greek poetry, sculptures and buildings still survive. They show the creativity of people long ago. Today there are also **modern art forms** such as cinema, television and photography.

Literature

Literature is written art. It includes **poetry**, **plays** and **novels**.

- The oldest poems and stories were told out loud, not written down. They were passed down by memory from one storyteller to another.

- When more people learned to read and write, stories were written down. Most books were written and illustrated by hand until printing became widespread in the 15th Century.

- The first story books for children were written in the 19th Century. *Swiss Family Robinson* and *Alice in Wonderland* were among the first children's stories ever published.

From left to right: quill pen, fountain pen, typewriter and word processor.

Visual arts

Visual arts include **painting**, **drawing** and **sculpture**.

- Prehistoric people painted pictures of animals and hunters on cave walls. Some have been found that were painted about 25,000 years ago.

- One of the world's best-known paintings is the 'Mona Lisa' painted by Leonardo da Vinci between 1503 and 1507. Now it is too valuable to be given a price.

Strange but true

- Decorated bones dug up in Germany may be the most ancient pieces of art ever found. They are about 35,000 years old.

- In 1517, Francis I, King of France, bought the 'Mona Lisa' to hang in his bathroom.

- The Globe Theatre in London had no roof. If it rained, performances were cancelled.

- Audiences at the Globe Theatre were noisy and rowdy. Fights often broke out in front of the stage.

1894 Paris: first public showing of moving pictures on a screen

1922 Berlin: first public showing of a film with sound added
1929 London: first TV sets for sale and first TV programmes broadcast

Drama

Plays are stories written for actors to perform. Today they are usually acted in purpose-built **theatres**.

• Ancient Greek plays were performed in open-air theatres. Actors wore masks and took part in plays that told stories about Greek gods and heroes.

• In Europe, about 500 years ago, people watched plays about Bible stories. Actors performed on open carts that could be moved from place to place.

• The world-famous playwright, William Shakespeare, lived in England in the 16th Century. Many of his plays were performed at the Globe Theatre in London.

• The Globe was circular in shape. Rich members of the audience sat on or around the stage. Poor people stood in front of the stage. Women were not allowed to act, so boys played women's parts.

Music

Here are some of the most common groups of **musical instruments**:

• Percussion instruments make a noise when they are tapped or hit.

• Some stringed instruments are played using a bow.

• Some stringed instruments are plucked with the fingers.

• Keyboard instruments have keys that you press with your fingers. Each key makes a different sound.

• These wind instruments are made of brass.

• These wind instruments have reeds that you blow across to make a sound.

Famous People

Columbus (1451-1506): explorer who sailed to the West Indies and Central America.

Only a small number of people from the past have become so **famous** that their names are still remembered long after their death. Some of these people became famous for their **daring deeds** and **leadership**. Others are famous for helping to **improve other people's lives**. Many are remembered because the stories of their lives are so **dramatic**.

Today, television, cinema and newspapers can quickly make people famous all over the world. In the past it was difficult to become well known. Here you can find out about some famous people from the past.

Tutankhamun

Tutankhamun was a **pharaoh**, or ruler, of ancient Egypt. He died in 1352 BC. He has become famous because, more than 3000 years after his death, his tomb was discovered containing gold, jewels and many other beautiful objects.

- Tutankhamun became pharaoh when he was 11 years old. He married an Egyptian princess.

- He died when he was about 18.

- In 1922 archaeologists discovered his tomb in Egypt in the Valley of the Kings.

- The pharaoh's body was mummified (preserved and wrapped in bandages) inside a coffin made of solid gold.

Queen Elizabeth I

Queen Elizabeth I lived from 1533 to 1603. She was one of the most famous **rulers of England**. Her court was well known for its poets, painters, musicians and playwrights.

- Elizabeth was born in 1533, the daughter of King Henry VIII and Anne Boleyn. When Elizabeth was a baby, her father had her mother beheaded.

- When she was a young girl she was locked up for a while in the Tower of London by her half-sister Mary. Mary thought Elizabeth was plotting against her.

- After Mary's death, Elizabeth came to the throne of England. She was 25 and reigned for another 45 years.

Napoleon Bonaparte

Napoleon, who lived from 1769 to 1821, was a famous French **leader** and **ruler**. He conquered large parts of Europe and made himself emperor over them.

- He was born on the island of Corsica and went to a military school in Paris.

- He became head of the French army and won many victories throughout Europe.

- He reorganized France by improving the law, banks, trade and education. He also encouraged the sciences and the arts.

- In 1804 he crowned himself Emperor of France. His wife, Josephine, was made Empress.

- When his enemies in Europe invaded France, Napoleon was sent into exile on Elba, an island off the coast of Italy.

- He escaped from Elba and returned to France, gathering an army. However, he was finally beaten at the Battle of Waterloo.

Abraham Lincoln

Abraham Lincoln lived from 1809 to 1865. He was a famous American politician. From a humble background he rose to become the sixteenth **president of the United States**, leading the country at a dramatic point in its history.

- Lincoln grew up as a farmer's son, living in a log cabin in Kentucky. He studied law and began to take an active part in politics.

- In 1860 he was elected President of the United States. The American Civil War broke out soon after. Lincoln led the Union generals during the war.

- He worked to change laws and to improve life for all Americans. In particular he brought about the end of slavery in the United States.

- Towards the end of the Civil War, Lincoln was shot dead by a political enemy while at the theatre.

Strange but true

- The Ancient Egyptians used to mummify animals such as cats, baboons, dogs and crocodiles as well as kings.

- Potatoes and tobacco were unknown in Europe until sailors brought them back from the Americas in the 16th Century.

- Abraham Lincoln went to school for less than a year. He taught himself to read and write.

Gandhi

Gandhi was an important **Indian leader**. He lived from 1869 to 1948. During his life he worked to bring peace and justice to the world. His ideas and courage made him admired in many countries.

- He was born in India and went to study law in London when he was 19.

- As a lawyer in South Africa and in India he worked to help the poor and suffering, trying to change laws that were unfair.

- Many Indian people called him 'Mahatma', which means 'great soul'.

- He led the Indian people in their struggle for independence from Britain.

- Gandhi believed there was no need to be violent to solve the world's problems. To draw attention to his beliefs he sometimes went on hunger-strikes that endangered his life.

- Shortly after India became independent, Gandhi was shot dead by an enemy at an open-air prayer meeting.

127

Inventions

Early humans learned to use simple stone tools over 2 million years ago. Since then people have gradually gathered **knowledge** and **skills**. Now there are many **inventions** that have changed the way people live.

The number of inventions has increased enormously in the 20th Century. People who lived only a hundred years ago would be amazed to see how it is now possible to send messages round the world in seconds, conquer diseases and even send people to the Moon!

Transport

Until about 200 years ago, **transport** was slow, difficult and uncomfortable. Since that time there have been many changes:

● Late 1700s: Road-building improved, so more people began to travel in horse-drawn coaches.

● 1783, France: First passenger-carrying hot air balloon.

● 1803, Great Britain: Richard Trevithick built the first steam locomotive to pull wagons.

● 1825, Great Britain: First steam public railway.

● 1885, Germany: First petrol-driven car.

● 1903, USA: First powered flight by Orville and Wilbur Wright's aeroplane, Flyer 1.

● 1950s, worldwide: First jet-engined airliners introduced, able to carry many passengers at high speed.

Communications

Ideas spread quickly when they can be easily passed on to other people. These are some important stages in the development of **communications**:

● Paper: In about 3500 BC the Egyptians invented paper called papyrus. It was made from reeds. The Chinese invented the modern kind of paper almost 2000 years ago.

● Printing: In 1450 Johannes Gutenburg of Germany invented a press that could print books easily. Books before this time were copied by hand.

● Telephone: In 1876 the inventor, Alexander Graham Bell, developed the telephone. For the first time people could speak to each other over long distances.

● Radio: In 1894 Guglielmo Marconi experimented with radio messages and used them to send messages without any wires being needed.

● Satellites: In 1957 the first satellite was sent into space by the USSR. Satellites now send telephone and TV signals around the world.

A modern telephone

Bell's telephone

Strange but true

● The abacus, a counting frame with beads, was first used about 5000 years ago. It is still used in parts of Asia.

● In 1909 the fastest any human being had flown was 54.7 km/h. By 1976 this had risen to 2193 km/h – a 4000 per cent increase!

● The longest recorded freight train had 500 trucks, 6 engines and was 6.4 km long.

Medicine

Here are some important developments in **modern medicine**:

● 1796: Edward Jenner made the first *vaccine* (a tiny amount of a disease). When injected with vaccine, the body is protected from catching that disease.

● 1846: Ether, the first successful *anaesthetic*, was used. Anaesthetics deaden pain and make surgery safer.

● 1867: Joseph Lister performed the first operation using *antiseptics*. They kill the germs that cause illness. Before their use, many patients died from infections.

● 1895: X-rays were discovered by Wilhelm Röntgen. X-rays are invisible waves of energy that pass through flesh but not through bone. This allows pictures to be taken of the bones of the body.

● 1939: Penicillin, the first *antibiotic*, was developed. Antibiotics are drugs that kill the bacteria that cause illness.

● 1967: The first heart *transplant* was performed. Transplant operations enable unhealthy organs such as hearts, lungs or kidneys to be replaced with healthy ones.

In prehistoric times, as people hunted for food, they learned to run and to throw. The **oldest sports** – running, throwing, archery and wrestling – grew out of hunting skills. As people began to settle into farming communities, they turned these skills into sports for **exercise** and **amusement**.

Soccer, the world's most popular team game.

Today there are thousands of different sports and games, each with their own **rules**. Some involve just one person testing out his or her skill against another. Some involve teams of people competing against each other. Taking part in games and sports is not only healthy exercise; it is fun, too. Even just being a spectator can be exciting.

The Olympic Games

The first **Olympic Games** were held about 2700 years ago at the Temple of Zeus, in Olympia, Greece.

● Soldiers in Ancient Greece were trained to run, jump and throw. They competed against each other in the Olympic athletic events.

● Winners of the ancient Games were given an olive branch and treated as national heroes.

● In Ancient Greece the Games were a festival of mind and body, and included poetry and music as well as athletics.

Team games

Many of the world's most **popular sports** involve two **teams** competing against each other. Here are some examples:

● Soccer (Association football)
Number in team: 11
Ball: round, leather
How ball is moved: kicked
Object: to score goals by kicking the ball into a netted goal area

● Rugby Union - Number in team: 15
Ball: oval, leather
How ball is moved: carried/thrown/kicked
Object: to gain points by scoring tries (touching ball onto ground in goal area) and goal (kicking ball over H-shaped posts)

● Baseball - Number in team: 9
Ball: small, horse-hide
How ball is moved: hit with long cylindrical wooden bat or thrown
Object: to score runs round a diamond-shaped pitch

Baseball

● Cricket - Number in team: 11
Ball: small, leather-covered
How ball is moved: hit with flat side of long wooden bat or thrown
Object: to score runs between two sets of wooden wickets

Chess: India,
about AD 200

Dominoes: China,
about AD 1100

Monopoly: USA,
1930

• After a gap of 1500 years, the Olympic Games were started again in 1896. They are now held every four years.

• Olympic competitors must be amateurs, which means they must not earn money from sport.

Olympic symbol

• The modern Games begin when a runner arrives with a flame that has been carried from Greece.

Strange but true

• One of the earliest known Olympic records was a long-jump of 7.05 metres. It was achieved in about 656 BC.

• In 1314, King Edward II of England banned soccer in London because the players and fans had become so rowdy.

• The longest running race was held in 1928 from New York to Los Angeles – a distance of 5507 km. The winner took 79 days!

Indoor games

Not all games involve physical strength. Many call for **mental skills**, or rely on **luck**. Here are some of the world's best-known **indoor games**:

• Chess: an ancient strategy game played on a board of 64 black and white squares. Each player has black or white pieces: 1 king, 1 queen, 2 bishops, 2 castles, 2 knights and 8 pawns.

• Draughts, or checkers: related to chess but older and simpler. It is played with round counters.

• Ludo, Snakes and Ladders: games of chance relying on luck. Moves of counters are controlled by throwing dice.

• Backgammon: a mixture of chance and skill. Players use a coloured board and have 15 counters each. They throw two dice and try to be first to move all their counters round and off the board.

Backgammon

Snakes and Ladders

Chess

• Playing cards: there are many games involving cards. Some are team games (e.g: Bridge). Some can even be played by one person on their own (e.g: Patience). Cards come in packs of 52, in four suits: Hearts, Spades, Clubs and Diamonds.

131

Limits and Records

There are many **feats of daring** that people have achieved over the centuries. They range from **explorations** of the world's most isolated places to **breaking records** by pushing human skills to the limit.

New records are being set all the time as humans strive to break barriers of endurance and achievement.

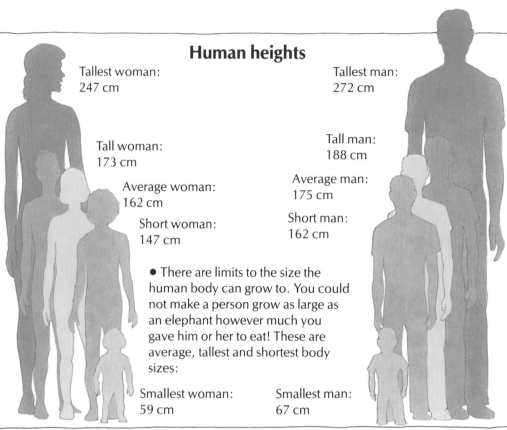

Human heights

Tallest woman: 247 cm

Tall woman: 173 cm

Average woman: 162 cm

Short woman: 147 cm

Tallest man: 272 cm

Tall man: 188 cm

Average man: 175 cm

Short man: 162 cm

● There are limits to the size the human body can grow to. You could not make a person grow as large as an elephant however much you gave him or her to eat! These are average, tallest and shortest body sizes:

Smallest woman: 59 cm

Smallest man: 67 cm

Exploring the world

Some people have been prepared to risk their lives and suffer great discomfort to be the first **explorers**. Here are some famous achievements of exploration:

● A Norwegian team first reached the South Pole in 1911 after a 53-day march.

● The first polar round-the-world trip began in 1979 in London. The explorers travelled to the South Pole, the North Pole, and back to London (a distance of 56,325 km). They reached home in 1982.

● On 21 July 1969, US astronaut Neil Armstrong became the first person to walk on the Moon.

● The longest recorded swim was 2938 km down the Mississippi River in 1930. The swimmer spent 742 hours in the water.

● The first people to climb Mount Everest, the highest mountain in the world, were Edmund Hillary and Tenzing Norgay, in1953.

Heights and depths

Modern technology has enabled people to reach the depths of the **ocean** and the heights of **Space**.

• Apollo 13 astronauts reached a height of 400,187 km above the Earth.

• The highest a hot-air balloon has flown is 34,668 metres over the Gulf of Mexico in 1961.

• The record depth for diving without breathing apparatus is 105 metres.

• The furthest anyone has reached into the sea depths is 10,916 metres, inside a submersible craft exploring the Pacific Ocean.

Strange but true

• The human brain is five times smaller than an adult elephant's brain.

• The record for balancing on one foot with no support is 34 hours.

• A baby's head is about a quarter of its total body length. An adult's head is only about one eighth of its total height.

Human limits

There are many things humans cannot do as well as some animals can:

• They are not as fast as cheetahs, which can run at 70 km/h.

• They are not as strong as a rhinoceros beetle, which can carry 850 times its own weight on its back.

• They cannot smell as well as the Emperor moth, which can detect smells 11 km away.

• They cannot hear as well as dolphins and bats, which can hear sounds too high-pitched for humans to hear.

• They cannot eat as much as the Polyphemus moth, which eats 86,000 times its own birth weight in 48 hours.

• They cannot make as much noise as South American howler monkeys, whose cries can be heard 16 km away.

Conflict and Crime

Through the ages, people have waged **wars** and committed **crimes**. This negative side of human nature is often caused by greed for money, property or power. Sometimes, though, people have been driven by poverty and injustice to be violent or break the law.

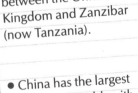

Strange but true

● The longest jail sentence passed was in the United States – 10,000 years for a triple murder.

● The shortest war on record lasted for just 38 minutes on 27 August 1896. It was fought between the United Kingdom and Zanzibar (now Tanzania).

● China has the largest army in the world, with over 2 million soldiers.

Weapons

Warfare has changed over the centuries. Here are some of the **weapons** people have invented to defend themselves and attack others:

● Hand weapons are used for stabbing or hitting. They are the oldest group of weapons, and include clubs, swords and spears.

● Catapults are early examples of shooting weapons. Guns and cannon came later. Modern versions include machine-guns, torpedoes and guided missiles.

● The first bombs, used in the 16th Century, were hollow metal balls filled with gunpowder. They were lit with a fuse.

● Booby-trap weapons probably originated from animal-trapping methods. Modern booby-traps include landmines that explode when touched.

● Modern bombs include the devastating nuclear bomb, which can poison the atmosphere with radiation.

Wars

Wars have been waged throughout history. Here are some facts about **warfare**:

● In the last 5500 years there have been only 292 years when no known war was being fought somewhere in the world.

● The longest war was fought between England and France. It lasted 115 years, from 1338 to 1453.

● World War II (1939-1945) cost approximately £1050 billion. That is more than all the world's previous wars put together.

● World War II also saw the greatest loss of life of any war. About 54 million people died.

● It is estimated that in 1988 the amount spent on weapons throughout the world was £460 billion. That is equal to £72 for every person.

Crime

All societies have **laws**. **Crimes** are acts that are forbidden and are punished by law. Here are some major crimes:

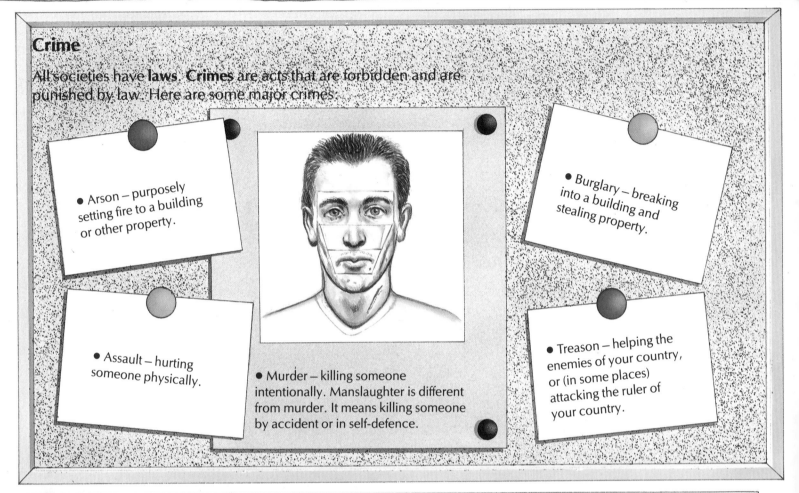

- Arson – purposely setting fire to a building or other property.

- Assault – hurting someone physically.

- Murder – killing someone intentionally. Manslaughter is different from murder. It means killing someone by accident or in self-defence.

- Burglary – breaking into a building and stealing property.

- Treason – helping the enemies of your country, or (in some places) attacking the ruler of your country.

Punishment

A person found guilty of a crime is punished. This is intended to **stop them offending** again, and to **discourage other people** from committing crimes. Here are some methods of **punishment**:

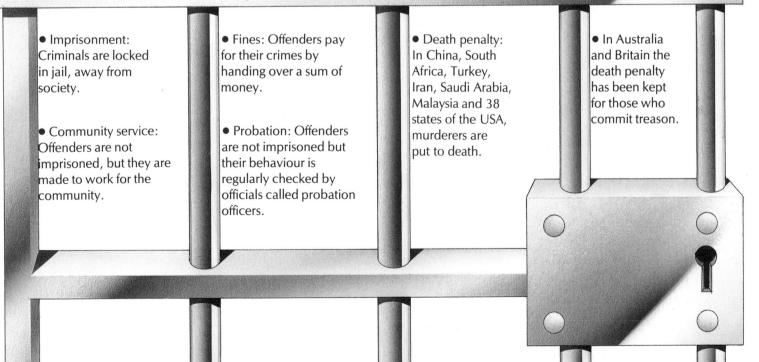

- Imprisonment: Criminals are locked in jail, away from society.

- Community service: Offenders are not imprisoned, but they are made to work for the community.

- Fines: Offenders pay for their crimes by handing over a sum of money.

- Probation: Offenders are not imprisoned but their behaviour is regularly checked by officials called probation officers.

- Death penalty: In China, South Africa, Turkey, Iran, Saudi Arabia, Malaysia and 38 states of the USA, murderers are put to death.

- In Australia and Britain the death penalty has been kept for those who commit treason.

The Future

Life on Earth has changed more during the last hundred years than at any other time since people lived on the planet. It is impossible to know what further changes will happen in the future, but it is clear there will be great **challenges** to meet.

One of the greatest challenges will be to preserve life on the planet from **pollution**. Ways will have to be found, too, of sharing out the **world's resources** more fairly.

Pollution

Pollution of the **environment** is threatening the world's water and air. International laws, together with conservation efforts by everyone, can help to limit the damage.

- The build-up of carbon dioxide gas in the Earth's atmosphere has resulted in global warming – the slow warming up of the air temperature.

- Acid rain contains poisonous substances leaked from factories and cars. It can quickly destroy plantlife. People can help limit acid rain by using unleaded petrol in cars.

- CFC gases (used in spray aerosols and refrigerators) seem to be damaging the Earth's ozone layer, a blanket of gas about 25 km above the ground.

- Oceans and rivers are sometimes polluted by poisonous industrial waste that can kill fish and affect drinking water. Many countries now have laws to limit this pollution.

- Carbon dioxide is released by burning fossil fuels such as coal, gas and oil. It also increases when forests are destroyed, because trees use up carbon dioxide.

Saving animals and plants

The actions of people have put many **animals** and **plants** in danger of **extinction**, which means that they may die out altogether. World organizations and governments are working to stop this continuing.

- Some of the world's rarest plant species are known by only one specimen.

- An animal is declared extinct if it has not been seen for 50 years.

Extinct dodo

- Each year an area of rainforest about the size of Switzerland disappears. The trees are cut for wood or cleared for mining or farming.

Strange but true

- A solar power station in California, USA, will soon be using the Sun's power to produce enough electricity to supply a million people.

- Throughout the world, almost 750 million people suffer from lack of food. This is twice the population of Europe.

- The Arabian oryx antelope became extinct in the wild but has been saved by zoos.

New sources of power

The world's supplies of coal, gas and oil are being used up rapidly as cities and industries develop. In the future, people may learn how to use **new sources of power** that do not run out:

- Wind power: electricity can be generated by using windmills that turn simply by the power of the wind.

- Water power: experiments are taking place to find out how to use the power of the world's oceans and rivers to produce electricity.

- New fuels: these can be made from tiny algae plants, from alcohol, and even from animal dung.

- Solar power: the Sun's rays can be used to produce power on Earth.

- Nuclear fusion: by joining atoms together, enormous amounts of power could be generated. This would be safer than the atomic power in use now.

Using Space

Space could be a very useful **resource**. Here are some possible future developments:

- Raw materials such as iron ore could be mined on the Moon.

- Giant solar power stations could orbit the Earth, sending down power gathered from the Sun.

A space station being built

- People may be able to live in Space, on space stations orbiting the Earth.

People Facts and Lists

Early people

These are the approximate dates when scientists believe our human ancestors lived:

Australopithecus: 1-8 million years ago
Homo habilis: 1.4-2.6 million years ago
Homo erectus: 250,000-1.6 million years ago
Homo sapiens: first appeared about 280,000 years ago
Neanderthal people: 35,000-140,000 years ago
Modern people: first appeared 30,000-50,000 years ago

Prehistoric remains of early people

Here are some of the most important prehistoric finds made by anthropologists:

Year found	Find	Where found	Dating from (years ago)
1856	Neanderthal skull and bones	Germany	120,000
1868	Cromagnon skeleton (Homo sapiens)	France	35,000
1924	Australopithecus skull	Botswana	1 million
1974	Australopithecus skeleton (Lucy)	Ethiopia	3-4 million
1975	Homo erectus skull	Kenya	1.5 million
1980	Homo sapiens	Tanzania	120,000

● Anthropologists who discovered the oldest Australopithecine skeleton called her Lucy after the Beatles song 'Lucy in the Sky with Diamonds'.

● Lucy died around 3 million years ago. She was about 20 years old when she died and only 106 cm tall.

Population

These are some of the most crowded countries in the world:

Country	People per square km in 1990
Monaco	14,681
Singapore	4369
Vatican City	2500
Malta	1117
Bangladesh	784
Bahrain	726
Maldives	718
Barbados	598
Taiwan	561
Mauritius	529

Some of the least crowded countries in the world are:

Country	People per square km in 1990
Greenland	0.1
Western Sahara	0.5
Mongolia	1.4
Mauritania	1.9
Australia	2.2
Botswana	2.2
Libya	2.4
Surinam	2.5
Canada	2.9
Iceland	3.2

● There are 235 people per sq km in Britain and 26 per sq km in the USA.

The human body

● Most people spend about a third of their lives asleep.

● A two-year-old child is about half the height it will reach as an adult.

● The heart beats about 70 times a minute. That is nearly 37 million times a year!

● The longest and strongest bone in the body is the femur, or thigh bone.

● There are about 650 muscles in the human body.

● There are four basic blood groups found throughout the world. They are called A, AB, B and O. Group O is the most common.

● Some people have such good colour vision that they can tell the difference between as many as 300,000 different shades of colour.

● The human ear can pick out more than 1500 different musical tones.

● It is impossible to sneeze with your eyes open!

People of the world

● Scientists who study the way the world's peoples are related to each other study the following, which can vary from group to group:

Skin	Blood group
Hair	Colour blindness
Language	Type of ear wax
Skeleton	Inherited diseases

Languages

These are the most widely spoken of the world's 5000 languages:

Language	Number of speakers
Mandarin Chinese	788 million
English	420 million
Hindustani	300 million
Spanish	296 million
Russian	285 million

● Other widely spoken languages include Arabic, Portuguese, Bengali, German and Japanese. They each have about 100-200 million speakers.

● The English and American languages are similar but not exactly the same. Here are some differences:

English	American English
Sweets	Candy
Cheque	Check
Draughts	Checkers
Bread roll or scone	Biscuit
Biscuit	Cookie
Cupboard	Closet
Nappy	Diaper
Chemist's shop	Drugstore
Lift	Elevator
Autumn	Fall
Tap	Faucet
Ground floor	First floor
Petrol	Gas
Handbag	Purse
Terrace house	Row house
Pavement	Sidewalk
Frying pan	Skillet
Braces	Suspenders
Drawing pin	Thumb tack
Vest	Undershirt
Waistcoat	Vest

Food

The energy content of food is measured in calories. This is how many calories some foods contain:

Food	Number of calories in 100 grams
Butter	740
White sugar	394
Wholewheat bread	318
White bread	233
Rice (boiled)	123
Potatoes (boiled)	80
Milk (non-skimmed)	65
Apple (raw)	46
Peas	41
Cabbage (boiled)	9

● An adult man needs an average of 3000 calories a day. A woman needs about 2200.

This is how many calories per day most people get, on average, in some countries of the world:

Country	Number of calories/day
USA	3600
Australia	3300
Brazil	2600
China	2600
India	2200
Chad (Africa)	1700

This is how many calories some activities use up:

Activity	Calories used per hour
Resting in bed	60
Driving a car	168
Washing up	230
Walking at 6 km/h	492
Cycling at 21 km/h	660
Running at 8 km/h	850
Swimming breaststroke at 56 strokes/min	1212

Clothes

These are some traditional clothes from around the world:

Clothing	Worn by Men/Women	Country
Aba – long robe	M	Nigeria
Dhoti – white cotton loin-cloth	M	India
Fustanella – pleated kilt	M	Greece, Turkey
Kaftan – long loose robe	M	Middle East and North Africa
Kilt – pleated skirt in the special colours of a family, or clan	M/W	Scotland
Kimono – long loose robe with wide sleeves and a sash	W	Japan
Parka – fur-lined padded coat	M/W	Arctic, Alaska
Poncho – cloak made of a blanket with a hole to put the head through	M/W	Mexico, South and Central America
Sari – long, wide strip of decorated cloth worn wrapped around the body and often also over the head	W	India
Sarong – decorated strip of cloth wrapped round the body	M/W	Far East

● In China, in the past, only wealthy people were allowed to wear yellow. Most people wore blue, because the blue dye was cheap.

● Traditionally, Chinese brides wore red. White was the colour for funerals.

● Levi Strauss made the first pair of blue jeans in 1850. They were intended as work trousers for American miners looking for gold.

● In Ancient Rome only important people wore purple clothes. This is because the purple dye came from a particular kind of shellfish and was very expensive.

People Facts and Lists

Religion

These are the world's most popular religions:

Religion	Number of followers
Christianity	1758 million
Islam	935 million
Hinduism	705 million
Buddhism	303 million
Sikhism	18 million
Judaism	17 million

● 233 million people throughout the world describe themselves as atheists (who do not accept any god) and a further 866 million people describe themselves as non-religious.

Government

British Kings and Queens

These are the most recent British monarchs:

George I	1714-1727
George II	1727-1760
George III	1760-1820
George IV	1820-1830
William IV	1830-1837
Victoria	1837-1901
Edward VII	1901-1910
George V	1910-1936
Edward VIII	1936 (abdicated)
George VI	1937-1952
Elizabeth II	1952-

US Presidents

These are the first five Presidents of the United States of America:

President	Years in office
George Washington	1789-1797
John Adams	1797-1801
Thomas Jefferson	1801-1809
James Madison	1809-1817
James Monroe	1817-1825

and the most recent Presidents:

President	Years in office
Lyndon Johnson	1963-1969
Richard Nixon	1969-1974
Gerald Ford	1974-1977
Jimmy Carter	1977-1981
Ronald Reagan	1981-1988
George Bush	1988-1992
Bill Clinton	1992-

Ten famous children's books

Hans Christian Andersen	Fairy Tales (including *The Emperor's New Clothes*)
J M Barrie	*Peter Pan*
Lewis Carroll	*Alice's Adventures in Wonderland*
Clive King	*Stig of the Dump*
Rudyard Kipling	*The Jungle Book*
C S Lewis	*The Lion, the Witch and the Wardrobe*
A A Milne	*Winnie-the-Pooh*
R L Stevenson	*Treasure Island*
Mark Twain	*The Adventures of Huckleberry Finn*
Roald Dahl	*The BFG*

Ten great writers

Here is a list of ten great writers and one of their best-known works:

Jane Austen	*Pride and Prejudice*
Charlotte Bronte	*Jane Eyre*
Emily Bronte	*Wuthering Heights*
Miguel de Cervantes	*Don Quixote*
Geoffrey Chaucer	*Canterbury Tales*
Dante	*Divine Comedy*
Charles Dickens	*Great Expectations*
Dostoevsky	*Crime and Punishment*
Jonathan Swift	*Gulliver's Travels*
Tolstoy	*War and Peace*

Painters

These are some of the world's famous painters:

Artist	Dates	Nationality	Major subjects
Sandro Botticelli	1444-1510	Italian	Religious pictures
Pieter Brueghel	1520-1569	Flemish	Pictures of village life
John Constable	1776-1837	English	English landscapes
Leonardo da Vinci	1452-1519	Italian	Mona Lisa
Paul Gauguin	1848-1903	French	People and landscapes of Tahiti, South Pacific
Michaelangelo	1475-1564	Italian	Religious pictures on the Sistine chapel ceiling, Vatican City
Claude Monet	1840-1926	French	Impressionist pictures
Pablo Picasso	1881-1973	Spanish	Many styles, including Cubism that changed modern art completely
Rembrandt	1606-1669	Dutch	Portraits
Joseph Turner	1775-1851	English	Landscapes
Vincent Van Gogh	1853-1890	Dutch	Landscapes, people and everyday objects

Ten famous composers

Composer	Dates	Nationality
Bach	1685-1750	German
Beethoven	1770-1827	German
Brahms	1833-1897	German
Britten	1913-1976	English
Chopin	1810-1849	Polish
Gershwin	1898-1937	American
Haydn	1732-1809	Austrian
Mozart	1756-1791	Austrian
Stravinsky	1882-1971	Russian
Tchaikovsky	1840-1893	Russian

Cinema

● The first film with sound, called a 'talking picture', was *The Jazz Singer*, made in 1927.

● The world's largest cinema is Radio City Music Hall, in New York, USA. It has 5874 seats.

● The world's largest cinema complex is in Brussels, Belgium. It has 24 screens and seats 7000 people.

Inventions

These are the approximate dates when some important discoveries were made:

Invention	When	Where
Pottery	7000 BC	Iran
Bricks	6000 BC	Jericho
Writing	4000 BC	Mesopotamia
The wheel	3200 BC	Mesopotamia
Glass	3000 BC	Egypt
Printing	770 BC	Japan
Gunpowder	AD 950	China

These modern objects were invented a surprisingly long time ago:

Knitting machine	1589
Microscope	1590
Thermometer	1592
Submarine	1620
Adding machine	1623
Pressure cooker	1679
Machine gun	1718
Lightning conductor	1752
Parachute	1783
Battery	1800
Burglar alarm	1858

Around the world

These are the times it took various craft to go round the world:

1500s **Sailing ship** 2 years

1929 **Airship** 21 days 7 hr

1957 **Boeing B-52** 1 day 21 hrs

1967 **Satellite** 80·5 minutes

Conflict and crime

● In 1988, there were about 57,000 prisoners in British prisons. By 1997 the total is expected to be more than 60,000.

● A survey in 1986 showed that more than 8 people per 100,000 in the USA were murdered that year. That was twice as many as in the next highest countries in the survey – Hungary, Israel and Australia. Norway had the fewest murders.

● During World War I, more than a million soldiers were killed or wounded at the first Battle of the Somme in 1916.

● About 2.5 million people died at the Battle of Stalingrad in 1942-43, fought between the Germans and the Russians during World War II.

● In all, about 55 million people were killed during World War II. Almost a half of these people were from the USSR.

These countries fought each other in the two World Wars:

War	Dates	Won by	Against
World War 1	1914-18	Belgium, Britain and the Empire, France, Italy, Japan, Russia, Serbia, USA	Austria-Hungary, Bulgaria, Germany, Ottoman Empire
World War II	1939-45	Australia, Belgium, Britain, Canada, China, Denmark, France, Greece, Netherlands, New Zealand, Norway, Poland, South Africa, USA, USSR, Yugoslavia	Bulgaria, Finland, Germany, Hungary, Italy, Japan, Romania

Olympic Games

● The first recorded Olympic Games were held in 776 BC, although they were probably held for many years before this.

● The ancient Games included running, jumping, wrestling, discus throwing, boxing and chariot racing.

● The first modern Games, held in 1896, had only 311 competitors, of whom 230 were from Greece.

These were the top medal-winning countries in the 1992 Olympic Games:

Country	Gold	Silver	Bronze
CIS (former USSR)	45	38	29
USA	37	34	37
Germany	33	21	28
China	16	22	16
Cuba	14	6	11
Hungary	11	12	7

Miscellany

● A scientist has calculated that about 60 billion people died between the years 40,000 BC and 1990. This means that about 9 per cent of all people who have ever lived are alive today!

● If the age of the Earth is likened to a single year, the following events take place on 31st December, the last day of the year:

4.15 pm: Appearance of human-like beings

11.10 pm: Arrival of earliest inhabitants in Europe

14 seconds before midnight: Birth of Christ

● Using this same comparison, the life span of someone who lived to be 120 years old would be just three-quarters of a second.

INDEX

Indexes to other sections are on pages 46, 94 and 190.

abacus 129
acid rain 136
actors 125
AD 102
adding machines 141
adolescence 109
aeroplanes 128
Africa
    ancestor worship 121
    governments 122
    Homo erectus 100
    languages 113
    population 102
    traditional clothes 117
    unusual foods 114
    wedding customs 111
ageing 102, 108, 109
alphabets 113
American Civil War 127
American English 139
American Revolution 123
Amnesty International 135
anaesthetic 129
ancestor worship 121
Ancient Egypt 126
    draughts 130
    mummies 126, 127
    paper 129
    shadow clocks 128
    writing 113
Ancient Greece
    art 124
    drama 125
    games 130, 141
    religions 121
Angkor Wat 120
animal skins
    for clothing 101, 116
    for shelter 100, 119
animals, extinction threatened 136
antibiotics 129
antiseptics 129
apartment blocks 118
Apollo 133
Arabian oryx 137
Arabic alphabet 113
archaeological discoveries
    bones 100
    mummies 126, 127
Arctic regions, igloos 118
Ark, Jewish 120
Armstrong, Neil 132
arson 135
arteries 105
artists 140
arts 124-25
    visual 124
Asia 119
    homes 119
    Homo erectus 100
    population 102
assault 135
Association football 130
atheists 140
athletics 130
atmosphere, protection 136-7
atomic clock 129
Australia
    death penalty 135
    exploration 133
    population 138
    urban population 103
Australopithecines 100, 138

axes 100, 101
Aztec religion 121

babies 108-9
    birth customs 111
    conception 108
    growth 109
    head size 133
backgammon 131
Bahrain, population 138
balancing on one foot 133
balloons 128
Bangladesh, population 138
Barbados, population 138
barter 101
baseball 130
batteries 141
Battle of the Somme 141
Battle of Stalingrad 141
Battle of Waterloo 127
BC 102
Belgium, cinemas 140
Bell, Alexander Graham 129
Bible 120
bilingual 112
birth 107
    customs 111
blood system 105, 138
body language 113
Boleyn, Anne 126
bombs 134
bones 104, 138
    decorated 124
    fossils 100
    needles 101, 116
    prehistoric remains 138
booby-trap weapons 134
books 124, 140
Botswana, population 138
boxing 141
boys 109
    clothes 117
Brahma 120
brains 106-7, 133
breaking records 132
brickmaking 141
bridge 131
Britain
    death penalty 135
    density of population 138
    inventions 128
    kings and queens 140
    life span 103
    parliamentary system 123
    prisons 141
    wedding customs 111
bronze tools 101
Brussels, cinemas 140
Buddha 121
Buddhism 121, 140
burglar alarms 141
burglary 135
burials 101
Burkina, population 103

calories 139
Cambodia
    alphabet 113
    temple 120
Canada
    clothes 117
    population 138
cannons 134
carbohydrates 115
carbon 109
carbon dioxide gas 136
cards 131
catapults 134
cave dwellings 100
cave paintings 124

Ceausescu 122
cells 104
Central America, unusual foods 115
CFC gases 136
chariot racing 141
Charles I 122
checkers 131
chess 131
children 110
    books for 124, 140
    clothes 117
    learning to speak 112
China
    ancestor worship 121
    army 134
    clothes 139
    communist government 122
    death penalty 135
    dominoes 131
    Mandarin language 112, 138
    Olympic medals 141
    paper 129
    picture symbols 113
    population 103
    silk 117
    unusual foods 115
christenings 111
Christianity 120, 140
cinema 124, 126, 140
    films with sound 125, 140
    first screening 125
CIS, Olympic medals 141
cities 118-19
    distribution of population 103
Civil War
    American 127
    English 122
clans 110
climate, clothing 117
clocks 128-29
clothes 116-17, 139
clubs 134
coaches 141
coal 136, 137
colour blindness 106
Columbus, Christopher 126
common-law marriage 111
communes 110
communications 129
    satellites 129
communism 122
composers 140
conception 108
conflict 134-135, 141
cooking food 100, 115
cotton fabric 117
countries 103, 138
    clothing for cold 117
    clothing for heat 117
    population 138
covered wagons 119
cricket 130
crime 135, 141
Cromagnon 138
Cuba
    communist government 122

da Vinci, Leonardo 124
death ceremonies 101
death penalty 135
democracy 122
depths of the oceans 133
desert tents 119
dialects 112
dictatorship 122
diet 114
digestive system 105
discus throwing 141

diving 133
divorce 111
dodo 136
Dolní Vestonice 102
dominoes 131
doublets and hose 117
drama 125
draughts 130
drawing 124

ears 107
Earth
    age 141
    pollution 136
Edward I 123
Elba 127
electricity 137
Elizabeth I 126
energy 105, 114
England, war with France 141
English Civil War 122
English language 113, 138
environment pollution 136
Esperanto 112
ether 129
Ethiopia, life span 103
Europe, population 102
exploration 132-33
extended families 110
eyes 107

fabrics 116, 117
families 110
famous people 126-27
    see also composers, monarchs, painters, writers
farmers 101
farming, population 103
fashion 117
fats 115
fertilization 108
fires for cooking 100, 115
fish, polluted 136
flight, speed 127, 141
Flyer I 128
food 114-15, 139
    and drinks consumed 104
    digestive system 105
    shortage 103, 137
football 130, 131
forests, polluted 136
former USSR
    communist government 122, 123
    satellites 129
fossil
    bones 100
    fuels 136
France
    invention of hot air balloons 141
    war with England 134
Francis I 124
French Revolution 123
fruits 114
    nutrients 115
fuels 136, 137
future 136-37

games 130-31
Gandhi 127
gas 136, 137
Germany
    decorated bones 124
    inventions 128
    Olympic medals 141
    printing 129
girls 109
    clothes 117

glands 107
glass making 141
global warming 136
Globe Theatre, London 124, 125
gods 120, 121
government 122-23
Great Britain see Britain
Greece
    alphabet 113
    Olympia 130
    wedding customs 111
    see also Ancient Greece
Greenland
    clothes 117
    population 138
guided missiles 134
gunpowder 141
guns 134
Gutenberg, Johannes 129

hair 104, 138
hand axes 101
Hawaii, traditional clothes 117
heart 104, 105, 138
    beats 138
    transplants 129
heights 133
Henry VIII 126
hieroglyphics 113
Hillary, Edmund 132
Hinduism 120, 140
Hindus
    attendance at festival 120
    temples 121
    wedding customs 110
Hindustani language 138
Hitler 122
holy places 120
homes 118-19
Homo erectus 100, 138
    remains 138
    tools 101
Homo habilis 100, 138
Homo sapiens 101, 138
Hong Kong, houseboats 119
hot air balloons 133, 141
House of Commons 123
House of Lords 123
houses 101, 118-19
    ancient styles 119
    igloos 118
    mud 119
    prehistoric 100
    on stilts 119
Houses of Parliament 123
housing shortage 103
human body 104-7, 138
    blood system 105, 138
    brain 133
    carbon 109
    compared to animals 133
    digestive system 105
    fat 108
    hearing 107, 138
    height 132, 138
    iron 109
    limits 133
    lungs 105
    seeing 107, 138
    sleeping 138
    smelling 109
    sneezing 138
    tasting 107
    temperature 104-5
    touching 107
    water 109
human rights 122
Hungary, Olympic medals 141
hunger-strikes 127

hunting 100

Iceland
    houses 118
    population 138
igloos 118
India
    chess 131
    elections 122
    independence 127
    wedding customs 110
Indo-European languages 112
industrial waste 136
instruments, music 125
intestines 105
inventions 128-29, 141
Iran
    death penalty 135
    tents 119
iron 109
Islam 121, 140
    Mecca 121

jail sentence, longest 134
Japan
    life span 102
    urban population 103
jeans 139
Jenner, Edward 129
Jericho 102
Jesus Christ 120
jet-engined airliners 128
Jewish Holy Law 120
Jews 121
    synagogues 121
Josephine Bonaparte 127
Judaism 101, 140
jumping 141

kebabs 115
Kenya, population 103
kings and queens, British 140
knitting machines 141
Koran 121

landmines 134
languages 112-13, 138-39
lavatories 118
laws 122, 135
    international 136
leather 116
Lewis and Clark 133
Libya, population 138
life span 102-3
lightning conductors 141
Lincoln, Abraham 127
literature 124
London
    Globe Theatre 124, 125
    population 103
ludo 131
lungs 105

machine-guns 134, 141
Magellan, Ferdinand 133
Mahatma 127
maize 114
Malaysia, death penalty 135
Maldives, population 138
Malta population 138
Mandarin Chinese 112, 138
manioc 114
manslaughter 135
Mao Tse-tung 122
Marconi, Guglielmo 129
marriage 111
    wedding rings 110
Mary, Queen 126
Mauritania, population 138

Mauritius, population 138
Mecca, Saudi Arabia 121
medicine 129
Mediterranean houses 119
men, height 132
menstruation 108, 109
Mexico, Aztec people 121
Mexico city, population 103
microscopes 141
Middle East
    cave dwellings 119
    unusual foods 115
minerals in food 115
modern art 124
Mona Lisa 124, 140
Monaco, population 138
monarchs 123, 126
Mongolia, population 138
monogamy 111
monopoly 131
Moon
    mining ore 137
    walking on 132
Mount Everest 132
movement 106
    see also muscles
Mozart, Wolfgang Amadeus 127
Muhammad 121
mummies 126, 127
murder 135
muscles 104, 138
music 125
musical instruments 125
Muslims 121

Napoleon Bonaparte 127
Neanderthal man 100, 101,138
needles, bone 101, 116
nerve cells 104
nerves 106
new fuels 137
New Guinea 113
New York
    apartment block 118
    population 103
    Radio City Music Hall 140
New Zealand, government 122
newspapers 126
Niepce, Joseph Nicéphore 124
nirvana 121
nomads 118
non-violent action 127
North America, exploration 132
North America
    traditional clothes 117
    wagons 119
noses 107
novels 124, 140
nuclear bombs 134
nuclear families 110
nuclear fusion 137
nutrients 105, 115

oceans
    exploration 133
    polluted 136
Odin 121
oil 107, 136, 137
old age 108, 109
Olympia, Greece 130
Olympic Games 130-31, 141
omnivorous 114
Oxfam 134
ozone layer 136

Pacific Ocean 133
painters 140
painting 124
palaces, largest 118

paper 129
papyrus 129
parachutes 141
parents 110
Parliament 123
Patience 131
pebble tools 100
penicillin 129
pens 124
periods 108, 109
pharaohs 126
Phoenicians 113
photography 124
Picasso, Pablo 127
places of worship 120-21
plant food 114
plants 136
playing cards 131
plays 124, 125
poetry 124
polar round-the-world trip 132
political parties 122
pollution 103, 136
polygamy 111
popular sports 130
population
    distribution 103, 138
    explosion 102
    problems 103
    rate of growth 102
potatoes 127
pottery 141
poverty 103
power, new sources 137
prehistoric people 101-2,138
prehistoric paintings 124
Presidents 123
    USA 127, 140
pressure cookers 141
printing 124, 129, 141
prisoners 141
proteins 115
puberty 109
punishment 135

quartz crystal 129
quills 124

radiation 134
radio 129
Radio City Music Hall, New York 140
railways 128
rainforests 136
records 132
Red Crescent 135
Red Cross 135
relatives 110
religion, ancestor worship 121
religions 120-1, 140
religious ceremonies 120
reproduction 108-9
republics 123
revolutions 122-23
rice 114
rivers polluted 136
road-building 141
robes 117
Rome 102
    clothes 139
    government 122
    Vatican City 103, 120, 138
    villas 119
Röntgen, Wilhelm 129
Rugby Union 130
running 141
    longest race 131
Russian language 138
Russian Revolution 123

sacred objects 120
Saddam Hussein 122
Sahara Desert, tents 119
St Helena 127
satellites 129
Saudi Arabia
    death penalty 135
    Mecca 121
sausages, longest 115
Scandinavia, Viking people 121
sculpture 124
sense organs 106
sewing thread 116
shadow clocks 128
Shakespeare, William 125
Shanghai, population 103
Shinto 120
shoes 117
shrines 120
Siberia, tents 119
Sikhism 140
silk 117
Singapore, population 138
single-parent families 110
skeleton 104, 138
skills 101
skin 107, 138
skins
    for clothing 101, 116
    for housing 100, 119
Snakes and Ladders 131
sneezing 138
soccer 130,131
solar power 137
Somme,Battle of the 141
South Africa, death penalty 135
South America
    houses 119
    unusual foods 115
South Pole exploration 132
Space, using resources 137
space exploration 133
Spanish language 138
spears 134
speech 107
speed of flight 129,141
sperm 108
spinal cord 106
sports 130-1
Stalin 122
Stalingrad, Battle of 141
staple foods 114
state ownership 122
steam locomotive 128
stomach 105
stone spears 101
stone tools 128
stories 124
Strauss,Levi 137
submarines 139
submersible craft 133
Surinam, population 138
sweat 107
sweet potatoes 114
swimming, longest swim 132
Switzerland, houses 119
swords 134
Syria, houses 118

Taiwan, population 138
Tasman, Abel 133
tastebuds 107
taxes 122
telephone 129
television 124,125,126
Tensing, Norgay 132
tents, desert 119
theatres 124,125
thermometers 141
thought 107

tobacco 127
Tokyo,population 103
tongues 107
tools 100 -1,128
Torah 120
torpedoes 134
towns 101
trading 101
trains 129
transplants of body organs 129
transport 128
treason 135
    death penalty 135
Trevithick, Richard 128
tribes 110
trousers 117
Turkey
    death penalty 135
    kebabs 115
    oldest fabric 117
Tutankhamun 126
typewriters 124

unemployment 103
uniforms 116
United Kingdom, urban
    population 102
United Nations 135
unleaded petrol 136
USA
    American Civil War 127
    American Revolution 123
    Congress 123
    death penalty 135
    density of population 138
    English language 139
    Executive 127
    exploration 133
    government 123
    House of Representatives
    123
    houses run on solar power
    119
    lifespan 103
    Monopoly 131
    Olympic medals 141
    powered flight 128
    Presidents 127, 140
    Senate 123
    states 123
    Supreme Court 123
    urban population 103
    use of solar power 137
USSR, see former USSR

vaccines 129
Valhalla 121
Valley of the Kings, Egypt 126
Vatican City 103,120
    population 138
vegetables 114
    nutrients 115
vegetarians 114
Victoria, Queen 127
Vikings
    children 110
    exploration 133
    religions 121
vision 106,107,138
visual arts 124
vitamins 115
voting 122,123

wars 134,141
Washington 123
waste heat 136
water 109
water power 137
Waterloo,Battle of 127
weapons 101,134

wedding customs 110-11
Western Sahara,population 138
wheat 114
wheel 141
White House,Washington 123
wildlife habitat 103
wind power 137
windmills 137
wireless 129
wombs 108
women
    actors 125
    birth cycle 108
    conception 108-9
    height 132
    trousers 117
wool 117
word processors 124
work,clothing 116
world
    exploration 132-3
    population 102,103,138
    religions 120 -1,140
    resources 136
World War I 134,141
World War II 134,141
wrestling 141
Wright,Orville and Wilbur 128
writers 140
writing 113,141

X-rays 129

yams 114

Zeus 121
    Temple of 130

SPACE

Part Four

SPACE

The Universe	148
The Stars	150
The Constellations	152
Galaxies	154
Space Oddities	156
The Sun	158
The Moon	160
Earth and the Solar System	162
The Nearest Planets	164
Asteroids, Comets and Meteoroids	166
The Giant Planets	168
Uranus, Neptune and Pluto	170
Ancient Astronomy	172
Modern Astronomy	174
The Space Age	176
Landing on the Moon	178
Satellites	180
Space Probes	182
The Future	184
Space Facts and Lists	186
Index	190

The term 'billion' in this Part means one thousand million

Introduction

Space contains our own planet, Earth, and our own star, the Sun. Both belong to a galaxy called The Milky Way, which contains about 100 billion stars. In this Part, you can find out about other planets, stars and galaxies, and discover what scientists know about Space.

Earth is one of nine planets that go round the Sun. Jupiter, the biggest, is so huge that all the other planets in the Solar System could fit inside it.

Scientists call the Sun a yellow dwarf star. You can read about other types of stars too, including some that seem to turn into mysterious black holes.

Not everything in Space is huge. Meteoroids are tiny fragments of rock that usually burn up near the Earth in flashes of light called meteors or shooting stars. More than 20 million meteoroids are thought to enter Earth's atmosphere every day!

People have been interested in the stars and planets from early times, but the Space Age didn't begin until the 1950s. Since then, space flights have helped astronomers to learn much more.

The Universe

The Universe goes on for ever. Most of it is **empty space**, with huge swarms of stars called **galaxies** shining out into the blackness. Our Sun belongs to a galaxy called the **Milky Way** containing about 100 billion stars. There are billions of galaxies in the Universe.

Our Sun is a star. Other stars may also have planets, comets and other space bodies circling round them. There are probably other planets like the Earth in the Universe.

The Solar System

The **Solar System** is the name given to our Sun and all the space bodies that revolve around it, including the Earth.

● There are nine planets and over 60 moons, or satellites, all spinning as they orbit or travel round the Sun.

Mercury
Venus
Earth
Mars
Sun
Saturn
Jupiter
Uranus
Neptune
Pluto

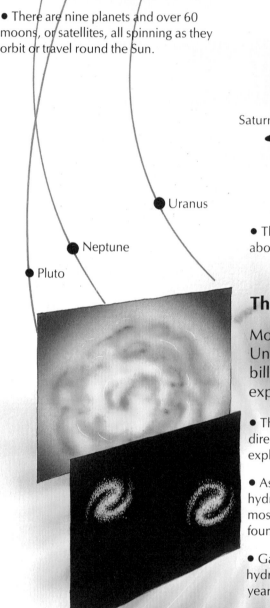

● The Solar System was probably formed about 5 billion years ago.

The Big Bang theory

Most scientists believe the Universe began about 14 billion years ago with a gigantic explosion they call the **Big Bang**.

● The bang blasted hot material out in all directions. It was far hotter than a nuclear explosion, or even the centre of the Sun.

● As this material cooled, it turned into hydrogen and helium. These are the two most common 'elements', or substances, found in the Universe.

● Galaxies and stars began to form out of hydrogen and helium about one billion years after the Big Bang.

Clues to the Big Bang

There are some **clues** to show that the Big Bang happened. Two of the most important clues are:

● The galaxies are flying further apart, as if from the force of an explosion.

● Space is still slightly 'warm' from the last traces of the explosion.

148

Theories about the future

There are **two main theories** about what will happen to the Universe in the future. They are:

● The Open Theory, which says that the Universe started with the Big Bang and the galaxies will carry on expanding for ever.

● The Closed Theory, which says that the Universe will stop expanding. The pulling force of gravity will slowly drag the galaxies back towards each other again until there is a Big Crunch!

● The latest observations made by astronomers show that the Open Theory is more likely to be the correct one.

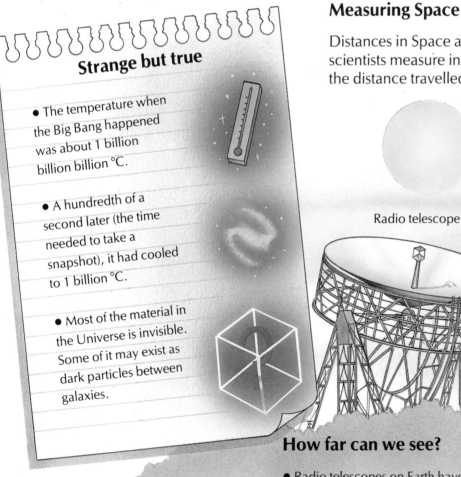

Strange but true

● The temperature when the Big Bang happened was about 1 billion billion billion °C.

● A hundredth of a second later (the time needed to take a snapshot), it had cooled to 1 billion °C.

● Most of the material in the Universe is invisible. Some of it may exist as dark particles between galaxies.

Earth

Gravity

Moon

Gravity

Gravity is the **pulling force** that exists between things. It is the force that keeps the Moon orbiting round the Earth.

● The Sun's gravity keeps the planets in orbit, and stops them from flying off into Space as they spin round.

● The Sun has a much greater pull of gravity than the Earth, because it has 333,000 times as much mass (amount of material) as Earth.

● Your weight is the force of the Earth's gravity pulling you down on to its surface.

Measuring Space

Distances in Space are too vast to be measured in kilometres, so scientists measure in **light-years**. A light-year is 9460 billion km – the distance travelled by light in one year.

● The nearest star to the Sun is called Proxima Centauri. It is 4.3 light-years away, which means it takes 4.3 years for its light to reach Earth.

Hubble space telescope (see p175)

Radio telescope

How far can we see?

● Radio telescopes on Earth have helped astronomers to detect very distant objects. The most distant galaxy so far observed by astronomers is at least 6 billion light-years away.

● Some telescopes have been put into Space. They can 'see' more clearly than telescopes on Earth and can detect invisible energy waves (see p151). One day they may discover new planets.

The Stars

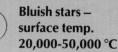
The stars in the sky look small because they are so far away. In fact they are huge. Each star is a glowing **ball of gases** held together by gravity. Most of this gas is **hydrogen**. In the hot fury of a star's 'core', or centre, hydrogen reaches a temperature of at least 10 million °C.

The heat inside a star changes hydrogen atoms into the atoms of another gas called **helium**.

When this happens there is an '**atomic reaction**' and a flash of energy is given out. Billions of these flashes of energy keep the star hot and make it shine.

The **Sun** is the nearest star to Earth. It is only a middle-sized star but it looks big to us because it is so close – only 150 million km away!

The birth and death of a star

Stars are born in clusters. A **cloud of gas and dust** called a **nebula** breaks up over millions of years into smaller clouds which are then pulled tighter and smaller by their own gravity. Eventually they heat up and start to shine.

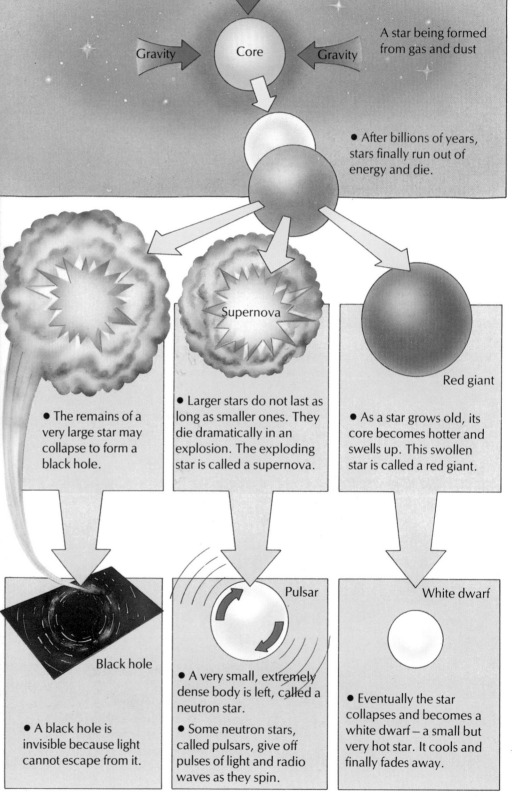

Gravity — Core — Gravity

A star being formed from gas and dust

• After billions of years, stars finally run out of energy and die.

Supernova

Red giant

• The remains of a very large star may collapse to form a black hole.

• Larger stars do not last as long as smaller ones. They die dramatically in an explosion. The exploding star is called a supernova.

• As a star grows old, its core becomes hotter and swells up. This swollen star is called a red giant.

Black hole

Pulsar

White dwarf

• A black hole is invisible because light cannot escape from it.

• A very small, extremely dense body is left, called a neutron star.

• Some neutron stars, called pulsars, give off pulses of light and radio waves as they spin.

• Eventually the star collapses and becomes a white dwarf – a small but very hot star. It cools and finally fades away.

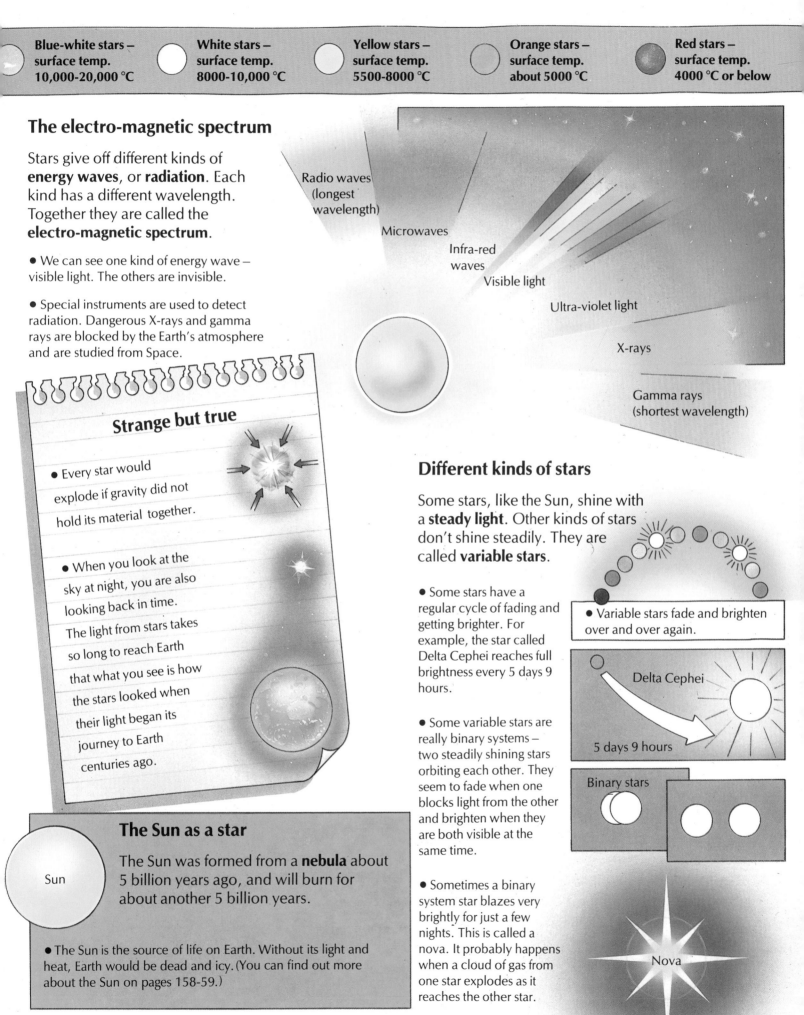

The electro-magnetic spectrum

Stars give off different kinds of **energy waves**, or **radiation**. Each kind has a different wavelength. Together they are called the **electro-magnetic spectrum**.

● We can see one kind of energy wave – visible light. The others are invisible.

● Special instruments are used to detect radiation. Dangerous X-rays and gamma rays are blocked by the Earth's atmosphere and are studied from Space.

Radio waves (longest wavelength)

Microwaves

Infra-red waves

Visible light

Ultra-violet light

X-rays

Gamma rays (shortest wavelength)

Strange but true

● Every star would explode if gravity did not hold its material together.

● When you look at the sky at night, you are also looking back in time. The light from stars takes so long to reach Earth that what you see is how the stars looked when their light began its journey to Earth centuries ago.

The Sun as a star

Sun

The Sun was formed from a **nebula** about 5 billion years ago, and will burn for about another 5 billion years.

● The Sun is the source of life on Earth. Without its light and heat, Earth would be dead and icy. (You can find out more about the Sun on pages 158-59.)

Different kinds of stars

Some stars, like the Sun, shine with a **steady light**. Other kinds of stars don't shine steadily. They are called **variable stars**.

● Some stars have a regular cycle of fading and getting brighter. For example, the star called Delta Cephei reaches full brightness every 5 days 9 hours.

● Variable stars fade and brighten over and over again.

Delta Cephei

5 days 9 hours

Binary stars

● Some variable stars are really binary systems – two steadily shining stars orbiting each other. They seem to fade when one blocks light from the other and brighten when they are both visible at the same time.

● Sometimes a binary system star blazes very brightly for just a few nights. This is called a nova. It probably happens when a cloud of gas from one star explodes as it reaches the other star.

Nova

The Constellations

Constellations are **patterns of stars** in the night sky. The shapes they seem to make were given names in ancient times, and many of these names are still used today.

The stars that make up constellations are not really close to each other. Sometimes the stars that look closest are really far apart – they just happen to be in line with each other and so look like a group when viewed from Earth.

Hemispheres

On maps, Earth is divided in half by an imaginary line called the **Equator**. One half is known as the **northern hemisphere**. The other is called the **southern hemisphere**.

Some northern hemisphere stars

- The constellation Taurus (the Bull) contains a group of stars called the Pleiades, or the Seven Sisters (although there are actually far more than seven stars). They are 400 light-years away.

Taurus

Pleiades

- The Andromeda galaxy (see p155) is a dim smudge in the Andromeda constellation. It is 2 million light-years away.

Andromeda

Andromeda galaxy

Northern hemisphere

Equator

Southern hemisphere

- Viewed from the Earth, stars appear to form patterns on the inside of a huge imaginary sphere. Like the Earth, this 'star sphere' is also divided into northern and southern hemispheres.

- The constellation Ursa Major (the Great Bear) is often called the Plough. It contains a group of seven bright stars.

The Plough

Ursa Major

- Polaris, the North Star, is in the constellation Ursa Minor (the Little Bear). It appears to be fixed in the sky, and so for centuries has helped travellers find north.

Polaris

Ursa Minor

Star drift

During the night, stars seem to **rise**, **move** across the sky and then **sink** out of sight. They do not really move, however. It is the **turning Earth** that makes the stars appear to move across the sky.

- Stars seen from the North and South Poles appear to move around the sky in level paths, without ever rising or setting at all.

- If photographic film is exposed to a starry sky for some hours, the stars leave trails on the film as they appear to move across the sky.

Star trails on photographic film

Canopus	Alpha Centauri	Arcturus	Vega
magnitude minus 0.7	magnitude minus 0.3	magnitude 0.06	magnitude 0.04
230 light-years away	4.3 light-years away	38 light-years away	27 light-years away

Some southern hemisphere stars

● Proxima Centauri, our nearest star apart from the Sun, is part of the Centaurus constellation. It is 4.3 light-years away.

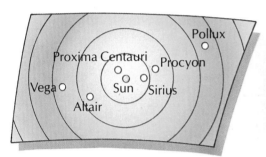

● The constellation called Canis Major (the Great Dog) contains Sirius, the brightest star in the sky. It is also called the Dog Star.

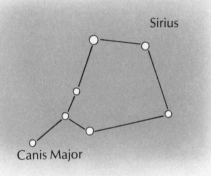

Sirius

Canis Major

● The Southern Cross is the smallest constellation. Two of its stars can be lined up to point due south, which is useful for navigation.

Southern Cross

South

● The Magellanic Clouds, two small irregular galaxies, are the Milky Way's closest companions in Space. They are about 200,000 light-years away.

Andromeda

Milky Way

Magellanic Clouds

Orion the hunter

Some constellations, such as **Orion**, belong to both the **northern** and the **southern hemispheres**.

● Orion was named after a famous hunter in ancient Greek mythology.

● Betelgeuse is a variable red giant star (see p150-51), in Orion.

Orion

● Three stars make up Orion's belt.

● The Horsehead Nebula is in Orion close to the 'belt'. It is a dark cloud of cold gas and dust, shaped like a horse's head.

Star brightness

The brightness of a star is called its **magnitude**. Astronomers have given each star a **magnitude rating**.

● The higher the number, the dimmer the star. The dimmest stars visible without a telescope have a magnitude of about 6. A magnitude 0 star is very bright. The brightest stars have minus numbers.

● Sirius, the brightest star in the sky, has a magnitude of minus 1.5.

Strange but true

● The African Dogon tribe say their ancestors knew about the invisible star Sirius B thousands of years before scientists discovered it in 1862.

Sirius B
Sirius

● In the constellation Corona Borealis there is a star that sometimes dims when tiny black particles hide it from view.

● North American Indians tested warriors' eyesight by seeing how many stars of the Pleiades they could spot!

Galaxies

Galaxies are **huge groups** containing hundreds of millions of **stars**. They were probably formed about a billion years after the Big Bang (see p148) when the Universe was quite young.

No-one knows how many galaxies there are in all, but there are probably billions.

Galaxies often move together in groups, called **clusters**. Our galaxy is in a cluster of about twenty galaxies, but there are much bigger groups containing thousands of galaxies.

The Milky Way

Our galaxy is called the **Milky Way**. It contains about 1000 billion stars. The **Sun** and the **Solar System** are more than halfway out from the centre of the galaxy.

● It takes light about 100,000 years to travel from one side of the Milky Way to the other. (Light takes only 8½ minutes to travel to Earth from the Sun.)

● The whole Milky Way rotates in Space. It takes the Sun 225 million years to revolve once around the centre of the galaxy. This is called a galactic year.

● The centre of our galaxy cannot be seen from Earth because it is hidden by dust and gas.

Colliding stars

● The central bulge of the Milky Way contains almost half of all the stars in the galaxy. They are much closer together than the Sun and its neighbouring stars.

● Although they are so close together in Space terms, stars collide with each other in the centre of the galaxy only rarely – perhaps one collision every 1000 years.

Galaxy shapes

These are the four main **galaxy shapes**:

Spiral

Barred spiral

- Spirals turn like a lit Catherine wheel, or cream swirling in a cup of coffee. Our galaxy is a spiral.

- Barred spirals look like two tadpoles joined at the head. They have a bar shape in the centre and two long arms.

Elliptical

Irregular

- Elliptical (oval) galaxies look like squashed circles. It is thought they contain older stars.

- Irregular galaxies contain a lot of dust and form no definite shape.

Strange but true

- There may be a huge black hole at the centre of our galaxy that is gradually sucking in the surrounding light and gas.

- The ancient Greeks called our galaxy the Milky Way because they thought it was made from drops of milk from the breasts of the Greek goddess Hera.

- Giant elliptical (oval) galaxies, found at the centre of large clusters, may be 'eating up' smaller galaxies.

Neighbouring galaxies

The **biggest galaxy** in our group is the **Andromeda Spiral**. It is about 2 million light-years away from Earth and contains about 400 billion stars.

- Andromeda can be seen from Earth with the naked eye.

- Our nearest galaxy neighbours are the Magellanic Clouds. These are two small irregular galaxies. The larger galaxy contains about 10 billion stars and is 180,000 light-years away. The other galaxy is much smaller and further away.

- The Magellanic Clouds were first sighted in 1521 by the explorer Ferdinand Magellan.

Red shift

As galaxies speed away from Earth, the light from them gets distorted so that it appears red. This is known as **red shift**. The faster a galaxy is moving away, the more red it will seem to be. The red colour cannot be seen by the eye. Astronomers study it using special instruments.

155

Space Oddities

Although scientists know much about the Universe, there are still many strange things in Space that have not been fully explained. **Black holes** are the most mysterious. It seems that they exist, but they can never be seen!

Anything that falls into a black hole can never come out again because gravity will crush it to nothing.

Quasars and **cosmic rays** are other space objects that still baffle scientists. If you think of the Universe as a giant jigsaw, only a few pieces have so far been fitted together.

Black holes

Some **very rare stars** contain as much material as fifty or more Suns. They are the brightest stars in the Universe yet they turn into **black holes** – the blackest objects in Space.

1 When these stars die (see p150) they keep on shrinking, because the pull of gravity is so strong.

2 They shrink down to a tiny speck, called a singularity or black hole.

3 Although tiny, the black hole contains all the material from the huge star.

4 A black hole's gravity is so strong that no light can escape from it.

5 Astronomers have not seen a black hole, but they have found stars they think may have a black hole nearby.

Quasars

Quasars are very distant objects that send out far more **light** than ordinary galaxies. They may also send out strong **radio waves**.

● Quasars seem to be sending out tremendous energy from a small space inside them. This could come from gas whirling around a giant black hole at the centre of the galaxy.

● The name 'quasar' is short for quasi-stellar (star-like) object.

● Quasars may have been a stage that some galaxies went through early in their lives. Because they are billions of light-years away, we are seeing them today as they were billions of years ago.

Detecting black holes

Some **binary star systems** (see p151) may contain a star that has turned into a black hole. Gas from the other star would swirl around the black hole before being pulled into it, giving off high-energy radiation, including X-rays.

Earth

● X-rays cannot travel through Earth's atmosphere, so they are studied by satellites that send information back to Earth.

● A hot supergiant star in the Cygnus constellation has an invisible companion called Cygnus X-1. It is probably a black hole.

● There are many other suspected black holes, including a giant one at the centre of our galaxy .

Strange but true

● If the Sun became a black hole, it would be only a few kilometres across – but it could swallow the Earth!

● A quasar turns out heat and light a billion billion times more efficiently than the Sun does.

● Cosmic rays can affect tree growth. Some astronomers have studied tree rings to find out how the number of cosmic rays reaching the Earth has changed over the centuries.

Cosmic rays and neutrinos

Cosmic rays are tiny **particles** that travel in Space at high speed and constantly shower Earth. They may come from exploding **stars**. Most of them do not penetrate Earth's atmosphere.

Exploding star

● Some cosmic rays bounce off into Space.

Cosmic rays

Earth's atmosphere

● Some cosmic rays reach the Earth's surface.

● Some cosmic ray particles are called neutrinos. These can pass right through the Earth itself as if it were not there!

● Several million neutrinos will pass through you as you read this page!

Neutrinos pass right through the Earth.

New planets?

There are nine planets in our Solar System. Scientists are trying to find **other planets** circling other stars.

● Throughout the Universe, there are probably millions of other stars with Solar Systems. Each could have its own planets.

● So far, no other planets have been found. Astronomers who thought they had found a planet outside the Solar System in 1991 later announced that they had made a computer error.

The Sun

The Sun, like all stars, is a ball of fiercely hot gas. Hydrogen gas deep inside it is constantly being turned into helium (see p150). This releases energy in the form of **light** and **heat.**

The Sun is the nearest star to Earth and the central body of the Solar System around which the planets revolve. The Sun has shone steadily for thousands of millions of years. If it went dim for only a few days, most lifeforms on Earth would perish.

Features of the Sun

These are some of the Sun's more **spectacular features:**

● Enormous eruptions of gas, called prominences, rise continually from the surface of the Sun. Some reach out into Space as far as 2 million km.

Arched prominences

Sunspots

● Sunspots are darker, cooler areas that appear on the Sun's surface from time to time. Some are much larger than the Earth and can last for months. Smaller ones last for only a few days or weeks.

● Every 11 years or so, sunspots become more common and then fade away. This is called the sunspot cycle.

Solar flares

● Solar flares are violent explosions of energy from the Sun's surface. They shoot particles at high speed out into Space. On Earth they can produce strange effects, such as the glowing lights, called aurorae, that sometimes appear in the night sky.

Sun facts

● The diameter or distance through the centre of the Sun is 1,392,000 km.

● The temperature at the core is believed to be about 14 million °C. At the surface it is 6000°C.

● A million bodies the size of the Earth could be squashed inside the Sun.

● The Sun is 92 per cent hydrogen. At the centre is a core of helium. Around this core 4 million tonnes of the Sun's material is turned into energy every second.

Different parts of the Sun rotate at different speeds

Different speeds

● Because the Sun is made of gases, different parts of it can rotate at different speeds. The centre part, or Equator area, rotates faster than the Poles.

● Energy from the core takes a million years to reach the Sun's surface, but only 8½ minutes to travel from the Sun's surface to the Earth.

Chromosphere – A layer a few thousand km deep that shines pink during an eclipse

Corona – The outer atmosphere that stretches millions of km into Space

WARNING Never look directly at the Sun. It can damage your eyes and blind you.

Solar eclipses

Occasionally the **Moon** passes in front of the Sun so that it **blocks out sunlight** from part of the Earth. This is called a **total solar eclipse**.

- If the eclipse is total, the Sun's faint atmosphere or corona shines out in the darkened sky. This is the only time it can be seen from Earth.

- During a total eclipse, prominences can sometimes be seen flaring out around the darkened outline of the Sun. Eclipses provide scientists with good opportunities for studying such things as prominences and the corona.

- When the Moon blocks out only part of the Sun's light, this is called a partial eclipse.

Area of partial eclipse

Earth

Moon

Sun's rays

Sun

Area of total eclipse

Total eclipse

Corona

Prominences

Sun

Moon

Partial eclipse

Strange but true

- The Sun is described by scientists as a yellow dwarf star.

- There may be a connection between the appearance of sunspots and changes in the weather on Earth.

- Sound waves produced inside the Sun make it swell and shrink by a kilometre or so every few minutes.

What will happen to the Sun?

Like all stars, the Sun is **changing**. This is what scientists believe will happen to it:

1 Several billion years from now, the Sun will have a crisis. The hydrogen supply around its core will start to run out, and our star will begin to collapse.

2 This collapse will put new energy into the core so the Sun will blaze hotter than ever.

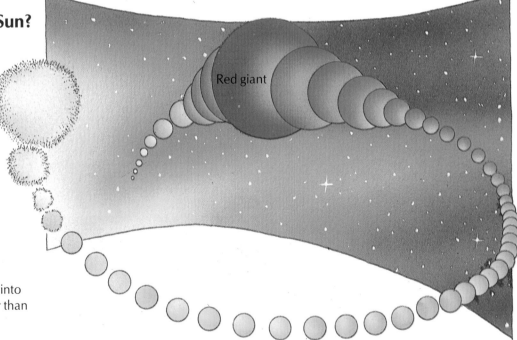

Red giant

3 The blast of energy will force the higher gas layers outwards. The Sun will become a red giant, 100 times its present diameter and 500 times brighter.

4 The red giant will fill Earth's sky. The great heat will melt the surface of the Earth into seas of lava.

5 Eventually the Sun will cool and shrink, becoming a white dwarf star (see p150) about the size of Earth.

The Moon

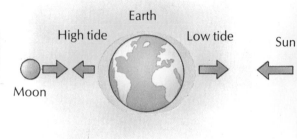

The Moon is an airless ball of **rock** about a quarter the diameter of the Earth. It circles round the Earth once every 27.3 days. It has no **light** of its own, but reflects light from the Sun.

The Earth and Moon shown to scale

The Moon has probably always been lifeless, but it has had a violent, turbulent history. Most of the **craters** on its surface were caused by solid space bodies called meteoroids crashing into it between 3 and 4 billion years ago. The darker areas are called **maria** (seas). They are made of lava that flowed out from inside the Moon about 3 billion years ago.

Gravity

The Moon is much smaller than Earth and so has much weaker **gravity**. Astronauts had to be weighted down to help them walk properly on the Moon's surface.

Astronauts on the Moon

Phases of the Moon

The Moon keeps the same **side** facing Earth all the time, so we only see this one side of it. As the Moon travels around the Earth, we see a varying amount of this side each day. These different amounts, or stages, are called the **phases of the Moon**.

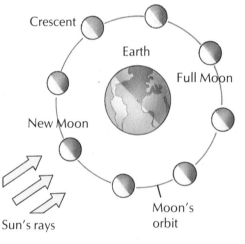

Crescent

Earth

Full Moon

New Moon

Sun's rays

Moon's orbit

● It is gravity that causes ocean tides on Earth to rise and fall. The gravity of the Sun and Moon pulls the Earth's oceans into bulges. The Earth rotates beneath these bulges, producing two high tides a day.

Earth

High tide   Low tide   Sun

Moon

● When the Moon is seen as a crescent, only a sliver of the side facing Earth is sunlit.

● As the Moon moves round the Earth, it appears half-lit and then finally fully lit (the Full Moon). At this stage the whole of the side facing Earth is sunlit.

● After Full Moon, the shape changes back to half and finally to a thin crescent. It then disappears for a few nights (New Moon) and the process begins again.

● It takes 29.5 days for the Moon to move through all its phases from New, through Full, and back to New again.

Crescent   Half Moon   Half Moon   Crescent

Waxing Moon   Full Moon   Waning Moon

● As the Moon grows from crescent to Full, it is called the waxing moon.

● As it shrinks back to a crescent, it is called the waning moon.

Diameter
3476 km

Temperature
on sunlit side 100°C
on dark side −170°C

Gravity
One-sixth as strong as
Earth's gravity

The Moon's surface

The Moon's **surface** is covered with craters, ridges, mountains and valleys. The dark maria are the smoothest parts because the lava that created them flowed over and covered old craters. These are some facts about the Moon's surface:

● The biggest Moon crater that can be seen from Earth is called Bailly. It is about 290 km across.

● The largest Moon crater is on the far side of the Moon and so cannot be seen from Earth.

● Because the Moon has no air or water to wear rocks away, the Moon's surface has remained unchanged for thousands of millions of years.

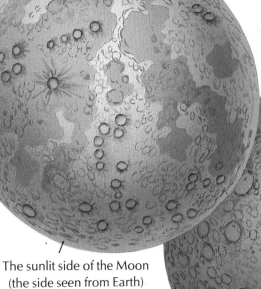

The far side of the Moon (the side that cannot be seen from Earth)

The sunlit side of the Moon (the side seen from Earth)

Where did the Moon come from?

The Moon and Earth are roughly the same age. Scientists are unsure where the Moon came from. Here are four theories:

1 The Moon and Earth formed together from the same dust and gas cloud.

2 The Moon was a wandering space body that came close to Earth and became trapped in Earth's orbit.

3 When the Earth was young and molten, it grew a bulge that spun off and became the Moon.

4 A small planet hit the young molten Earth and threw material into orbit, which got drawn together to form the Moon.

Strange but true

● The Moon is moving slowly away from Earth at the rate of 3 cm per year.

● The far side of the Moon was not seen until 1959 when the Soviet spacecraft, Luna 3, flew by and took pictures of it.

● Earth's gravity has pulled on the side of the Moon that faces Earth, causing a bulge several kilometres high.

● It would take 81 Moons to weigh the same as Earth.

Lunar eclipses

The Earth casts a long **shadow** in Space on the side away from the Sun. A **Lunar eclipse** happens when the Moon passes into the darkest part of this shadow. During a total Lunar eclipse, the Moon looks dark brown colour.

Sun

Earth

Moon

Earth's shadow

Earth and the Solar System

Earth is a smallish, rocky planet. It is in just the right place in the Solar System to allow **life** to be supported. If Earth were nearer to the Sun, it would be too hot for life as we know it to survive. If it were further away, it would be too cold.

Seen from Space, Earth is a beautiful **bluish disc** with swirling white clouds. It looks blue because so much of its surface is ocean.

Earth seen from Space

Strange but true

● The Icelandic island of Surtsey was formed between 1963 and 1966. It began when an underwater volcano suddenly erupted, shooting columns of lava high into the air.

● Some underwater volcanoes are higher than Mount Everest.

● The Himalayan mountains were formed when India (then an island) collided with the rest of Asia.

Earth's position in the Solar System

Earth is the third planet from the Sun. Its closest neighbours are Venus and Mars.

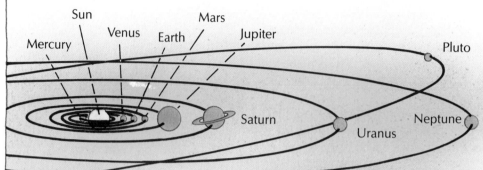

Sun, Mercury, Venus, Earth, Mars, Jupiter, Saturn, Uranus, Neptune, Pluto

How Earth began

Earth was formed about 4.6 billion years ago, from **small rocky bodies** that collided with each other as they whirled around the Sun.

● These collisions gave out so much energy that the Earth glowed red-hot as further rocky bodies crashed into it.

● After several hundred million years, Earth reached its present size. The collisions died down and the Earth started to cool.

● The metal in the Earth sank to the centre, forming the core, with the lighter rocks forming the mantle and crust.

Crust, mantle and core

This is what the Earth might look like inside. At the centre is the **core**, surrounded by the **mantle**. The **crust** is a thin outer layer.

Mantle

Crust

Outer core

Inner core

● The Earth's core is about 7000 km across and is probably made of iron and nickel. The outer part is liquid and the inner part solid.

● The mantle is made of rock. It contains most of the Earth's material.

● The crust is made of lighter rocks that floated to the top when Earth was molten. It varies from 6 to 40 km thick.

Earth's atmosphere

Earth is surrounded by an **atmosphere**, which enables life to survive on the planet. This is what the atmosphere does:

- Provides the air we breathe.

- Protects Earth from harmful rays from Space (see p151).

- Protects Earth from space debris, such as meteors.

- Stops Earth getting too cold at night or too hot in the day.

Layers of the atmosphere

The atmosphere can be divided into these **different layers**:

- Exosphere (500-8000 km above the Earth) Weather satellites orbit in this layer.

- Ionosphere (80-500 km above the Earth) This layer protects the Earth from harmful rays.

- Mesosphere (48-80 km above the Earth) Unmanned balloons have measured the temperature of this layer.

- The ozone layer is part of the stratosphere, at about 40 km high.

- Stratosphere (10-48 km above the Earth) Jet aircraft fly in this layer.

- Troposphere (From the ground to 10 km high) We live in this layer and all Earth's weather happens in it.

Exosphere — 700 km
— 600 km
— 500 km
Ionosphere — 400 km
— 300 km
Auroras — 200 km
— 100 km
Mesosphere
Ozone layer
Stratosphere
Troposphere

Volcanoes

Volcanoes are openings in the Earth's crust where molten (melted) rock from inside bursts through the surface. Some molten rock (called **lava**) spills out. It can build up round the opening to form a **mountain**.

Lava

Molten rock

- Earth has more than 1300 active volcanoes, many of them under the sea.

- The islands of Hawaii and Iceland are made of rock that erupted out of the sea from underwater volcanoes.

- Most volcanoes are found near where the plates of the Earth's crust (see below) collide with each other.

Plates

The Earth's **crust** is not an unbroken shell. It is a jigsaw of about 15 huge **rocky pieces** called **plates** that continually push and slide against each other.

- When two plates collide, the rocks they are made of can get squashed and pushed up into the air. Some mountains were formed that way.

Plates of the Earth's crust

- Earthquakes are caused by the plates of the Earth's crust sliding against each other.

- The surface of the Earth is changing all the time as rocks wear down and plates move.

163

The Nearest Planets

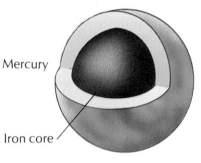

Mercury
57.9 million km

The nearest planets to Earth are **Mercury**, **Venus** and **Mars**. They all have a solid, **rocky surface**, like Earth's.

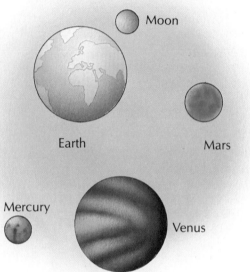

Moon

Earth

Mars

Mercury

Venus

Space probes have taken photographs of Venus, Mars and Mercury and studied their surfaces. Some people thought there was a slight chance of finding **life** on Mars, but no sign of life was found on any of the planets.

Mercury facts

Mercury is the **closest planet** to the Sun. It has:

- Extremely hot days, with temperatures of 350°C, because it is so close to the Sun.

- Very cold nights, because there is no atmosphere to trap the daytime heat.

- An iron core, like the Earth's.

Mercury

Iron core

- Earth is 2½ times bigger than Mercury.

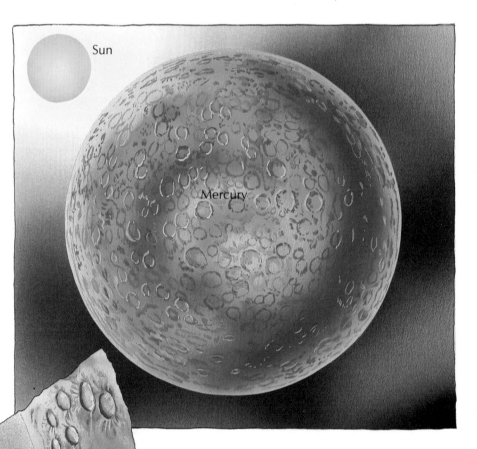

Sun

Mercury

- A dry and cratered surface, a bit like the Moon's. The craters were made by rocky bodies crashing into the planet thousands of years ago.

- A day that lasts for 176 Earth days. Its year is 88 days long – about a quarter of Earth's year.

- Mercury spins round the Sun faster than any other planet. This is how it came by its name. In Ancient Roman mythology Mercury was the swift messenger of the gods.

Venus
108.1 million km

Earth
150 million km

Mars
228 million km

Venus facts

Venus is the closest planet to Earth. Sunlight reflecting from it makes it the **brightest planet** in the night sky. It has:

● Heavy, swirling clouds that hide the mountains and craters on its surface. The clouds trap the Sun's heat, raising the temperature to around 480°C.

● Three large highland areas surrounded by deserts. These have been seen only by radar, as clouds cover them from view.

● An atmosphere of mainly unbreathable carbon dioxide. There are constant thunderstorms, with drops of sulphuric acid in the clouds.

Venus

● Venus is similar in size to the Earth.

● Ishtar Terra, a highland area of Venus, is larger than the USA.

Mars facts

Mars is the furthest inner planet from the Sun. It looks red from Earth, which is why it was named after Mars, the god of war. Mars has:

● A barren, dusty surface with reddish soil and rocks. There are deep canyons and high volcanoes.

● A day that lasts for 24 hours, 37.5 minutes – almost the same as Earth's. Its year, however, is nearly twice as long as Earth's – 687 Earth days.

● A thin atmosphere of carbon dioxide that does not block the Sun's harmful radiation. It is cold, with temperatures averaging −23°C.

● Occasional large dust storms that are visible through a telescope from Earth.

● Spectacular white icy caps at its north and south poles. These grow and shrink depending on the Martian seasons.

● A long time ago, some astronomers thought there might be intelligent life on Mars, because regular lines on the planet's surface looked as if they had been made by intelligent beings.

Strange but true

● Venus' day is longer than its year. It takes 243 Earth days to spin once, and only 225 Earth days to go round the Sun.

● Clouds on Venus spin round the planet in only four Earth days.

● Mars has the largest volcano in the Solar System. It is called Olympus Mons and rises to 25 km. The picture shows only one of its summits.

Mars' surface

● Mars has two very small natural satellites, or moons, called Phobos and Deimos. Phobos is 22 km across. Deimos is 14 km across.

Phobos

Deimos

Asteroids, Comets and Meteoroids

Asteroids are mini-planets that orbit the Sun. Most of them are less than 1 km across. **Comets** are lumps of dirty ice, dust and rock. Most of them move in long oval-shaped orbits around the Sun. **Meteoroids** are rocky fragments, mostly varying in size from a grain of sand to fragments a few centimetres across. If they enter Earth's atmosphere they usually burn up in flashes of light known as **meteors.** However, larger meteoroids are not always destroyed and may land on Earth. Then they become known as **meteorites.**

The asteroid belt

The **asteroid belt** lies between the orbits of Mars and Jupiter. It probably contains at least 40,000 **tiny planets** over 1 km across, revolving round the Sun.

● Astronomers once thought asteroids were fragments of one mini-planet that broke up. Evidence now suggests they are fragments of smaller bodies that collided with each other.

● The asteroid belt makes journeys dangerous for spacecraft, which can be destroyed if they hit even a tiny object. Fortunately, the asteroids are several kilometres apart!

Comets

Comets are made of crumbly **rock** and **ice.** Most travel in long orbits that stretch from near the Sun to the outer part of the Solar System.

● When a comet is near the Sun, the heat turns some of the ice to gas. It streams out behind the comet's head in a glowing tail that may be tens of millions of kilometres long.

● Comets freeze down to a small, dark core when they are far from the Sun.

● Some comets go right round the Sun every few years. Others take thousands or even millions of years to do so because their orbits are so huge.

● Halley's Comet takes 76 years to orbit the Sun. It was last seen in 1986, although it was much less spectacular than on its previous appearance in 1910.

Strange but true

- Halley's Comet was seen in 1066, before the Battle of Hastings. William the Conqueror believed it was a sign that he would win the battle.

- In Greenland, people dig up meteorites and use the iron in them to make tools.

- In 1908, forests in Siberia were flattened by a strange explosion. It may have been caused by a small comet hitting the Earth.

Meteors

Meteors are the **bright streaks** seen when **meteoroids** burn up as they hurtle through the atmosphere at up to 50 km/sec. They are often called **shooting stars.**

- Shooting stars (meteors) are seen more often when the Earth travels through a swarm of meteoroids in its path round the Sun. This is known as a meteor shower. The most famous meteor shower is called the Perseids.

- More than 20 million meteoroids are thought to enter Earth's atmosphere every day. Most burn up.

Meteorites

Meteorites are large **meteoroids** that do not burn up completely in the Earth's atmosphere. They fall to the ground.

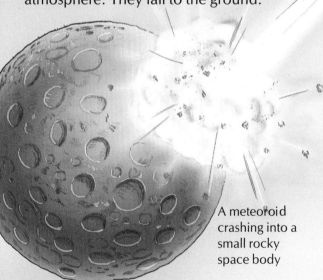

A meteoroid crashing into a small rocky space body

- Meteorites land with such force that they can make holes in the ground called craters. Craters can be seen on many planets and their satellites.

- The biggest known meteorite weighed 60 tonnes. It fell in prehistoric times in Namibia, Africa, where it still lies.

- The most famous meteorite crater on Earth is in Arizona, USA. It is more than a kilometre wide.

- Not all meteorites are so large. In May 1991 a meteorite weighing only 0.5 kg fell into a garden in southern England. Some meteors fall as dust onto the ground.

The Giant Planets

The giant planets, **Jupiter** and **Saturn,** are the largest planets in the Solar System. Their surfaces are not solid and rocky but are made up of a mixture of turbulent, swirling **gas** and **ice**.

Jupiter

Jupiter, the biggest planet, is so huge that all the other planets in the Solar System could fit inside it.

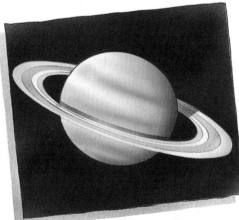

Saturn

Saturn is smaller than Jupiter, but is very large. It is surrounded by brightly shining rings.

Jupiter facts

- Its day is only 9 hours 50 minutes long.

- Its year is 11.9 Earth years long.

- Its diameter (through the Equator) is about 142,800 km.

- There is a very faint ring around it, made of rocky particles. The ring is too faint to be seen from Earth.

- Its atmosphere is made of hydrogen and helium.

Strange but true

- Jupiter's gases change colour so often that the planet looks different each night when seen through a telescope.

- Until the Voyager 1 space probe passed it in 1979, astronomers did not know Jupiter had a ring round it.

- Winds on Saturn blow at about 1400 km/h. Tornadoes on Earth blow at only 300-600 km/h.

The Great Red Spot

Jupiter's **Great Red Spot** is a swirling **tornado** that has been raging for at least 100 years. It is about 40,000 km long and 11,000 km wide. That is more than three times the diameter of Earth!

Inside Jupiter

Jupiter is made mainly of **hydrogen.** Its four major layers are:

- A very small rocky core

- An inner layer of hydrogen

- A shell of liquid hydrogen and helium

- A swirling surface of icy clouds

Saturn's rings

Saturn's **rings** are **bands of ice** and **rock** whirling round the planet. The largest rocks are several metres across.

- There are three main rings containing thousands of separate ringlets.

- Saturn's rings are huge but very thin. A sheet of paper 4 metres across would give you a scale model of their depth (the thickness of the paper) compared to their width (the width of the paper).

Voyager space probe

- Voyager probes photographed Saturn's rings and found new satellites.

Saturn facts

- Its day is only 10 hours 14 minutes long.

- Its year is 29.5 Earth years.

- Its diameter (through the Equator) is about 120,000 km.

- Its diameter measured from one side of the ring system to the other is 272,000 km.

- Its atmosphere is made of hydrogen and helium.

- A bright white area appeared on the surface in September 1990. It is as large as Jupiter's Great Red Spot.

The satellites

Jupiter and Saturn have natural **satellites**, or **moons**, orbiting them. Jupiter has at least 16 moons and Saturn at least 19.

Jupiter's main satellites

- Callisto, the outermost, is an icy and cratered satellite much bigger than Earth's Moon.

- Ganymede is larger than the planet Mercury. Its surface is icy, with grooves and streaks.

- Europa is smaller than Earth's Moon. It is smooth and icy with very few craters.

- Io, the innermost, is slightly larger than the Moon. It has a red, volcanic surface.

Io

Europa

Callisto

Ganymede

Some of Saturn's satellites

- Mimas (pictured below) is one of the innermost satellites. It has a crater on its surface over 100 km wide. That is nearly two-thirds of its diameter!

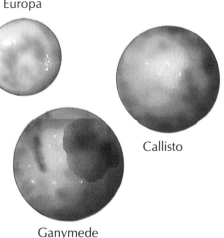

- Titan, the largest satellite, is bigger than Mercury. It has a cloudy atmosphere of nitrogen gas, and may have oceans made of liquid methane.

Uranus, Neptune and Pluto

Uranus, Neptune and Pluto are the **furthest planets** from the Sun. They are all icy cold. Uranus and Neptune are quite similar to each other and look greenish in colour from Earth. Pluto, the tiniest of all the planets, is a dim speck.

In 1985 and 1989, the space probe **Voyager 2** flew past Uranus and Neptune. It took spectacular pictures of the planets, showing details never seen before. It also showed the **rings** around both planets, and discovered an amazing number of new **satellites** – ten for Uranus and six for Neptune.

Uranus

Uranus was discovered in 1781 by **William Herschel**, an amateur astronomer, using a home-made telescope. At first he thought he had found a comet.

● Uranus is made up mostly of hydrogen and helium. The gas methane is also present in its atmosphere, which makes Uranus look green from Earth.

Uranus' satellites

Uranus has 15 satellites altogether. The five main ones are Miranda, Ariel, Umbriel, Titania and Oberon. The largest, Oberon and Titania, are about 1500 km across.

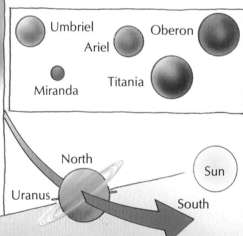

Umbriel
Ariel
Oberon
Miranda
Titania

North
Uranus
Sun
South

● Uranus spins on its side instead of almost upright, like the other planets. Because of this, the poles of the planet can sometimes face the Sun. When this happens, they are warmer than the planet's equator!

Uranus

Herschel's telescope

● The diameter of Uranus is 51,000 km. Its day is about 17 hours long, and it takes 84 Earth years to travel round the Sun.

● Until 1986, only nine rings had been counted round Uranus. On its fly-past, however, Voyager 2 found four more rings, making 13 in all.

Strange but true

● Uranus' small satellite Miranda may have been shattered in a collision with another body. It seems to have broken up into large pieces which collected together again.

● The cycle of seasons on Triton, Neptune's largest satellite, takes 680 years.

● During the 1990s, Pluto is the nearest it can get to Earth, so it is a very good time to study it. This will not happen again until the 23rd century!

Neptune

Neptune was discovered in 1846. It cannot be seen with the naked eye. Through a telescope it looks like a faint blue-green star. Like Uranus, it is surrounded by **rings**.

- Neptune is colder than Uranus. It is about −220°C.

- Neptune is slightly smaller than Uranus, measuring 48,400 km across.

Neptune

Triton

- Neptune's day is about 18 hours long. Its year, however, is 164.8 Earth years long.

Neptune's satellites

Neptune has **eight satellites**. The two main ones are called Triton and Nereid. Triton, the larger, is smaller than Earth's Moon. Very unusually it orbits Neptune in the opposite direction from the planet's own spin.

Nereid

Pluto

Pluto is the **smallest planet**. Because of its orbit (see below) it is usually the furthest away from the Sun. It was not discovered until 1930 and is very difficult to see, even with a telescope.

Pluto

- Pluto's diameter is 2200 km which means it is smaller than our Moon.

- Pluto's day lasts for just over six Earth days, and its year lasts 247.7 Earth years.

Charon

Pluto's satellite

Pluto has **one known satellite**, Charon. It is 800 km across and was discovered in 1978.

Pluto

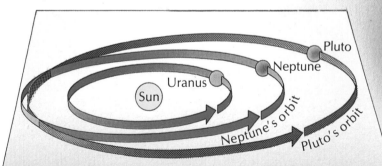

Sun
Uranus
Neptune
Pluto
Neptune's orbit
Pluto's orbit

- Pluto is usually the furthest planet from the Sun. However, its orbit sometimes takes it inside Neptune's orbit. This is happening now, so from 1979 until 1999 Neptune is the 'outermost planet'.

Planet X?

Astronomers used to think that Uranus and Neptune 'wandered' in their orbits because they were pulled by the **gravity** of an unknown space body. They thought there might be another planet – **Planet X** – beyond Pluto. However, this now seems unlikely.

Ancient Astronomy

From early times, people have been interested in the stars and planets. They have tried to understand Space and how it affects human life. Great **stone circles**, such as Stonehenge in England (built about 3500

years ago) may have been used to study how the Sun and Moon moved through the sky.

More than 2000 years ago, the **Chinese**, **Egyptians**, **Babylonians** and **Greeks** were all skilled astronomers.

The Babylonians

About 3000 years ago, the **Babylonians** (who used to live in what is now Iraq) studied the stars. They invented **astrology** - the belief that people's lives are influenced by the position of the stars and planets.

● This Babylonian boundary stone shows the importance of the Sun, Moon and planets to this ancient civilization.

● The Babylonians invented the twelve signs of the zodiac that are still used in astrology.

The Ancient Greeks

The **Greeks** were fine astronomers and mathematicians. In about 240 BC, Eratosthenes, a Greek mathematician, accurately worked out the **size of the Earth**.

● Here are four of the star groups or constellations (see p152-53) named by the Greeks:

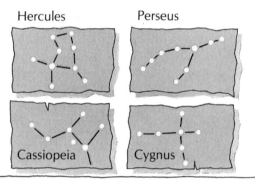

Hercules   Perseus

Cassiopeia   Cygnus

Pioneers of astronomy

Many ancient astronomers added a great deal to our understanding of Space. Some were **persecuted** for their discoveries because they went against the teachings of the Christian Church.

● Ptolemy of Alexandria was born in AD 120. He believed the Earth was at the centre of the Solar System and that the Sun, Moon and planets circled round it.

● Ptolemy's idea of the Solar System was accepted for 1300 years.

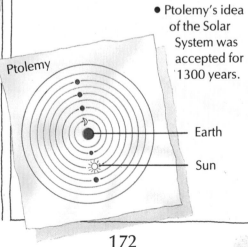

Ptolemy

Earth

Sun

● Nicolaus Copernicus (1473-1543) was a Polish astronomer and mathematician. He published a book that said the Sun, not Earth, was the centre of the Solar System. His book was officially banned until 1835.

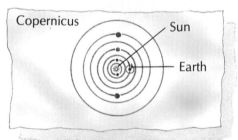

Copernicus

Sun

Earth

● Tycho Brahe (1546-1601) was a Danish astronomer. He wrongly placed Earth back in the centre of the Solar System but accurately observed and measured stars, planets and comets.

Brahe

Sun

Earth

Early equipment

Before the **telescope** was invented, all astronomy was done with the **naked eye.** However, there were some **instruments** to help astronomers when they studied the sky.

● Quadrants and sextants were instruments that enabled astronomers to work out the position of stars and planets.

● Observatories were built to study the sky. This stone-built observatory in India was designed to help people measure the movements of stars and planets, and foretell eclipses.

● Ancient Greek sailors studied the stars and the Sun to help them navigate.

Not to scale

● Ancient people knew only five planets: Mercury, Venus, Mars, Jupiter and Saturn.

A modern sextant

An astronomer working out a star's position in the sky by reading the degrees marked on a quadrant.

● Johannes Kepler (1571-1630), a German mathematician, put the Sun back in the centre of things. He drew up three Laws of Planetary Motion, which are still used today.

Ellipse

● Kepler correctly showed that a planet's orbit is an ellipse (a squashed circle) rather than a true circle.

● Galileo Galilei (1564-1642), an Italian mathematician, was persecuted for saying that the Sun, not Earth, is the centre of the Solar System. He made many discoveries, such as sunspots and Jupiter's four large satellites.

● In 1609, Galileo made one of the first drawings of the Moon's surface.

Galileo's drawing

● Galileo was one of the first to use a telescope. This is one of his instruments, which he built soon after telescopes were invented at the beginning of the seventeenth century. He even made the lenses himself. The most powerful of his telescopes magnified, or enlarged, an object thirty times.

Galileo's telescope

Modern Astronomy

The invention of the telescope made it possible to see objects in Space more clearly. But the Earth's atmosphere makes them appear blurred and blocks out some important radiation coming from stars and galaxies.

Now there are space telescopes that, outside the haze of Earth's atmosphere, can 'see' much more clearly than Earth-based telescopes. They have instruments for detecting X-rays and other invisible radiations. They can tell astronomers more about such things as galaxies and black holes.

Telescopes

Telescopes make distant things seem nearer. Light from a distant object enters the tube and the image of the object is then **magnified** (made larger). There are two main kinds: reflector and refractor.

Binoculars

Binoculars are good for giving a **wide, general view** of the night sky, and for tracking moving objects such as satellites.

REFLECTOR — Light — REFRACTOR

Lens — Eyepiece — Mirror — Mirror — Eyepiece

- Reflectors: Light is bounced off mirrors into an eyepiece.
- Refractors: Light is focused by lenses.
- Both types of telescope produce upside-down images.

- Binoculars make distant things look closer but do not magnify as powerfully as telescopes.

Earth-based astronomy

There are many powerful **telescopes on Earth** that provide a good view of Space.

- Large optical telescopes produce images that can be analyzed by computer They are put in buildings on high ground so they can avoid the lights and polluted air of towns and cities.

Radio telescope

Kitt Peak observatory

- The MMT (Multiple Mirror Telescope) on Mount Hopkins, Arizona, USA, has six mirrors, all 1.8 metres wide.

Optical telescope

- Radio telescopes pick up radio waves from Space that are usually produced by clouds of gas or dust. Radio waves are one of the few kinds of space radiation that can pass through Earth's atmosphere.

- There are several telescopes on Kitt Peak in Arizona, USA, including a reflector 4 metres across. It also has the world's largest solar telescope (for observing the Sun).

MMT

- The largest single radio telescope dish in the world is at Arecibo in Puerto Rico. It is 305 metres across.

Arecibo

Space telescopes

Space telescopes revolutionized astronomy. They can now be launched by **Space Shuttle** and other craft.

Space telescopes have monitored the **Sun** and invisible **radiation**. They have also observed **stars** and **galaxies** that could never be studied before.

The Hubble telescope

The Hubble space telescope was launched by the USA on 24 April 1990. It can detect **ultra-violet** and **infra-red waves** (see p151) as well as **visible light.**

● If all had gone well, Hubble would have transmitted pictures of distant objects never seen before, and stunningly clear images of closer objects.

Space Shuttle

● Unfortunately, Hubble does not work properly. One of its two mirrors is two-thousandths of a millimetre too flat — enough to make all its images out of focus.

● The fault happened because the equipment used to test the mirror was out of adjustment by just one millimetre!

Telescope

Solar panels

The Hubble space telescope

Strange but true

● The satellite IRAS discovered the closest known comet to pass Earth for 200 years.

● The radio telescope at Arecibo, Puerto Rico, can pick up signals from up to 15 billion light-years away.

● An astronomer called James Lick, who died in 1876, is buried in the base of the telescope at the Lick Observatory in the USA.

● Despite problems, the Hubble telescope has been successful. Pluto and its satellite Charon, were seen clearly for the first time from its pictures.

● The Hubble telescope had other problems after the launch. The telescope wobbles twice for several minutes in each orbit.

● Scientists hope to send astronauts to mend the Hubble telescope. Three similar space telescopes are planned for the future.

The Space Age

Here is a selection of different rocket designs:

Lambda-4S-5: the first Japanese rocket, launched in Japan in 1970

The Space Age began on 4 October, 1957, when the USSR launched the satellite **Sputnik 1**. This was a small metal sphere with four thin antennae. It contained a radio transmitter.

Sputnik 1

The development of **spacecraft** has moved incredibly quickly. **Probes, satellites, rockets** and **space stations** have been successfully launched and have helped astronomers learn much more about the Solar System and beyond. Satellites also have many other uses for people on Earth (see p180-81).

Getting off the ground

The invention of the **rocket** made space exploration possible.

● As early as 1903, a Russian teacher called Tsiolkovskii suggested using liquid fuel for rockets and proposed rocket-building in separate parts, called stages.

V2

● Weapons called V2 rockets were developed by a German research team and used near the end of World War II. Space rockets were developed from them.

Vostok 1

Laika

● The USSR sent a small dog, called Laika, into orbit in Sputnik 2 in November 1957. She orbited Earth for a week and became the first animal in Space.

● In 1961, Yuri Gagarin, a Soviet cosmonaut, became the first person in Space. He orbited Earth once in the spacecraft Vostok 1, landing safely after a 108-minute flight.

Space Shuttle

In 1981, the first **Space Shuttle**, Columbia, was launched in the USA. For the first time a spacecraft could go into Space and return to Earth, landing like a plane. It could then be used again for another flight.

1 The Shuttle plane, called an orbiter, is launched attached to a giant fuel tank and two solid-fuel boosters.

Orbiter

Boosters

Fuel tank

2 The boosters drop off at a height of 43 km. They drop into the sea and are rescued for re-use.

3 At 115 km high, the fuel tank separates and burns up as it falls through Earth's atmosphere. It is the only part of the Shuttle that is not re-used.

How do rockets work?

Rockets need a great deal of **power** to escape from Earth's gravity. Most have from two to four fuel-burning parts, called **stages**, that lift the rocket into orbit. The stages separate from the rocket as their fuel runs out. Then they burn up in the Earth's atmosphere.

Liquid fuel

Propellant

1 Liquid-fuel rockets work by burning a mixture of fuel and a propellant.

2 The propellant makes the fuel catch fire with an explosive blast that pushes the rocket upwards.

3 The rocket then builds up enormous speed – many times faster than Concorde.

An Apollo Saturn V rocket, the one used to take people to the Moon (see p178-79).

Stage 1

Stage 2

Stage 3

Capsule

Stage 1 separated from the rocket at a height of about 61 km.

Stage 2 took the rocket up to about 183 km.

Stage 3 took the Apollo capsule into Earth orbit and then to the Moon.

4 The Space Shuttle carries a large cargo. Once in Space, the astronauts can repair or rescue satellites, launch new ones, or carry out experiments.

Satellite cargo

5 After the mission, the Shuttle re-enters Earth's atmosphere. The protective tiles glow red-hot at a temperature of 1260°C.

6 It glides down to Earth and lands on a long runway, like an ordinary aeroplane.

Payload bay

● In 1986, the Space Shuttle Challenger exploded 73 seconds after blast-off. All seven astronauts were killed. It happened because of a tiny fault in one of the solid-fuel boosters.

Strange but true

● Yuri Gagarin survived the first manned spaceflight but was killed in a plane crash seven years later.

● Astronauts become a little taller in Space! There is less gravity, so their bones are less squashed together.

● As it comes back into Earth's atmosphere, the Space Shuttle reaches a temperature of 1260°C.

Landing on the Moon

The Moon is the only place in the Universe that **people** have **visited**. The effects of the journey on the astronauts, along with their experiments and rock samples, taught scientists a great deal about the Moon.

The **first Moon mission**, *Apollo II*, blasted off on 16 July 1969. The enormous Saturn 5 rocket carried the three American astronauts into Space with the power of 160 jumbo jets. Four days later, Neil Armstrong stepped on to the Moon's surface and said the famous words: ''That's one small step for a man, one giant leap for mankind.''

The first Moon landing

Stacked at the top of the **Saturn 5 rocket** were the **Command Module**, the **Service Module** and the **Lunar Module**. Once in orbit round the Moon, the Lunar Module separated to start its journey to the Moon's surface.

● One astronaut, Michael Collins, stayed behind in the Command Module. Neil Armstrong and Edwin Aldrin were in the cramped Lunar Module.

● Minutes away from landing, Neil Armstrong took the controls, as the automatic navigation was taking them towards rocky ground. They landed safely on the 'Sea of Tranquillity'.

Lunar module

Command module

Service module

The rocket as it was at take-off

The Lunar Module coming down to land on the Moon

Other Apollo missions

There were six **Apollo missions** between 1969 and 1972, and 382 kg of Moon rock were collected for analysis.

● On the last three missions, the astronauts used a Moon buggy called the Lunar Rover.

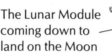

The Soviet missions

● In 1959, the Soviet unmanned probe, Luna 1, flew close to the Moon. A few months later Luna 2 was the first Earth-made object to land on the Moon.

Luna 3

● Soon after, Luna 3 flew past the far side of the Moon and took the first pictures of it.

● In 1966, Luna 9 landed on the Moon's surface and took the first close-up pictures of it.

Luna 9

• The Moon-walk lasted for only 2½ hours. During that time, the astronauts collected samples of dust and rock.

• They also put up a US flag, which they had to stiffen with wire as there is no wind on the Moon to blow it!

• The Moon has six times less gravity than Earth. This means that on the Moon astronauts weigh only a sixth of their normal weight. They could jump and spring about with ease, but it was difficult to walk.

• The astronauts tried to sleep in the Lunar Module, but it was much too cold. At night, temperatures on the Moon reach −150°C.

• The astronauts had to use special tools to collect rock samples because they could not bend over in their spacesuits.

Moon discoveries

On Earth the surface is changing all the time. The Moon, however, is a dead place with **no atmosphere** and **no weather** to erode and change the landscape. So Moon dust and rock have lain in the same positions for millions of years. The youngest **Moon rock** analyzed was 3.1 billion years old.

Moon rock	Moonquake detector	The Moon
• One sample of Moon rock was found to be about 4.6 billion years old – about the same age as Earth.	• Instruments detecting 'moonquakes' found them to be much weaker than earthquakes.	• Because of the Apollo missions, the Moon has now been mapped more accurately than before.

Strange but true

• Astronauts' footprints and Lunar Rover tyre tracks will stay on the Moon for millions of years as there is no wind to blow them away.

• The Moon is completely quiet, because there is no air to carry sound.

• Nothing can grow on the Moon, but plants did grow in Moon-soil on Earth.

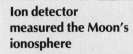

Satellites

There are about 200 **artificial satellites** whirling round the Earth. There is also lots of junk in Space, such as the remains of old satellites. Thousands have been launched and worked for a while before being replaced.

Satellites do all sorts of different jobs. Some can study Earth's **land** and **weather**, or beam **television pictures** and **telephone calls** around the world. Others can analyze **space radiation** that cannot penetrate the Earth's atmosphere. Some are used to **spy** on other countries.

A satellite photo of Earth

Getting into orbit

Satellites are taken into Space by **rockets** or by **Space Shuttle**. They are carried in the Shuttle's cargo, or payload, bay and then launched into orbit in Space.

● These are some of the kinds of orbit a satellite might use:

● Sometimes a robot arm, controlled by a Shuttle astronaut, lifts a satellite out of the payload bay and launches it.

● Most satellites have their own rocket launchers that boost them into orbit when they are at a safe distance from the Shuttle.

Geostationary orbit: the satellite orbits at the same speed as Earth's spin. It is always above the same point over the Equator, at a height of about 36,000 km.

Polar orbit: the satellite orbits Earth from north to south, and can cover most of the Earth within a day. This orbit is usually at a height of about 1000 km.

Eccentric orbit: the satellite flies low over parts of the Earth before swinging out to complete the orbit.

Different kinds of satellites

Communications satellites (comsats) beam telephone calls and television pictures from one part of the world to another. They receive a picture from Earth and send it on to its destination.

A Molniya satellite

Intelsat 6

● In 1965, Russian Molniya satellites began the world's biggest network of comsats.

● Intelsat 6 carries 120,000 telephone circuits and three television channels.

Power from Space

Satellites have large **solar panels** to trap energy from the Sun.

● Satellites store the Sun's energy in batteries and use it to power their equipment.

Space stations

Space stations are also called satellites, because they orbit the Earth. The Mir station was launched by the USSR in 1986. It now has three other sections added to the main station.

- Astronauts live and work for a few months at a time on space stations.

- Astronauts on space stations can use the lack of gravity to do experiments such as crystal-growing or making lenses and new kinds of medicines.

- Space stations have laboratories, living quarters and docking ports for other spacecraft.

Strange but true

- To run their equipment, satellites need only about the same amount of power as a one-bar electric fire.

- Space rubbish, such as bits of old satellite, are a hazard for spacecraft. The Space Shuttle has already been hit.

- Some people think that one day there may be huge space stations with many people living on them. They could travel far from Earth.

- ERTS (Earth Resources Technology Satellites) were launched to monitor sea and land. Landsats gave information on crops, forests and changing coastlines. Seasat studied the sea and provided information about such things as the sea bed, ocean currents, storms and the movement of fish shoals.

- SAGE (Stratospheric Aerosol and Gas Experiment) was launched to monitor the ozone layer (see p163) and the effects of pollution on it.

- IRAS (Infra-red Astronomy Satellite) was launched in 1983. During the 10 months that it operated it taught scientists a great deal about space objects. It could pick up infra-red radiation from galaxies hundreds of millions of light-years away (see p151). IRAS discovered a cloud of dust round the bright star, Vega, which could possibly turn into a new Solar System.

Landsat 3

Seasat

IRAS

Space Probes

S pace probes have been some of the most successful developments of the Space Age. They have taught astronomers a great deal about the **Solar System** by visiting all the planets except Pluto. Scientists now have much more information about **planets** and their **satellites**, as well as amazing pictures.

In 1959, the Soviet probe **Luna 1** was the first to bypass the Moon. Thirty years later, in 1989, **Voyager 2** sent back the first detailed pictures of Neptune. The US probe **Galileo**, launched in 1989, will reach Jupiter in 1995. It will orbit the planet and send a probe into its deadly atmosphere.

Probes to the nearest planets

In 1974-5 the US probe **Mariner 10** flew past Mercury three times. It took 8000 pictures, all showing the same side of the planet. These are some other probes and their achievements:

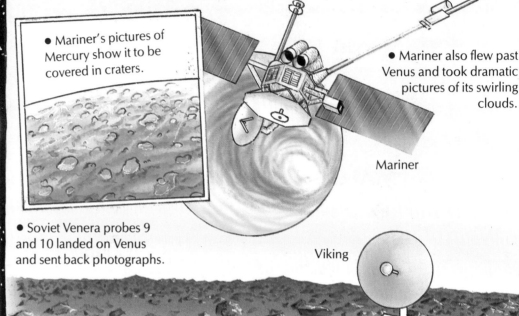

- Mariner's pictures of Mercury show it to be covered in craters.

- Mariner also flew past Venus and took dramatic pictures of its swirling clouds.

Mariner

- Soviet Venera probes 9 and 10 landed on Venus and sent back photographs.

Viking

- In 1976, two Viking probes landed on Mars, studied the climate and tested the soil for signs of life. They found none.

- More Mars probes are planned. They may lead to people landing on Mars within the next 50 years.

Pioneer probes

- Pioneers 10 and 11 were the first probes to brave the dangers of the Asteroid Belt on their journey to Jupiter and Saturn.

- Pioneer 10 flew past Jupiter in 1973, sending information back to Earth by radio signals. It is now further than Pluto from the Sun.

- Giotto found that the comet's solid nucleus was 15 km wide.

- The Giotto probe intercepted Halley's comet in 1986. It flew right into the comet's tail. Despite being damaged, it was able to send back information.

Mapped 84 per cent of Venus' surface

 Photographed swellings, called coronae, some of them 200 km wide

 Discovered that Venus is volcanic and covered in lava flows

Voyager probes

The two **Voyager** probes, launched in 1977, have given stunning new information about the **outer planets**. Both probes flew past Jupiter and Saturn, and Voyager 2 sent back the first detailed pictures of Uranus, Neptune and their satellites.

Jupiter

Voyager 1

● Voyager probes carried TV cameras and special equipment to measure such things as heat and magnetic fields on planets. They each had a large radio antenna and carried experiments on a central work ring.

● Voyager 1 flew past Jupiter in 1979 and Saturn in 1980 before flying out of the Solar System.

Saturn

Voyager messages

Both Voyagers carry **messages** in case they are intercepted by **aliens**. They include:

● Pictures of a man, woman and child and a map of the Solar System, showing where Earth is.

● A record containing music and greetings in various languages. There are 118 pictures of Earth stored on the record.

Strange but true

● Pioneer and Voyager probes may survive for millions of years, drifting in Space.

● Voyager 2 discovered huge 5 km-high ice cliffs on Miranda, Uranus' satellite.

● If Voyager had existed a few years earlier, it might have been possible to send it to visit Pluto as well, when Pluto was nearer the other outer planets.

● Voyager 2 flew past Jupiter in 1979, Saturn in 1981, Uranus in 1986 and Neptune in 1989. It discovered ten satellites of Uranus and six of Neptune.

● Voyager probes could visit so many planets because between 1979 and 1989 the planets furthest from the Sun were lined up together. This happens only once every 175 years.

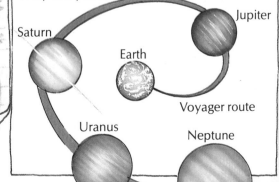

Saturn

Jupiter

Earth

Uranus

Voyager route

Neptune

Uranus

Neptune

● Voyager photographed Neptune's Great Dark Spot – a storm similar to Jupiter's Great Red Spot (see p168).

The Future

Space exploration is hugely expensive. Nevertheless, plans are underway for large orbiting **space stations** and **permanent bases** on the Moon and Mars. Eventually, people may live on a planet other than Earth. It might even be possible to travel to other stars and set up bases in their solar systems.

Materials from outside Earth would be used to build bases on nearby planets. Rocks from the Moon and asteroids, for example, could be used for building materials. Astronauts would be sent to work on these projects.

Moon base

A Moon base could become a reality in the fairly near future, with astronauts living and working there for long periods.

Mars base

Within the next 50 years or so, people may have walked on Mars. They may even have started building the first **Mars base**.

The cost of exploration

How much new space exploration takes place will depend on whether governments can afford the **cost**:

● From 1961-72, the USA spent about 25.5 billion dollars on getting astronauts to the Moon.

● From 1958-73, the USSR spent about 45 billion dollars on its space programme.

● At first, an observatory with powerful radio telescopes may be set up on the far side of the Moon. This would enable deep Space to be studied, away from radio interference from Earth. People at the observatory could also study the Moon and do experiments.

● Eventually, a permanent base could be set up on the Moon. The main industry would be mining Moon rock.

● A Moon base could help scientists plan manned landings on Mars. This is why the Moon was called a 'bridge between two worlds' by the US National Commission on Space.

● A base on Mars would be slow to build. It would take many missions, and many years, for astronauts to complete the work. They would have to spend eight months travelling in Space before they reached the planet.

● Some scientists believe that it may be better to set up a base on Phobos, Mars' larger satellite. Because of Phobos' weak gravity, it would be easier for spacecraft to approach and land there.

Near-future spaceflight

Britain, the USA, Japan and Germany all have plans for a new hypersonic **aerospace plane**. It would take off rather like a jet fighter, burning **oxygen** from the atmosphere rather than propellant (see p177). Rockets would then fire to take it into orbit.

- The new space planes could carry three times more than the Shuttle, either as passengers or as cargo. The planes would also be completely reusable.

Freedom space station

The USA hopes to launch the first part of its planned **Freedom space station** in 1995. It will be the biggest-ever space station, and the first permanent one.

- The Space Shuttle will take parts of the station into orbit over the course of 20 missions.

- Much research could be done on the station, ranging from monitoring the long-term effects on people of living in Space, to growing near-perfect crystals in the low gravity.

- Astronauts will assemble the station in Space.

- Russia has cancelled some space projects because political changes have made space exploration too expensive.

Power from Space

New sources of power for people on Earth could be found in Space. **Space power stations** would be built to do this.

- A gigantic solar panel could be sent into orbit to capture the Sun's energy and beam it back to Earth.

An artist's impression of what the space power station might look like

- The power station would probably have to be built in Space.

- One idea is to set up a 'factory' in a low orbit. Completed parts would then be moved into a higher orbit and used to build the station, which would orbit above one place on Earth.

Strange but true

- One idea for a space power station includes an orbiting solar panel that would be 21 km long and 5 km wide!

- In 1865 the French writer Jules Verne wrote a story about people travelling to the Moon from a launch site in Florida. A hundred years later, Apollo astronauts did exactly that!

- There could be millions of inhabited planets like Earth. Nobody knows what the inhabitants might look like!

Space Facts and Lists

Stars

- About 1500 stars are visible at night with the naked eye in a clear, dark sky.

- There are 88 constellations altogether.

- The smallest star measures about 1700 km across. It is a white dwarf called LP 327-16.

Supernovae

Supernovae are exploding stars. Here are four recorded supernovae explosions seen with the naked eye. The first one was recorded by the Chinese, who said that the supernova was visible for two years.

Date	Constellation	Brightness
1006	Lupus (Wolf)	−9.5 (very bright)
1054	Taurus (Bull)	−4
1572	Cassiopeia	−4
1604	Ophiuchus (Serpent-Bearer)	−3

- At its brightest, a supernova can be 500 million times as bright as the Sun.

- There was a supernova in 1987 in the Large Magellanic Cloud – our closest galaxy.

- A cloud of dust and gas called the Crab Nebula is the remains of the supernova seen in 1054.

Galaxies

These are the nearest galaxies to the Milky Way.

Name	Distance	Diameter
	(Light-years)	
Large Magellanic Cloud	180,000	30,000
Small Magellanic Cloud	190,000	16,000
Ursa Minor dwarf	250,000	2000
Draco dwarf	250,000	3000
Sextant dwarf	280,000	6000
Sculptor dwarf	280,000	5000
Fornax dwarf	420,000	7000
Carina dwarf	550,000	3000
Leo I	750,000	2000

Solar eclipses

- The longest total eclipse of the Sun was recorded on 20 June 1955. It lasted for 7 minutes, 8 seconds.

- The first recorded eclipse of the Sun was in China on 22 October 2136 BC.

- There are usually two to four solar eclipses each year. However, occasionally there are five. This last happened in 1935.

Here are the dates of the eclipses of the Sun between 1992-2000.

Year	Visible in	Kind of eclipse
1992		
4/5 January	Central Pacific	Annular
30 June	S.Atlantic	Total
24 December	Arctic	Partial
1993		
21 May	Arctic	Partial
13 November	Antarctic	Partial
1994		
10 May	Pacific, Mexico USA, Canada	Annular
3 November	Peru, Brazil S.Atlantic	Total
1995		
29 April	S.Pacific, Brazil Peru, S.Atlantic	Annular
24 October	Iran, India, E.Indies, Pacific	Total

Year	Visible in	Kind of eclipse
1996		
17 April	Antarctic	Partial
12 October	Arctic	Partial
1997		
9 March	Russia, Arctic	Total
2 September	Antarctic	Partial
1998		
26 February	Pacific, South of Panama, Atlantic	Total
22 August	Indian Ocean E.Indies, Pacific	Annular
1999		
16 February	Indian Ocean Australia, Pacific	Annular
11 August	Atlantic, England, France, Turkey, India	Total

- An annular eclipse happens when the Moon is too far away to cover the Sun completely. A ring of light appears round the Moon.

The Moon

- The biggest 'sea' on the Moon is the Mare Imbrium (Sea of Showers), which is 1300 km across.

- The biggest Moon crater visible from Earth is Bailly, which is 295 km wide and 4 km deep.

- The deepest Moon crater is Newton, which is over 8 km deep.

- There are about 1500 moonquakes a year. They are usually 700-1100 km below the surface and are much weaker than earthquakes.

Lunar eclipses

These are the dates of Lunar eclipses between 1992 and 2000.

Date	Type	Mid-point of eclipse
1992		
15 June	Partial	4.58 am
9 December	Total	11.45 pm
1993		
4 June	Total	1.02 pm
29 November	Total	6.26 am
1994		
25 May	Partial	3.32 am
1995		
15 April	Partial	12.19 pm
1996		
4 April	Total	12.11 am
27 September	Total	2.55 am
1997		
24 March	Partial	4.41 am
16 September	Total	6.47 pm
1999		
28 July	Partial	11.34 am
2000		
21 January	Total	4.45 am
16 July	Total	1.57 pm

Comets

● Halley's Comet is the brightest comet seen regularly. It passes the Sun every 76.1 years.

● People used to believe that a comet's appearance signalled an important event about to happen on Earth.

● Comet West, which was visible in daylight in 1976, may take a million years to orbit the Sun.

● The comet with the shortest orbit is Encke's. It takes 3.3 years to travel round the Sun.

● The biggest comet was recorded in 1811. The head was 2 million km in diameter and the tail was 160 million km long.

● The Great Comet of 1843 had the longest recorded tail – 330 million km.

These are some comets that have been observed more than once:

Name	Years taken to circle the Sun
Encke	3.3
D'Arrest	6.2
Wolf-Harrington	6.6
Shajn-Schaldach	7.3
Smirnova-Chernykh	8.5
Slaughter-Burnham	11.6
Temple-Tuttle	32.9
Pons-Brooks	71
Halley	76.1
Herschel-Rigollet	156

Meteors

● Every year the Earth passes through groups of meteoroids. As Earth passes through them, showers of meteors can be seen in the sky.

● To see meteors, you need patience and a clear night sky, away from city lights and with no moonlight.

● The most spectacular meteor shower that takes place each year is called the Perseids. They are visible around 12 August.

● During the Perseids meteor shower, several dozen meteors can be seen every hour for several hours.

Meteorite craters

These are the names and sizes of some meteorite craters on Earth:

Name	Diameter (metres)
Meteor Crater, Arizona, USA	1265
Wolf Creek, Australia	850
Henbury, Australia	200
Boxhole, Australia	175
Odessa, Texas, USA	170
Waqar, Arabia	100
Desel, Estonia	100
Campo del Cielo, Argentina	75
Dalgaranga, Australia	70
Manicouagan Crater, Canada	70

These are the weights of some of the biggest meteorites ever found:

Meteorite	Weight
Hoba west, Grootfontein, South Africa	60 tonnes
Armanty, Outer Mongolia	20 tonnes
Willamette, Oregon, USA	14 tonnes
Campo del Cielo, Argentina	13 tonnes
Mundrabilla, Australia	12 tonnes

Asteroids

● The biggest asteroid is Ceres, with a diameter of 940 km.

● The smallest known asteroid is probably Hathor. Its diameter is about 0.5 km.

● Vesta is the brightest asteroid. Arethusa is the darkest.

● The asteroid Hermes came within 800,000 km of Earth on 28 October 1937.

● An asteroid called the NORC was named after an electronic calculator. Most asteroids are named by their discoverers, who can choose any name they like.

Space Facts and Lists

Astronomy dates

1543
Copernicus published the book in which he stated that the Sun, not Earth, was the centre of the Solar System.

1576-1596
Tycho Brahe drew up the most accurate star catalogue ever made without a telescope.

1600
Giordano Bruno was burned at the stake for publicly stating that the Earth goes round the Sun.

1604
Kepler's Star was the last supernova to be seen in our galaxy, to date.

1608
The telescope was invented in Holland by Hans Lippershey.

Newton's telescope

1668
Isaac Newton made the first reflecting telescope.

1758
Halley's Comet returned, as had been predicted for the first time.

1781
The astronomer William Herschel discovered Uranus.

1801
Ceres was the first asteroid to be discovered.

1846
Neptune was discovered, using the predictions of its position made by John Adams and Urbain Leverrier.

1850
The first successful photograph of a star (Vega) was produced.

1908
There was a mysterious explosion in Tunguska, Siberia, which was thought to be caused by a meteorite landing.

1930
Astronomer Clyde Tombaugh discovered Pluto.

1937
The first radio telescope dish was built. It measured 9.4 metres across.

1963
Quasars were identified for the first time.

1967
Pulsars were discovered.

1986
Halley's Comet returned as predicted. The probe Giotto passed through the comet's tail and sent back information about the comet's head.

1990
The Hubble space telescope was launched.

Space Age firsts

● The first object to orbit Earth was Sputnik 1, launched by the USSR in October 1957.

● The first animal in Space was the Soviet dog, Laika, in November 1957. It died on the flight.

● The first animals to survive an orbital spaceflight were the Soviet dogs, Strelka and Belka, launched in Sputnik 5 in August 1960.

● The first person to orbit Earth was Yuri Gagarin, from the USSR, in April 1961.

● The first American to orbit Earth was John Glenn in February 1962.

● The first woman in Space was Valentina Tereshkova, from the USSR, in June 1963.

Some space rockets and their heights

Titan 33 metres • Vostok 38 metres • Ariane 47 metres • Soyuz 51 metres

● The first docking in Space of two manned spacecraft was in January 1969. The spacecraft were the Soviet Soyuz 4 and 5. Two cosmonauts spacewalked to Soyuz 4.

● The first person to walk on the Moon was Neil Armstrong in July 1969.

● The first vehicle on the Moon was the unmanned Soviet Lunokhod Rover in November 1970.

● The first landing on Venus was by the Soviet Venera 3 probe in March 1966.

● The first space station to be launched was the Soviet Salyut 1 in April 1971.

● The first space probe sent to the outer planets was Pioneer 10, launched in March 1972. It passed out of the Solar System after its mission.

● The first US space station, Skylab 1, was launched in May 1973.

● The first Space Shuttle, Columbia, was sent into orbit by the United States in April 1981.

● The first US woman in Space was Sally Ride in 1983.

● The first astronaut to fly untethered in Space, using a self-propelling backpack called a Manned Manoeuvring Unit (MMU), was American Bruce McCandless in February 1984.

● The first British person in Space was Helen Sharman in May 1991.

Rocket launch centres

Here are the world's main rocket launch centres:

USA:
 Cape Canaveral, Florida
 Vandenberg Air Force Base, California
 Wallops Station, Virginia
Former USSR
 Baikonu Cosmodrome
 Plesetsk
 Kapustin Yar
JAPAN:
 Kagoshima Space Centre
 Tanegashima, Osaki
CHINA:
 Jiuquan Satellite Launch Centre
 Xi Chang Satellite Launch Centre
 Taiyuan Satellite Launch Centre
ESA (European Space Agency):
 Guiana Space Centre, Kourou, French
  Guiana
ITALY:
 San Marco Launch Platform, Formosa
  Bay, Kenya
INDIA:
 Sriharikota Launching Range (SHAR)
ISRAEL:
 Palmachim Air Force Base

Giant telescopes

These are the biggest telescopes in the world:

Reflectors

Name	Aperture
Keck Telescope, Hawaii	982 cm
Mount Semirodriki, Russia	600 cm
Palomar, California, USA	508 cm
Mount Hopkins, California	440 cm
La Palma, Canary Islands	420 cm
Cerro Tololo, Chile	401 cm
Kitt Peak, Arizona, USA	401 cm
Siding Spring, Australia	389 cm

Refractors

Name	Aperture
Yerkes, Williams Bay, USA	102 cm
Lick, California, USA	91 cm
Meudon, France	83 cm
Potsdam, Germany	81 cm
Alleghany, Pittsburgh, USA	76 cm
Nice, France	76 cm

Radio telescopes

● The biggest non-steerable radio dish is in Arecibo, Puerto Rico. It measures 305 metres across.

● The biggest steerable radio dish is in the Max Planck Institute, Bonn, Germany. It is 100 metres across.

● The biggest group, or array, of radio antennae is in New Mexico. There are 27 antennae, all 25 metres wide. The array is Y-shaped and each arm measures 20.9 km.

Manned Moon missions

All manned missions to the Moon to date were made by US astronauts in Apollo spacecraft during the late 1960s and early 1970s.

Date	Mission	Astronauts
July 1969	Apollo 11	Neil Armstrong
		Edwin Aldrin
		Michael Collins
Nov 1969	Apollo 12	Charles Conrad
		Richard Gordon
		Alan Bean
April 1970	Apollo 13 (abandoned)	James Lovell
		John Swigert
		Fred Haise
Feb 1971	Apollo 14	Alan Shepard
		Stuart Roosa
		Edgar Mitchell
July 1971	Apollo 15	David Scott
		James Irwin
		Alfred Worden
April 1972	Apollo 16	John Young
		Thomas Mattingly
		Charles Duke
Dec 1972	Apollo 17	Eugene Cernan
		Ronald Evans
		Harrison Schmitt

Space probes

Here are some of the main space probes that have been launched:

1959
Luna 1, 2 and 3 (USSR) became the first successful probes to the Moon.

1965
Mariner 4 (USA) took pictures of Mars.

1966
Luna 9 (USSR) landed on the Moon.

1967
Venera 4 (USSR) landed on Venus

1971
Mariner 9 (USA) was put into orbit round Mars and took photographs of the surface.

1976
Vikings 1 and 2 (USA) landed on Mars.

1978
Veneras 11 and 12 (USSR) and two Pioneer probes (USA) visited Venus.

1979
Voyager 1 (USA) by-passed Jupiter.

1980
Voyager 1 (USA) by-passed Saturn.

1986
Voyager 2 (USA) by-passed Uranus. Five probes, including Giotto (USA), were sent to intercept Halley's Comet.

1989
Voyager 2 (USA) by-passed Neptune. Phobos 2 (USSR) entered orbit round Mars. Galileo (USA) was launched, eventually bound for Jupiter.

1991
Magellan (USA) sent back detailed information about Venus after mapping most of its surface by radar.

189

INDEX

Indexes to other sections
are on pages 46, 94 and 142.

Adams, John 189
aerospace planes 185
Aldrin, Edwin 178, 189
Alpha Centauri 153
Anaxagoras 173
Andromeda 155
Andromeda galaxy 152, 155
Andromeda Spiral 155
animals in space 188
Apollo II 178, 189
Apollo missions to the Moon 178, 189
Apollo Saturn V rocket 177
Arcturus 153
Arecibo, Puerto Rico 174, 175
Arethusa 139
Ariane rocket 177, 188
Ariel 170
Aristarchus 173
Armstrong, Neil 178, 188, 189
asteroid belt 166, 182
asteroids 166, 167, 187
astrology 172
astronauts 177, 179, 181, 184, 188
    working in space 184, 185
astronomy
    ancient 172-73
    modern 174-75
atmosphere of Earth 163
atomic reaction 150
aurorae 158

Babylonian astronomers 172
Betelgeuse 153
Big Bang, temperature 149
Big Bang theory 148
binary star systems 151, 157
binoculars 174
black holes 150, 155, 156
    detecting 157
boosters 176
Brahe, Tycho 172, 188
Bruno, Giordano 188
Bull 152

Callisto 169
Canis Major 153
Canopus 153
Carina dwarf 186
Cassiopeia 172
    supernova 186
Centaurus constellation 153
Ceres 167, 187, 189
Challenger 177
Charon 171, 175
Chiron 167
chromosphere 159
Closed Theory of future of the Universe 149
clusters 154
Collins, Michael 178, 179
Columbia 176-77, 188
Comet West 187
comets 166, 187
    orbits 166, 187
    tails 166
command module 178
communication satellites 180
comsats 180
constellations 152-53, 172, 186
    ancient names 186
Copernicus, Nicolaus 172, 188
corona 159

Corona Borealis 153
COS-B space telescope 175
cosmic rays 156
    and neutrinos 157
    and tree growth 157
Crab Nebula 186
crystals, growth in low gravity 185
Cygnus 172
Cygnus constellation 157
Cygnus X-1 157

D-1 rocket 177
D'Arrest's Comet 187
deep space 184
Deimos 165
Delta Cephei 151
Dog Star 153
Draco dwarf 186

Earth 148, 162-3, 177
    core 162
    crust 162
    diameter 148, 163
    distance from Sun 165
    effect of gravity on Moon 161
    formation 162
    gravity 149, 160
    mantle 162
    size 172
    surface 163
    weight 163
Earth Resources Technology Satellites 181
earthquakes 163
eclipses
    of the Moon 161, 187
    of the Sun 159, 186
electro-magnetic spectrum 151
Encke's Comet 187
Energiya 177
Equator 152
Eratosthenes 172
ERTS 181
Europa 169
Exosat space telescope 175
exosphere 163

former USSR
    Moon missions 178
    space exploration curtailed 185
    space programme 176, 177 180, 184
Fornax dwarf 186
Freedom space station 185

Gagarin, Yuri 176, 177, 188
galactic year 154
galaxies 148, 154-5, 175, 186
galaxy shapes 155
Galileo, space probes 182, 189
Galileo Galilei 173
Ganymede 169
Giotto space probe 182, 189
Glenn, John 188
GM-2 181
gravity 149, 161
    effect on body 177
    Moon 160
Great Bear 152
Great Comet 187
Great Dog 153
Great Pyramid of Cheops, Egypt 173
great red spot of Jupiter 168,183
Greek astronomers 172

Halley's Comet 166-67, 182, 187,189
Hathor 187
helium 148, 150, 158
hemispheres 152
Hercules 172
Hermes 185, 187
Herschel, William 170, 189
Herschel-Rigollet's Comet 187
Herschel's telescope 170
Himalayan mountains 162
Horsehead Nebula 153
Hubble space telescope 149, 175
    hydrogen 148, 150, 158, 168
    temperature 150
hypersonic space plane 185

INEWS 181
Infra-red Astronomy Satellite 175,181
infra-red waves 151, 175
instruments 173
Intelsat 180
Io 169
ion detector 179
ionosphere 163
IRAS 157, 175, 181

Japanese rocket 176
junk in space 180, 181
Jupiter 168, 173
    atmosphere 168
    distance from Sun 169
    great red spot 168, 183
    satellites 169, 173
    size 168
    space probes 182, 183

Kepler, Johannes 173
Kepler's Star 188
Kitt Peak observatory 174

Lambda-4S-5 rocket 176
Landsats 181
Large Magellanic Cloud
    supernova 186
lava 163
Laws of Planetary Motion 173
Leo I 186
Leverrier, Urbain 189
Lick, James 175
Lick Observatory 175
life on Earth 162
light-years 149, 151
Lippershey 188
Little Bear 152
LP 327-16 186
Luna 3 161, 178
Luna probes 182, 189
lunar eclipses 161, 187
lunar module 178, 179
Lunar Rover 178, 179
Lunokhod Rover 188
Lupus supernova 186

M51 155
M77 155
M81 154
M87 155
M104 155
Magellan space probe 182-3, 189
Magellanic Clouds 153, 155, 186
magnetometer 179
magnitude rating 153
Mare Imbrium 186
maria 160, 161

Mariner, space probes 182, 189
Mars 162, 165, 173
    atmosphere 165
    distance from Sun 165
    manned landings 184
    no life 164, 165, 182
    satellites 165
    space probes 182, 189
    space stations 184
    temperature 165
    volcano 165, 175
Mercury 173
    distance from Sun 164
    orbit 164
    space probes 164, 182
    temperature 164
mesosphere 163
meteor showers 167, 187
meteorites 166, 167
    craters 167, 187
    size 167
    weights 167, 187
meteoroids 160, 166, 167
meteors 166, 167, 187
Meteosat 181
methane 170
microwaves 151
Milky Way 148, 154, 155
Mimas 169
Mir space station 181
MMT 174
Molniya satellites 180
Moon 160-1,186
    age 179
    atmosphere 179
    craters 161, 186
    diameter 161
    distance from Earth 160
    drawing by Galileo 173
    eclipses 161, 187
    effect of Earth's gravity 161
    gravity 149, 160, 161, 179
    landing 178-9, 188
    mapping 179
    orbit round Earth 160
    phases 160
    rock mining 184
    rocks 178, 179, 184
    space stations 184
    studies 184
    temperature 161, 179
    waxing and waning, 160
    weather 179
Moon buggy 178
Moon missions 178-9
    USA 178, 179
    USSR 189
Moon walk 179, 188
Moonquake detector 179
Mount Hopkins, Arizona 174

National Aero-Space Plane 185
nebula 150
Neptune 170,171,189
    distance from Sun 171
    Great Dark Spot 183
    rings 171
    satellites 171, 183
    size 171
    space probes 182, 183
    temperature 171
Nereid 171
neutrinos 157
neutron stars 150
Newton, Isaac 189
Newton's telescope 188
NORC 187
North Star 152
northern hemisphere star 152

novas 151

OAO 157
Oberon 170
observatories 172-3
Open Theory of future of the
   Universe 149
Ophiuchus supernova 186
optical telescopes174
orbiters 176
orbiting astronomical
   observatory 157
orbits, satellites 180
Orion 153
OSO satellites 175
ozone layer 163, 181

Perseids 167, 187
Perseus 172
Phobos 165,184
   space probe 189
photosphere 158
Pioneer 10 188
   space probes 182, 183, 189
Planet X 171
planets 148 ,162, 164-5
   inhabited 185
   see also Earth, Jupiter, Mars,
   Mercury, Neptune, Pluto,
   Saturn, Uranus, Venus
planets of other stars 157
plates of the Earth's crust 163
Pleiades 152, 153
Plough 152
Pluto 170, 171, 175, 188
   closest to Earth 170
   distance from Sun 171
   orbit 171
   satellite 171
   size 171
   space probes 183
Polaris 152
Pons-Brooks Comet 187
prominences 158, 159
Proxima Centauri 149, 153
Ptolemy 172
pulsars 150, 188

quadrants 173
quasars 156, 157, 188

radiation 151, 175
radio telescopes 148, 174, 175
   188, 189
radio waves 151, 156, 174
red giant 150, 159
red shift 155
Ride Sally 188
Ring of Brodgar, Scotland 173
rocket launch centres 189
rockets 176-7, 188

SAGE 181
Sanger Project 185
satellites 180-1
Saturn 169, 173
   atmosphere 169
   distance from Sun 169
   rings 169
   satellites 169
   size 168, 169
space probes 182, 183
Saturn 5 rocket 178
Sculptor dwarf 186
Seasats 181
service module 178
Seven Sisters 152
Sextant dwarf 186
sextants 173
Shajn-Schaldach's Comet 187

shooting stars 167
singularity 156
Sirius 152,153
Sirius B 152
Skylab 188
Slaughter-Burnham's Comet 187
Small Magellanic Cloud 186
Smirnov-Chernykh's Comet 181
solar eclipses 159, 186
solar flares 158
solar panels 180
solar panels in Space 185
Solar System 148
   ancient view 172
   centre of 172
   and Earth 162
   in Milky Way 154
   new 181
   size 149
   space probes 182
solar wind spectrometer 178
Southern Cross 153
southern hemisphere stars 153
Soviet see former USSR
Soyuz rocket 188
Space
   deep 184
   exploration 184-5
   measurement 149
   power stations 185
   radiation 180
   rubbish 181
   satellites 176
space planes 185
space probes 164, 176, 182-3,
   188, 189
space rockets 176-7
Space Shuttle 176-7, 185, 188
   hit by rubbish 181
space stations 176, 181
   experiments 181
   exploration 184
space telescopes 149, 157, 175
   188
spacecraft 176
   docking 188
Sputnik 1 176,188
spy satellites 180
standing stones 172,173
star drift 152
star sphere 152
stars 150-1, 175, 186
   aid to navigation 173
   binary 151, 157
   colliding 154
   death 150, 156
   energy waves 151
   exploding 186
   formation 150
   internal heat 150
   magnitude rating 153
   surface temperature 150-1
   variable 151
Stonehenge 172
stratosphere 163
Stratosphere Aerosol and Gas
   Experiment 181
Sun 148,158-9
   distance from Earth 150, 158
   gravity 149
   position in Milky Way 154
   size 158
   speed of rotation 158
   as a star 151
   sunspots 173
   temperature 158
sunspots 158
supernovae 150, 186, 188
Surtsey 162

Taurus 152
Taurus supernova 186
telescopes 174-5,189
   Galileo 173
   Herschel 170
   Hubble 149, 175
   multiple mirrors 174
   Newton's 188
   optical 174
   radio 149, 174-75, 188,
      189
   solar 174
   space 149, 157, 175, 188
television satellites 180
Telstar 180
Temple-Tuttle's Comet 187
Tereshkova, Valentina 188
tides 160
Titan 169
Titan rocket 188
Titania 170
Tombaugh, Clyde 188
Triton 170, 171
troposphere 163
Tsiolkovski 176

ultra-violet light 151
ultra-violet waves 175
Umbriel 170
Universe 148-9
   future 149
Uranus 170, 189
   distance from Sun 171
   rings 170
   satellites 179, 183
   size 170
Ursa Major 152
Ursa Minor 152
Ursa Minor dwarf 186
USA
   Moon missions 176
   space programme 176-7,
      184
USSR see former USSR

V2 rockets 176
variable stars 151
Vega 153, 181, 188
Venera space probes 189
Venus 162, 165, 173
   atmosphere 165
   distance from Sun 165
   landing 189
   mapping surface 189
   space probe 182, 183, 189
   temperature 165
Vesta 187
Viking space probes 182, 183,
   189
visible light 151, 175
volcanoes 162, 163
Vostok 1 176, 188
Voyager 1 space probe 168, 169
Voyager 2 space probe 170
Voyager
   messages to aliens 183
   photographs of planets 183
   space probes 182, 183, 189

weather satellites 180
white dwarfs 150, 159
Wolf-Harrington's Comet 187

X-rays 151, 157

ziggurats 173
zodiac signs 172

This book was created and produced by
Blue Banana Books Ltd
The Barn, Randolph's Farm
Hurstpierpoint
Sussex BN6 9EL

Writers: Moira Butterfield, Dee Turner, Pam Beasant
Editors: Tony Potter, Dee Turner, Nicola Wright
Additional text contributions: Catriona Macgregor
Designers: Margaret Howdle, Chris Leishman, Brian Robertson, Iain Ashman
Illustrators: Mainline Design, Peter Bull, Sandra Hill, Ruth Lindsay,
Shelagh McNicholas, Guy Smith, Michael Steward

෪

This edition specially produced for Bookmart Ltd

Originally published in four separate volumes
Copyright ©1992 first editions, Times Four Publishing Ltd
Copyright ©1994 revised edition, Blue Banana Books Ltd

BRITISH LIBRARY CATALOGUING IN PUBLICATION DATA
A catalogue record for this book is available from The British Library

ISBN 1 874647 70 4

10 9 8 7 6 5 4 3 2 1

Colour origination by RCS Graphics Ltd, Leeds
Printed in Italy